I0114066

Imperfect Union:
How Errors of Omission Threaten Constitutional Democracy

Lawrence Goldstone

Imperfect Union:
How Errors of Omission Threaten Constitutional Democracy

Lawrence Goldstone

Academica Press
Washington~London

Library of Congress Cataloging-in-Publication Data

Names: Goldstone, Lawrence (author)
Title: Imperfect union : how errors of omission threaten constitutional democracy | Goldstone, Lawrence.
Description: Washington : Academica Press, 2024. | Includes references.
Identifiers: LCCN 2024930036 | ISBN 9781680538434 (hardcover) | 9781680538458 (paperback) | 9781680538441 (e-book)

Contents

Acknowledgments

My deepest thanks to Paul du Quenoy, President and Publisher of Academica Press, who immediately saw the importance of what I was trying to achieve and has supported the entire process with enthusiasm, intelligence, and good humor. To Judy Miller, both for introducing me to Paul and for recognizing that it can sometimes be as important to see what is left out as what is put in. Larry Sabato made a key suggestion that set me on the right path. Margaret McKeown had some terrific insights and gave me a better subtitle than I had thought of myself. Farley Chase helped immensely in crystalizing my thoughts and improving the line of the narrative, then made a noble effort to find the right home for the book. My daughter Lee was, as always, totally fabulous. But my biggest thanks goes, once again, to Nancy, who is so wonderful that words fail me ... and words are supposed to be my business.

Prologue

Negative Space

"The most important thing in communication is hearing what isn't said."
– Peter Drucker

From May 25 to September 17, 1787, a federal convention met behind locked doors on the ground floor of the State House in Philadelphia with the aim of refashioning the increasingly unworkable Articles of Confederation. Congress had petitioned all thirteen states to send representatives to this meeting, and eventually fifty-five men from twelve states did take part, with only Rhode Island refusing to participate. While a few of the men who attended, most notably James Madison and Alexander Hamilton, saw the convention as an opportunity to scrap the Articles entirely and start from scratch, most assumed that the Philadelphia conclave would be just another in a string of feeble attempts at reform.

Attendance was spotty at best, and many of those who attended regularly, including George Washington and Benjamin Franklin, said little for the entire four months. A small percentage of delegates dominated the debates, and although thirty-nine of them eventually signed the Constitution of the United States, perhaps only a dozen could legitimately be called "framers."

The less zealous members did not realize the role history had staked out for them, since most expected to retain both the form of the existing government and the power and prerogatives of the individual states. In 1787, national identity was nascent—overwhelmingly, Americans' first loyalty was to the state in which they lived, not the United States as a whole.

A key misconception among many Americans is that the delegates came to Philadelphia to ensure "liberty," be it personal, political, or religious. Americans already had liberty under the Articles of Confederation—a good deal more liberty, in fact, than they would be granted under the new Constitution. Citizens of each state in the Articles' "compact of friendship" had almost total control over their own destiny. Every state had its own constitution, legal system, trade regulations, monetary system, voting and naturalization rules, and all the other trappings of an independent nation. They guarded these institutions jealously. Participation in the central government was just short of voluntary.

Under the Articles, the nation lacked an effective means of common defence, the ability to raise money, and the consistency of laws necessary to promote trade and commerce. In order to acquire these advtantages and create a functional nation, Americans needed to be willing to *sacrifice* individual liberty rather than gain it. The key question was how much and in what areas.

"For most Americans, indeed, national politics mattered little ... When Americans thought about politics at all, they directed their concerns toward local and state issues. These were the levels of governance whose decisions affected their daily lives."[1] Finding a way to give the central government more power without sacrificing state sovereignty did not promise to be a gratifying exercise, especially since any new plan would need to be ratified by the very states whose continued authority would come under threat.

In addition, reform, however necessary, meant navigating uncharted waters. Under the Articles, by which the fledgling United States had been governed since 1781, the government consisted of only one branch, the legislative, with only a single house of Congress. To get almost anything done, nine states' agreement was required, and any alteration or amendment to the Articles demanded unanimous assent. The United States had no executive branch and no national judiciary. If the government were to be strengthened, almost everyone agreed that both missing branches would be required. Deciding how to establish each of these new departments and what powers to give them, however, was a thornier matter.

With the executive, the chief stumbling block was lack of even a fundamental prototype for a head of state. No institution in place could serve as a model. A monarch was out of the question, of course, but how to construct an executive was a conundrum. Would the executive be one man or three? How long should he serve? Should he be eligible for re-election? How should he be elected? What powers should he exercise? What should be the limitations on those powers? All of these questions would be brought to the floor, discussed, voted on, then scrapped, only to have the process begin again. More than sixty separate votes were ultimately required to complete Article II of the Constitution.

A national judiciary faced a different set of obstacles. Although the need for some form of national *court* was apparent, most Americans opposed a national court *system*. Each state already had a functioning legal apparatus whose powers and responsibilities would necessarily be diminished as those of national courts were enhanced. The delegates, therefore, were reluctant to grant a national judiciary too broad a mandate. Moreover, as state courts were already seen by many as tools of the rich, the instrument by which creditors enforced their claims on debtors—often struggling farmers—creating a national court system to buttress judicial authority drew immense suspicion. In addition, ceding local or state control over the judiciary to a national court that might not contain a single member from one's own state would seem akin to many Americans to asking them to sit in judgment before foreigners.

Finding a workable structure for government was far from the only problem facing the delegates. There were vast disagreements on any number of critical issues, including but not limited to the future of slavery and the slave trade. How would the nation raise money? Could it afford or did it even want a standing army? Who should be able to vote and for what offices? How would citizenship be determined? Did the rights of citizens and even states need to be delineated?

Given the breadth and magnitude of the disagreements, to avoid creating a document so provocative that states would never agree to adopt it, the delegates chose to leave many key elements of governance vague and omitted some altogether. These were no inadvertent oversights but a conscious strategy, often the result of pragmatic compromises fashioned to render the finished product as inoffensive as possible to powerful interest groups whose demands could not be fully satisfied. In addition, to make the new plan more likely to succeed, the delegates required only nine states to ratify the document, rather than ask for the unanimity that the Articles required. Unclear was what would happen to the holdouts if only nine states agreed, especially if either Virginia or New York, where resistance was deep, refused to join the new Union.

The delegates were not unaware that any document they produced would be necessarily incomplete. The hope was that Congress, after it was defined and constituted, would fill in the gaps. While to some degree, this strategy was successful—the Constitution was both approved in Philadelphia and ultimately ratified by all thirteen states—abdication proved to have a serious price. Almost from the moment the United States Constitution was signed on September 17, 1787, debate raged as to what the document actually said. In recent years that debate has reached a crescendo, endangering the very survival of the system of government the Constitution was created to define.

As has often been the case in the past, each side of the current ideological divide is convinced that the other's misinterpretation of the text is the primary cause of the nation's ills. With both employing incendiary rhetoric, and neither willing to concede even a sliver of ideological or semantic turf, it has become almost impossible to effectively address the very real problems confronting the United States. It is ironic that a constitution drafted to ensure "a more perfect union" has instead begat dysfunction and disunion. That the political process has become ossified is in good part due not to what the Constitution says, but rather from what it fails to say.

Although flaws of omission had enormous impact on the nation's development and continue to be felt today, like Sherlock Holmes's dog who did nothing in the nighttime, they are elusive and often evade analysis. Nonetheless, overlooking the areas in which the Constitution failed adequately to provide either proper guidance, rules of procedure, or limitations on power will impede both understanding the document's true meaning and finding the means to correct the flaws.

These include:

– Failure to create adequate rules for legislative apportionment and the national census.

– Failure to create a national standard for voting rights or rules for elections.

– Failure to define citizenship, either in terms of eligibility or naturalization. (There is not even a mention of who would be a citizen after ratification).

– Failure to provide standards for the creation of Congressional districts.

– Failure to specify what role the Supreme Court would play in deciding whether laws passed by Congress and signed by the president comported to the Constitution.

– Failure to define a national court system or if, beyond the Supreme Court, one would even exist.

– Failure adequately to define how the Electoral College would work and to create specific standards on how state votes would be tallied, certified, and transmitted to Congress.

– Failure to define the nature of the national government's control over state militias, or whether those militias would be considered part of a national army or navy.

– Failure to specify limits or conditions on "necessary and proper" in Article I, Section 8, which seemed to create an open-ended power for Congress to do whatever it pleased. Since the 10th Amendment did not yet exist, this meant the federal government might have unfettered power over the states. Even with the 10th Amendment, the line between federal and state power remained vague.

– Failure to provide a workable means of amending the Constitution, one of many concessions to Southern planters, who feared the document would be altered to outlaw slavery.

Each of these failures has caused one or more crises, all of which have limited the effectiveness of government and worked at the expense of the principles espoused by those who drafted the Constitution and worked for its ratification. Not dealing with these issues when the Constitution was being written made the document and the system of government that it attempted to create more fragile, and that fragility has been exploited by those who would bypass constitutional guarantees and institute a government that is a democracy in name only, to the point where the very survival of the system of government it enshrined is uncertain.

A vast body of work examines both the Constitution and the process by which it was created. Some explore the political philosophies of the framers, as did Jack Rakove or Gordon Wood; focus on the creditor/debtor dichotomy, like Michael Klarman or Charles Beard; the role of natural law, as examined by Andrew Napolitano; the impact of slave economics, as I did in *Dark Bargain* in 2005; and even includes the magisterial clause by clause analysis done by Akhil Amar in *America's Constitution: A Biography*. Then there are the dozens and dozens of other books that would be strictly thought of as Constitutional Law. Each approach has value and is crucial to fully grasping why events played out as they did. But investigating what delegates chose to exclude also yields important, perhaps unique, insight, since understanding where the gaps are provides a practical starting point in creating a means to fill them.

What this book attempts to do, therefore, is not to replace the other studies but rather to provide an additional perspective, to expand the assumptive boundaries of Constitutional analysis.

Chapter 1

The States of the Union: The Lack of National Identity

"*We must, indeed, all hang together or, most assuredly, we shall all hang separately.*"
– Benjamin Franklin, at the signing of the Declaration of Independence (apocryphal)

"*It is the long history of humankind (and animal kind, too) that those who learned to collaborate and improvise most effectively have prevailed.*"
– Charles Darwin

It was an improbable war, a group of insurgent farmers and other irregulars led by a man whose chief claim to fame was a battle in which he had led his soldiers into disaster, matched against the finest and best-trained army in the world. To make matters worse, that first group, called the Continental Army, was drawn not from a dedicated, united population, willing to suffer innumerable hardships in pursuit of victory, but rather from thirteen different political entities that often disagreed with one another and with the army's commanding general. Worse yet, these thirteen entities, whose leaders had pledged to support the war with both soldiers and money, delivered on their promises only grudgingly and sporadically, if at all.

By early 1776, the year after the war began, it became clear that political changes were required if the thirteen American colonies were to have any chance of victory against Great Britain. They had already defied expectations. George Washington, who as a British officer, had presided over a humiliating defeat at Fort Necessity in the Pennsylvania backcountry that helped ignite the Seven Years War, had proved himself a deft and able commander and, although the American colonists could hardly be described as winning, they had not been routed, as the British leaders in London had fully expected.

But an army needs both men and materiel, and both were proving hard to come by. It was clear to the political leaders of the rebellion, who had formed a supervisory group called the Continental Congress, that a means of both providing for domestic oversight and gaining foreign assistance was vital. For that, some mechanism was needed to centralize authority and allow the thirteen colonies to speak with one voice to foreign powers who needed to be persuaded to back a war whose outcome was at best uncertain.

In 1775, Benjamin Franklin had presented Congress with a plan for confederation—"a firm League of Friendship"—but it had never been considered.[2] Silas Deane had followed with another proposal that had been similarly ignored, and a third effort, drawn up by the Connecticut congressional delegation, likely written by Roger Sherman, was shelved as well. But by June 1776, two indisputable facts had become clear. First, there would be no foreign assistance except to an independent nation, and second, if the colonies delayed in creating a stronger central government, the war would almost surely be lost.

On June 7, 1776, Richard Henry Lee, a congressional delegate from Virginia, submitted a resolution: "That these United Colonies are, and of right ought to be, free and independent States, that they are absolved from all allegiance to the British Crown, and that all political connection between them and the State of Great Britain is, and ought to be, totally dissolved. That it is expedient forthwith to take the most effectual measures for forming foreign Alliances. That a plan of confederation be prepared and transmitted to the respective Colonies for their consideration and approbation."[3]

Lee's resolution was accepted, and on June 11, 1776, the Congress appointed three concurrent committees in response. To draft a formal declaration of independence, Congress appointed a committee of five, which included Franklin, John Adams, Roger Sherman, New York's Robert Livingston, and Thomas Jefferson. Jefferson, considered the group's most adept and elegant writer, was asked to pen the actual draft.

Another committee of five, which also included Adams and Franklin, was appointed to create a plan to negotiate treaties, and a third committee, consisting of one delegate from each colony, was asked to draw up a plan for confederation. The actual draft was assigned not to Franklin or Adams, but rather to the committee's chairman, John Dickinson of Pennsylvania.

Dickinson, born in Delaware, was also an accomplished writer and had been dubbed the “Penman of the American Revolution” for his 1767 and 1768 essays, “Letters from a Farmer in Pennsylvania.” The twelve essays defended resistance to the Townshend Acts, which had placed import taxes on a number of items, including tea. “They were an astounding success. The Farmer was toasted and praised throughout the colonies.”[4] Dickinson later served as president of both Delaware and Pennsylvania.

Dickinson’s task was formidable. Not one of the thirteen colonies was willing to abandon its status as an independent political body, and squabbling over such issues as slavery, claims to western lands, freedom of commerce, and taxation showed no sign of being subordinated to the need for national union. Only the threat of a return to British rule, likely to become a good deal more draconian if the war were lost, prevented inevitable rejection of any plan Dickinson came up with.

Realizing that he needed to tread softly on state prerogatives, Dickinson created “Articles of Confederation and Perpetual Union,” which, borrowing Franklin’s hopeful phrase, he also described as a “firm league of friendship.” He called this new political body the “United States of America,” although how united they would be remained unclear, since Article III stated, “each Colony shall retain and enjoy as much of its present Laws, Rights and Customs, as it may think fit, and reserves to itself the sole and exclusive Regulation and Government of its internal police, in all matters that shall not interfere with the Articles of this Confederation.”[5]

Dickinson’s draft, presented to Congress on July 12, 1776, caused a good bit of consternation, which anticipated some of the issues that would roil the Constitutional Convention a decade later. Article XI declared, “all Charges of Wars and all other Expenses that shall be incurred for the common Defence, or general Welfare, and allowed by the United States in General Congress assembled, shall be defrayed out of a common Treasury, which shall be supplied by the several Colonies in Proportion to the number of Inhabitants of every Age, Sex and Quality, except for Indians not paying Taxes.” It also mandated a triennial census of “white inhabitants,” the result to be transmitted to Congress.[6]

Slave owners categorically rejected that wording. Not only had Dickinson insultingly not distinguished between whites and slaves, except in the census, but he had also suggested that states be assessed population-based taxes that included slaves, whom slave owners insisted were property, no different than cows or horses, as they would later describe them. The North, the South pointed out, could not have it both ways—if taxes were to be assessed by population, it should be whites only; if by property, the value of land and improvements should be the basis.

As a result of these and other contentious provisions, Dickinson's draft was not adopted. It would be the first of six submitted to Congress, and it would not be until November 1777, with Washington's army under increasing pressure and the nation desperate for an alliance with France, that the oft revised document was approved and sent to the states for ratification. In the final version the state sovereignty article was shorter but equally potent. Article II stated, "each state retains its sovereignty, freedom and independence, and every Power, Jurisdiction and right, which is not by this confederation expressly delegated to the United States, in Congress assembled."[7] As Jack Rakove points out, "the adoption of this...provision can be taken as evidence that the Articles were intended to create a confederation of sovereign states, individually free to accept or reject congressional measures as each saw fit."[8]

Slave states won the taxation battle as the final draft would assess taxes "in proportion to the value of all land within each state, granted to or surveyed for any Person, as such land and the buildings and improvements thereon shall be estimated, according to such mode as the united states, in congress assembled, shall, from time to time, direct and appoint."[9] While a census for a population based formula might yield an inexact result, an estimate of value without strict agreed-on standards would so subjective as to be meaningless. Even worse, Congress would not have the power to levy or collect those imposts. "The taxes for paying that proportion shall be laid and levied by the authority and direction of the legislatures of the several states within the time agreed upon by the united states in congress assembled."

Slave owners were also successful in forcing the inclusion of the nation's first fugitive slave clause. Article IV stated, "If any Person guilty of, or charged with, treason, felony, or other high misdemeanor in any state, shall flee from Justice, and be found in any of the united states, he shall upon demand of the Governor or executive power of the state from which he fled, be delivered up, and removed to the state having jurisdiction of his offence."[10]

But taxing and apportionment were only two of the disagreements that threatened to scuttle the plan. As Maryland's Samuel Chase wrote Philip Schuyler in early August, "when we shall be confederated States, I know not. I am afraid the Day is far distant, three great Difficulties occur—The Mode of Voting, whether by Colonies, or by an equal Representation; The Rule by which each Colony is to pay its Quota, and the Claim of several Colonies to extend to the South Sea, a considerable Diversity of opinion prevails on each Head."[11]

The third of these would prove the most contentious. States with claims to western lands, which included Massachusetts, Connecticut, North Carolina, New York, Georgia, and Virginia, were adamant about retaining as state property territory that had been granted them in a variety of often overlapping and sometimes questionable royal charters. States without such claims, especially New Jersey, Delaware, Rhode Island, Pennsylvania, and Maryland, demanded that western lands revert to the nation as a whole, if there was ever to be a nation as whole. Since most of the grants lent title to all land as far as the South Sea—the Pacific Ocean—landless states would eventually be reduced to insignificance.

Pennsylvania's James Wilson questioned the "extravagant" land claims. "The grants were upon Mistakes. They were ignorant of the Geography. They thought the S[outh] Sea within 100 miles of the Atlantic Ocean. It was not conceived they extended 3000 miles."[12]

The landed states countered that the landless states wanted federal control to ease the way for speculators to profiteer in the disputed areas, an accusation with some truth in it, although the landed states had no shortage of speculators of their own. In August, Connecticut's Roger Sherman offered a tentative compromise whereby "no Lands to be separated from any State, which are already settled, or become private Property," but it failed to break the logjam. Virginia's Benjamin Harrison retorted simply, "By its Charter, Virginia owns to the South Sea."[13]

The dispute was not resolved—the western lands were simply too valuable for either side to concede. Even without windfall profits, sale or lease of some of the territory would enable landed states to pay off their war debts. The landless states, therefore, were unwilling to bankrupt themselves in the effort to break away from Great Britain, all so that the landed states could amass riches after the war was concluded.

With neither side willing to budge, Article IX continued to give the landed states title through to the Pacific Ocean. "No breakthroughs on the major issues preceded the final (and hurried) deliberations of October 1777. The delegates simply realized that a confederation had to be completed even at the risk of leaving specific groups of states unhappy with the solutions that had to be imposed on the most difficult issues."[14]

Bypassing the most contentious issues simply transferred the disputes to the ratification process, as would be the case in 1787. But to put the Articles into place required unanimous consent, which would be slow in coming. All the while, Congress was descending into irrelevance, with attendance poor and little accomplished. "Of the thirteen delegates who composed the committee that prepared the Dickinson plan of 1776, for example, only two—Samuel Adams and Thomas McKean—were present for the final debates of 1777. As one Massachusetts delegate complained in July 1777, confederation had fallen a "martyr to the change in Delegation which takes place between the periods of second and third distant discussions upon the same point."[15]

Ratification went as slowly as nationalists had feared. Not until June 1778 did Congress have sufficient acceptance by the states—eight had ratified—to solicit the five holdouts. Landed Georgia and North Carolina ratified in July, but landless New Jersey, Delaware, and Maryland refused. Maryland, in particular, promised to be a difficult sell—its delegates proposed two amendments to alter the manner in which western lands could be claimed by individual states, both of which would protect Maryland speculators. Both were defeated.[16] New Jersey also objected to the clause in Article IX that "provides that no state shall be deprived of territory for the benefit of the United States," with which Maryland and Delaware heartily agreed.[17]

Although the landless states' objections were still not incorporated into the document, Delaware and New Jersey, facing both economic and military emergencies, ratified the Articles by early 1789. But Maryland continued to refuse. Since it could scuttle the entire plan, Maryland found itself in a strong bargaining position, although its demands had to be balanced against its needs.

Maryland played its cards well, but its delegation's phrasing contained a good bit of false altruism. "The back lands, if secured by the blood and treasure of all, ought in reason, justice, and policy to be considered a common stock, to be parceled out by the Congress into free, convenient, and independent Governments, as the wisdom of that body, shall hereafter direct."[18] They did not feel the need to mention that they intended to exclude from this "common stock" land granted to or surveyed by speculators before the war began.

With the outcome of the war uncertain and the need for concerted action paramount, on October 10, 1780, an increasingly desperate Continental Congress resolved that unsettled land in the west be "formed into distinct republican States, which shall become members of the federal union, and have the same rights of sovereignty, freedom, and independence as the other States."[19] Almost immediately, New York, Connecticut, and, most importantly, Virginia rescinded their claims to western lands, although Virginia attempted to exact a bit of revenge by including a clause that nullified any claims made by Maryland speculators.

At first, Virginia seemed to have miscalculated, for that clause caused Maryland to continue to balk and hold ratification hostage. Only after Benedict Arnold, now fighting for the British, provided additional incentive by threatening an attack on Chesapeake Bay, did Maryland "rise above their principles" and agree to ratify the Articles. And so, on March 1, 1781, "while Greene was leading Cornwallis on his fatal chase across North Carolina," the United States of America was officially born.[20]

By the time they were approved, the Articles, none too strong to begin with, had been rendered into a remarkably weak governing document. The new national government lacked both an executive and a judiciary, voting was by state, with nine assents required to pass laws that could not be enforced, and unanimous consent was needed to alter the document in any way.

Granting each state equal influence rankled many large state delegates, including Benjamin Franklin, who groused, "Let the smaller Colonies give equal Money and Men, and then have an equal Vote. But if they have an equal Vote, without bearing equal Burdens, a Confederation upon such iniquitous Principles, will never last long."[21] There would, however, be no compromise, although the same question would be debated heatedly in Philadelphia in 1787.

Although one of the main goals in creating the Articles was to finance the war better, with Congress given no power to collect the taxes it had apportioned, states could ignore the requisitions, which they regularly did. This was by design. "A government possessed of coercive taxing authority could, for example, finance a standing army to oppress the people in their liberties."[22]

Without the power to demand payment, only about one-quarter of the funds requested from the states made it to the Treasury. Even when states did pay, the national currency used to facilitate either payment to the troops or purchase of goods from foreign nations was virtually worthless, while states remained free to coin currency of their own. Nor was there an effective means to regulate foreign and interstate commerce, although disputes between states about rules for trade and tariffs were common. Each state could even have its own military.

Although disputes between individual states would continue unabated, with nine states required to pass even mundane legislation, sectionalism became an additional impediment to nation building.

The United States, such as it stood, was divided into three distinct economic groups, with competing priorities. The North held the centers of shipping and commerce, the Upper South had a tobacco-based economy, and Lower South cultivated rice and indigo.[23]

Although the latter two economies were slave-based, their interests had diverged. In the Lower South—Georgia and South Carolina—although the staple crop, rice, was immensely profitable, it was grown in fetid, leech and snake infested swamps. Slaves had to work thigh-deep in standing water all summer long, with mosquitoes, disease, humidity, and exhaustion constant companions. Slave mortality was extremely high with many slaves surviving only two or three years. South Carolina therefore needed a constant influx of able-bodied male slaves to overcome the attrition, and by far the cheapest place to get them was Africa. The rice planters then, were not only committed to slavery as an institution but also to a continuation of the slave trade.

Virginia and the Upper South grew tobacco, which was cultivated in open country under what by comparison were bucolic conditions. As a result, slaves bred rather than died, and that eventually resulted in a crippling oversupply to tobacco growers. As the convention began, the most reliable population estimate had slaves in Virginia outnumbering whites. One of the downsides of the slave system, the tobacco planters discovered, was that they could not fire their workers—they were stuck with them from birth to death and had to feed and clothe them and provide basic medical care, even if the slaves were too young or too old to work.

In addition, since property equaled wealth and slaves were property, planters were more than a little reluctant to part with them, unless of course it was for a price. The best place to get a good price was South Carolina, where supply needed constant replenishment. But as long as the cheaper Africa option was available, Virginia was stuck, and so, while the Upper South remained committed to slavery, the planters were anxious to end the slave trade.

The North built, financed, and shipped. They brought rice and tobacco to Europe and returned with all the fineries that the Southern planters needed to support their lifestyle (to say nothing of side trips to the west coast of Africa for return cargo of a different sort.) So long as Northerners could ensure the free flow of commerce, their wealth would increase. Northerners were outspoken—at least in public—about their revulsion of slavery and especially the slave trade, but to a significant extent, their financial well-being was built around the opportunities created by the plantation system to the south. This left the Upper South, especially Virginia, in a precarious bargaining position.

Another key sectional issue was fought both state-by-state and within states themselves. As the nation expanded westward, access to the Mississippi and the port of New Orleans became vital to settlers west of the Appalachians as a route to both ship what they produced and receive the goods that were too cumbersome to carry overland. New Orleans and the Mississippi were controlled by Spain, which grew increasingly uneasy about the burgeoning number of settlers staking out claims near the Mississippi's eastern shore. The Spanish threatened to close both the river and the port to American commerce unless the United States granted them clear title to the river.

At the same time, Spanish merchants were all too happy to access the new American market through Atlantic ports, and American shippers, particularly in the Northeast coveted trade with Spanish New World colonies, which had been forbidden under British rule. To the Northerners, therefore, access to the Mississippi meant little. In theory, the Articles would allow the United States, as a single entity, to negotiate a commercial treaty with Spain, but this power would turn out to have a significant downside. In addition, the Articles did not prohibit individual states from cutting their own trade deals with foreign nations, which undermined the authority of a congress that had little of it to start with.

While sectional crises simmered and European nations saw a weak United States, vulnerable to pressure, the new Confederation Congress continued to prove itself unequal to the problems that the Articles had been meant to address. Washington's army was being held together almost exclusively by the force of his personality. Soldiers had not been paid, and replacement troops requested of the states rarely materialized. Food for many troops had become so scarce that starvation was often a genuine possibility.

Congress was helpless to address the crisis because it could neither enforce conscription nor compel states to pay their requisite taxes or deliver provisions that Congress demanded. Instead, Congress authorized the printing of paper money, which soon became little more than scrap paper and therefore did little to soothe the anger of unpaid troops.[24] Washington was furious. As he would write later, "Requisitions are a perfect nullity where thirteen sovereign, independent, disunited states are in the habit of discussing and refusing compliance with them at their option."[25] Already a strong nationalist, Washington became committed to creating a more powerful central government, even at the expense of the autonomy of his native Virginia.

With the recognition that Congress, under the Articles, was not all that much of an improvement over Congress before the Articles, attendance began to flag. Even after the great victory at Yorktown in October 1781, Congress was often an afterthought. And so it remained, even when presented with a treaty to mark the nation's victory. "In November 1783, American diplomats sent Congress the final version of the Treaty of Paris, which formally ended America's war with Great Britain. A quorum of nine states had to be present for Congress to ratify the treaty, yet throughout December scarcely that number was present. Weeks passed, the treaty sat, and Congress remained unable to act upon it. Some desperate congressmen went so far as to contemplate holding Congress in the sickroom of an ailing delegate, to add him to their numbers."[26]

When American leaders lost interest in a toothless national government, Europe saw the opportunity to pounce. Despite a provision in the Treaty of Paris that called for the withdrawal of all British troops, they maintained six forts in New York and the Northwest and did not withdraw their forces from New York City for months. When the last redcoat departed, Washington triumphantly rode in, and New York was declared the nation's capital. Washington would be inaugurated there as the nation's first president in 1789. (The following year, the nation's capital would move to Philadelphia.)

While British forts were a potential threat, the closing of the Mississippi became an immediate one. To prevent United States expansion and maintain its dominance in the region, Spain had "encouraged American immigration in the hope of drawing in settlers in small groups that could then be integrated into the Spanish system." That policy proved a mistake when English-speaking settlers virtually took over the important river ports, among them Natchez and New Madrid. As a result, in 1784, "Count Floridablanca, the foreign minister, decided to close the Mississippi to all but Spanish ships, to issue a formal statement in regard to Spain's position in North America, and to send Don Diego Gardoqui to America to negotiate a treaty."[27] Gardoqui had one task—persuade, cajole, or threaten the United States into giving up its claims to the Mississippi. To sweeten the deal, Gardoqui was authorized to make trade concessions in return, sure to appeal to at least part of the United States.

Facing off against Gardoqui would be America's Secretary for Foreign Affairs, John Jay, described as a "brilliant and almost pathologically honest New York aristocrat, a dedicated nationalist and also a pompous and pathetically vain man."[28] Jay had previously traveled to Spain in 1779, hoping to persuade the Spaniards to officially recognize American independence and perhaps agree to a treaty of alliance. He was also seeking financial aid. The mission got off to a rocky start when Jay became violently seasick and "suffered exceedingly at least five weeks," unable to even attend to his correspondence.[29]

Matters did not improve on land. Although Jay spent more than a year in Spain, his mission, "difficult and fruitless," was largely a failure. Spain refused to recognize the United States as an independent nation and would not conclude a treaty or commercial agreement. In November 1780, he wrote to Congress that Americans would "always be deceived if we believe that any nation in the world has or will have any disinterested regard for us" and that the nation should "endeavor to be as independent on the charity of our friends as on the mercy of our enemies."[30] Preventing the journey from being a total disaster, Jay did succeed in obtaining a loan of $170,000.

In this new negotiation, Jay was instructed not to give up claims to the

Mississippi, regardless of any incentives offered by Spain. Personally, of course, Jay identified with the Northeast and would have been more than willing to grant the Spanish title to the river in exchange for broader commercial concessions, a point of view with which the Spaniards were likely familiar.

Gardoqui, with whom Jay had met with often in 1780, arrived in North America in 1785. He was as charming and urbane as Jay was intense and humorless. A deft diplomat and skillful negotiator, Gardoqui, aware of with whom he was dealing, first set out to charm Jay's wife, Sarah, ten years his junior, with whom Jay was smitten and called "my Sally." Sally Jay, according to Gardoqui, "likes to be catered to and even more to receive presents." He added, "A skillful hand which knows how to take advantage off of favorable opportunities, and how to give dinners, and above all to entertain with good wine, may profit without appearing to pursue them."[31] And so, the Spanish aristocrat proceeded to escort Mrs. Jay to affair after affair, bestowing compliments and foisting gifts on both husband and wife. When time allowed, he and Jay (whom he had referred to as a "very self-centered man") negotiated for rights to the most important trading route in North America.

After a good deal of wrangling, Jay, as Gardoqui had anticipated, agreed to cede all claims to the Mississippi for thirty years in return for gaining access to Spanish ports in Europe and the New World, most importantly Havana. For all Gardoqui's ministrations, Jay had negotiated a deal that was not at all bad for the United States, or to be precise, for a particular part of the United States—the Atlantic states. American claims to the Mississippi had been questionable at best, so Jay may well have only given up territory that the nation had no right to in the first place. Trade through Havana, on the other hand, would be a windfall for New England shippers. For the South, and particularly settlers in the Southwest, however, the proposed treaty appeared to be a sellout.

Since Jay had been sent into the negotiations with specific instructions from Congress not to surrender use of the Mississippi, he was forced to request permission to change his authorization. He pushed hard for his treaty. "It appears to me," he said in a speech to Congress in August 1785, "that a proper commercial treaty with Spain would be of more importance to the United States than any they have formed or can form with any other nation." Jay continued, "At a time when other nations are showing us no extraordinary marks of respect, the court of Spain is even courting our friendship by strong marks, not only of polite and friendly attention, but by favors not common for her to hold out or bestow; for I consider the terms she proposes as far more advantageous than to be found in her commercial treaties with other nations."[32]

Jay also noted what might happen if the treaty were rejected. "The Mississippi would continue shut; France would tell us our claim to it was ill-founded; the Spanish posts on its banks, and even those out of Florida in our country would be strengthened, and nation would there bid us defiance with impunity, at least until the American nation shall become more really and truly a nation than it at present is."[33]

Jay's warning had little impact on Southerners, although the issue had jogged delegates out of their lethargy and when the vote to change Jay's authorization was called, twelve of the thirteen states were present. All five Southern states voted no, which rendered the seven Northern states' aye votes moot.[34] Even James Madison, generally one of staunchest nationalists, committed to bridging sectional divides, sided with the southern states on this issue. "The use of the Mississippi," he wrote, "is given by nature to our western country and no power on earth can take it from them."[35]

Sentiment among settlers in the southwest was even more extreme. Some threatened to secede, others to march on Congress, still others to align with Spain, or perhaps England, or perhaps to seize New Orleans for themselves. Regardless of the advantages that might accrue to the nation as a whole, sectionalism won out and the Jay-Gardoqui treaty was never adopted. Eventually Spain bowed to the inevitable and opened the Mississippi and New Orleans to American shipping on payment of a duty, but the distrust engendered between North and South could not be so easily bought off.

The Mississippi was not the only territorial dispute. An ineffectual Congress encouraged bickering over borders. After the war formally ended, Virginia and Maryland resumed their feud. Maryland, still smarting over the abuse it had received over its refusal to ratify the Articles, struck the first blow. According to the charter granted in 1632 by King Charles I to Cecil Calvert, 2nd Lord Baltimore, the new colony of Maryland extended up Chesapeake Bay to the mouth of the Potomac, then westward, following the river "from shore to shore." In other words, the boundary between Maryland and Virginia was not in the middle of the Potomac, but on the bank of the Virginia side. Maryland, therefore, claimed to own the entire river.

In 1688, however, a grant by James II to Thomas Colepeper, 2nd Baron Colepeper, pronounced the boundary of the new colony of Virginia as the "Potomac River," without specifying in what part of the river the boundary would be drawn. In 1776, Virginia appeared to acknowledge Maryland's claim. "In her republican constitution [Virginia] settled the longstanding territorial controversy between herself and Maryland by acknowledging the latter's claims through her charter, but she reserved the free navigation and use of the rivers Potomac and Pocomoke."[36] In addition, Virginia held what seemed clear title to Chesapeake Bay.

The agreement soon broke down and, in 1784, after years of wrangling, Maryland threatened to close the Potomac to Virginia. Virginia responded by threatening to close Chesapeake Bay to Maryland. If both states carried through, commerce through Chesapeake Bay and up the Potomac would cease, a terrible blow since that was precisely the moment when the Spanish had virtually closed off the Mississippi. Faced with such a cataclysm, both states agreed to resolve the dispute through negotiations.

But there was a question of whether they could legally formalize an agreement. The Articles clearly stated, "No two or more states shall enter into any treaty, confederation, or alliance whatever between them, without the consent of the united states, in congress assembled, specifying accurately the purposes for which the same is to be entered into, and how long it shall continue." But since "congress assembled" was an ephemeral notion and the Articles were being taken none too seriously, Maryland and Virginia decided to ignore the prohibition and negotiate a private agreement.

A meeting was arranged for March 1785 in Alexandria, Virginia, then the primary port for traffic up the Potomac, in which Virginia's representatives, Alexander Henderson and George Mason, met with Maryland's Samuel Chase, Daniel of St. Thomas Jenifer, and Thomas Stone. James Madison, who had little respect for the Articles as a governing document, was also appointed to the Virginia delegation, as was Edmund Randolph, but the state's governor, Patrick Henry, failed to inform them of the date of the meeting. Madison's and Randolph's absence was made up for. "George Washington (though not a commissioner), dropped in on the conference by accident (or design) and invited the members to adjourn to Mount Vernon."[37]

Because of the enormous problems a weak central government had caused him as commanding general, Washington had emerged as the nation's most prominent nationalist. In December 1784, he had written to Virginia Governor Harrison, "The disinclination of the individual States to yield competent powers to Congress for the Federal Government, their unreasonable jealousy of that body and of one another, and the disposition which seems to pervade each, of being all-wise and all-powerful with in itself, will, if there is not a change in the system, be our downfall as a nation. This is as clear to me as A. B. C."[38]

In addition, Washington had long viewed the Potomac, not the Mississippi, as the best route to open the West. Although many states would eventually benefit from navigation along the Potomac, Virginia, in particular, would garner an immense revenue boon. Washington, an inveterate speculator, intended to personally profit from whatever monies were generated by the commercial traffic. Not coincidentally, he also owned 32,000 undeveloped acres on or near the Ohio River. Because he would have a financial interest in the meeting's outcome, Washington did not actively participate in the negotiations.

Although no treaty was finalized, the two states agreed to manage the Chesapeake-Potomac waterway through a joint entity they called the Patowmack Company, in which each state would buy a block of stock and leave the rest to private investors. On March 28, they signed what was called the "Mount Vernon Compact," in which each state vowed to respect the navigation rights of the other while establishing each state's jurisdiction and creating formulas for tariffs and currency exchange. "Compact" was employed as a euphemism to get around the treaty prohibition in the Articles. The capital the company raised would be used clear a channel upriver and dig canals to avoid the Potomac's treacherous waterfalls and other sections of the river that would be difficult or impossible to navigate.[39] Washington immediately put in a bid to purchase shares. The compact was ratified by both states' legislatures, with an added stipulation introduced by Maryland, "That currencies should be regulated; that duties and imposts should be the same in both states; that commissioners should be annually appointed to regulate commerce; that Delaware and Pennsylvania should be notified and requested to join with Virginia and Maryland."[40]Only after the agreement had been consummated did Virginia and Maryland seek official approval from Congress.

It turned out that the compact was also an attractive notion to Delaware and Pennsylvania. In November 1785, Maryland invited those two states, and any others that might be interested, to attend a meeting in Annapolis to determine if the agreement might be expanded.

Madison, who had been trying for some time to convince the Virginia assembly to press Congress into expanding its control over interstate commerce and trade with foreign nations, had a more ambitious plan. He proclaimed the success of the Mount Vernon conference as a demonstration of the benefits of cooperation, until then in quite short supply, which he insisted would increase trade and profits for all.

Washington was also touting the success of the conference. In a December 1785 letter to Richard Henry Lee, then president of Congress, Washington, with what was described as "unwonted enthusiasm," wrote, "The Assemblies of Virginia and Maryland have now under consideration the extension of the inland navigation of the Rivers Potowmac and James and opening a communication between them and the western waters. They seem fully impressed with the political as well as the commercial advantages, which would result from the accomplishment of these great objects; and I hope will embrace the present moment to put them in a train for execution."[41]

The following month, at Madison's urging, the Virginia assembly passed a resolution that he had first introduced the previous October, inviting the other twelve states to send delegations to special meeting in Annapolis in September 1786 to discuss revising both interstate and foreign commercial regulations. He timed his attempt well. Not only had Washington made it plain that the nation must adapt to current conditions, but the Jay-Gardoqui fiasco had just concluded, leaving a sour taste in everyone's mouth.

Madison was not deluding himself and saw the meeting as at best a good start to remedying the "vices" of the Articles. "The efforts for bringing about a correction thro' the medium of Congress have miscarried. Let a Convention then be tried. If it succeeds in the first instance [commerce] it can be repeated as the defects force themselves on the public attention, and as the public mind becomes prepared for further remedies."[42]

But nor was Madison leaving anything to chance. As he would do the following year in Philadelphia, he arrived in Annapolis a week early, took rooms at Mann's Inn, where the conference would meet, and sketched out a plan for getting the states to bypass Congress and come to agreement independently. But his plotting was for naught. Instead of the national conference he had hoped for, only eleven men from four other states, New York, New Jersey, Pennsylvania, and Delaware, showed up. Maryland, the host, did not even choose to appoint commissioners. Four of the states that had named a delegation failed to make an appearance. But among those who did attend were Hamilton, Dickinson, and Randolph, a powerful core group of nationalists. He had already twice called for a constitutional convention, in 1780 and 1782, and, as did Madison, was seeking a vehicle to bring that goal to fruition.[43] Increasing the possibility of success was the giant shadow of Washington, which fell over the proceedings.

Those proceedings were not extensive. With so skimpy a turnout, the convention lasted but three days. Hamilton, not known for hiding his feelings, was assigned to write a report on what had been achieved, which of course was nothing. It did not promise to be favorable. In 1782, with acid dripping from his quill, he had written, "There is something noble and magnificent in the perspective of a great Federal Republic, closely linked in the pursuit of a common interest, tranquil and prosperous at home, respectable abroad; but there is something proportionably diminutive and contemptible in the prospect of a number of petty states, with the appearance only of union, jarring, jealous and perverse, without any determined direction, fluctuating and unhappy at home, weak and insignificant by their dissentions, in the eyes of other nations."[44] His draft here was equally scathing, so much so that Madison and Dickinson persuaded him to soften the tone. But the main thrust was not the opportunity that had been lost, but the one that had been created.

In his revised report to the attending states, which was signed by all twelve participants and submitted by Dickinson to Congress, Hamilton noted, "Your Commissioners submit an opinion, that the Idea of extending the powers of their Deputies, to other objects, than those of Commerce, which has been adopted by the State of New Jersey, was an improvement on the original plan, and will deserve to be incorporated into that of a future Convention."[45] New Jersey had, indeed, suggested in its charter to their deputies that the Annapolis convention not confine itself to purely commercial issues, but rather seek to remedy other of Articles' shortcomings.

That was all the opening Hamilton, Dickinson, and Madison needed. Hamilton added:

> That there are important defects in the system of the Federal Government is acknowledged by the Acts of all those States, which have concurred in the present Meeting; That the defects, upon a closer examination, may be found greater and more numerous, than even these acts imply, is at least so far probable, from the embarrassments which characterise the present State of our national affairs—foreign and domestic, as may reasonably be supposed to merit a deliberate and candid discussion, in some mode, which will unite the Sentiments and Councils of all the States. In the choice of the mode your Commissioners are of opinion, that a Convention of Deputies from the different States, for the special and sole purpose of entering into this investigation, and digesting a plan for supplying such defects as may be discovered to exist, will be entitled to a preference from consideration, which will occur, without being particularised.

Leaving nothing to chance, the report suggested the proposed federal convention meet "at Philadelphia on the second Monday in May next, to take into consideration the situation of the United States, to devise such further provisions as shall appear to them necessary to render the constitution of the Federal Government adequate to the exigencies of the Union."

And so, a call for a federal convention to revise the Articles had been officially made.

Of course, calling for a convention was no guarantee one would be held. Sentiment to make serious changes in the manner of governance was lukewarm at best. "Sectional rifts in Congress over commercial policy and navigation of the Mississippi had exposed fault lines along which the Union might divide … while the idea that the Union might devolve into regional confederacies still seemed incredible, events since 1783 had called into question the very idea of a national interest."[46] And so, the nationalists were going to need help, a spur to convince reluctant sectionalists and state supremacists that their prosperity, perhaps even their survival, depended on forfeiting some of their authority to attain the strength that a more powerful union would provide. They would get it late in 1786 from a ragtag band of farmers, debtors, and ne'er-do-wells in western Massachusetts, one of whom was an army veteran named Shays.

Chapter 2

The Road to Philadelphia: One Revolution Was Enough

"If three years ago any person had told me that at this day, I should see such a formidable rebellion against the laws & constitutions of our own making as now appears I should have thought him a bedlamite—a fit subject for a madhouse."

– George Washington on Shays's Rebellion.

"There is no clear or meaningful difference between insurgency and civil war, or between national terrorism and civil war for that matter."

– Anthony Cordesman, former Director of Intelligence Assessment for the Secretary of Defence.

Americans who anticipated the end of the Revolution as the beginning of untold prosperity were quickly disillusioned. "The United States endured a serious depression in the wake of the Revolutionary War—described by many historians as the worst economic climate suffered by the nation until the Great Depression of the 1930s."[47] A good deal of fertile land had been rendered unusable to farmers, British markets had been closed off, British shippers were prohibited from buying American-built ships, the war debt was immense, and the gold and silver required to pay off most individual debt in extremely short supply. As a result, the gross national product plummeted while foreclosures, especially for unpaid army veterans, and sentences to debtors' prison skyrocketed.

As in every financial crisis, however, hardship was not distributed equally. Massive tax increases imposed to restore state treasuries fell heaviest on yeomen farmers and others not in the merchant class. The nation soon divided into creditors and debtors, neither of which had anything good to say about the other, especially when creditors resisted debtors' calls to issue paper money to ease repayment. Paper money would, of course, depreciate the value of the underlying currency, but would allow many indebted farmers to maintain title to their land.

To the debtors, opponents of paper money were "'flint-hearted misers' who were 'lying in wait to buy our lands [at auction] for less than a quarter of their real value.'" Creditors saw debtors as having brought their misfortune on themselves through indolence, sloth, and the willingness to live "upon the sweat of their neighbors' brows." Richard Henry Lee, for example, asserted that private debt "almost universally arises from idleness and extravagance," and the remedy was "industry and economy," not debtor relief.[48]

As a result, as became true in a number of former colonies, Massachusetts had devolved into two de facto states. On the Atlantic Coast lay Boston and the prosperous, cosmopolitan, mercantile East, where shippers such as John Hancock and James Bowdoin grew wealthier by the day. Inland, away from the ports, was the agrarian West, where gruff, laconic, debt-ridden farmers were regularly hauled into court to be deprived of their land or sent to prison. "As farm prices slowly declined and the wages of farm laborers shrank to a low of 40 cents a day by 1787, farm mortgages were foreclosed in rapidly increasing numbers and debtors were imprisoned or even sold into servitude."[49] It was easy for the farmers to see where to direct their anger. "In Hampshire County from July 1784 to December 1786, [merchants] sent to jail, for an average two-month term, seventy-three men with relatively small debts."[50]

The Bostonians had little sympathy for their plight. They thought the westerners uneducated louts, unworthy to have a voice in state governance. By a happy coincidence—at least for them—the westerners had next to no voice in it. The westerners, on the other hand, looked on Boston as a den of iniquity, populated by rich, overfed merchants whose high living was made possible by extortionate taxes, state fees, and repossessed property of patriotic farmers and army veterans. The westerners were incensed at exorbitant court costs and legal fees, which made it almost impossible for anyone who was not rich to protect their rights effectively. "Widespread insolvency and uncertainty during the postwar recession from1783 to 1785, propelled creditors to the courts in droves. High court fees meant that litigation to collect subjected debtors to obligations vastly increased over their original debts."[51]

Most galling, however, were the property seizures. "Living in a community-oriented society, [farmers] were indignant at the plight of friends and relatives. 'To see a collector distrain upon one of their neighbors and carry off his hog or his colt for the payment of taxes, this startles them exceedingly,' wrote one commentator."[52]

The westerners demanded relief through the issuance of paper money, a route chosen, albeit reluctantly, by seven other states. A previous attempt to introduce paper, in May 1785, had been defeated in the Massachusetts legislature by a 93-23 vote, and subsequent efforts had met similar fates.[53] Governor Bowdoin refused this time as well.[54] He had no intention of adopting a monetary system that would effectively write down debts by as much as ninety percent.

In mid-1786, the westerners' frustrations boiled over. "Impatient with the failure of their legislators to enact relief measures, men all over the state, and particularly in Hampshire County, began to talk sedition. Gathering in the rural taverns, they aired their grievances and demand whether this was the liberty and justice for which they had fought and which had been guaranteed to them the Declaration of Independence."[55]

That June, an ad hoc group of angry farmers, many of them veterans, marched to Taunton and, using a prerevolutionary tactic, blocked the local court, demanding that the judges, clerks, tax collectors, and lawyers leave and go home. As some of the farmers were armed and seemed willing to put their weapons to use, the court personnel agreed and left the building. Similar protests at other courts followed and by midsummer had spread through western Massachusetts. The farmers then convened county conventions at which petitions demanding a redress of grievances were drafted and forwarded to Boston.

The protestors began to organize. Calling themselves "Regulators," angry farmers and veterans took up arms and began drilling in the countryside.[56] On August 29, more than 1,500 protestors marched on the Court of Common Pleas in Northampton and threatened the judges and clerks with unnamed consequences if they convened. The docket contained a number of cases that would have resulted in property forfeiture or prison for local farmers and the protestors made it clear that they would allow neither. The court personnel agreed to suspend proceedings. One week later, three hundred Regulators descended on the Worchester courthouse, and soon afterward Regulator groups shut down courts from Concord, just outside Boston, all the way west to Great Barrington.

The success of these disruptive operations seemed to demonstrate a vulnerability of creditor class, and the creditors' fear became palpable. In a September edition of the *Hampshire Gazette*, one essayist lamented, "A collection of restless people, stimulated by wicked agents and unjustifiable motives, have made a desperate onset upon us and upon the commonwealth at large, in forcibly interrupting the courts of justice and in a neighboring county by the additional violence of opening the public jail and discharging the prisoners … It is a duty then which we owe to ourselves forthwith to delay the efforts of violence and stop the fury of insurrections and teach our eager and misjudging brethren that smaller or doubtful evils are not to be remedied by indecent clamors and hostile attacks on the government."[57]

Calls to cease the insurrections had the opposite effect. The emboldened Regulators decided to escalate the pressure on Boston to reform not only the judicial system, but the totality of state government. They renewed their call that the state issue paper money, and the longer they waited, the more they grew prepared fight to achieve change.

As the insurgents became more militant, their compatriots in other New England states watched with interest. Although at first the protest groups in the other states did not take the sort of drastic action as in western Massachusetts, the Regulators' continuing success spurred some to more aggressive action. On September 20, 1786, "200 militants surrounded the state house in New Hampshire and held the governor and the assembly prisoners for over five hours."[58] Armed militants in Connecticut planned to attack the court in New Haven in October, and courts were attacked in Vermont.

In Massachusetts, the rebels continued to step up the pressure on state government, albeit under a different name. One of the Regulators was a forty-year-old former captain in the Continental Army named Daniel Shays. Although he had a distinguished war record, including service at Lexington, Bunker Hill, and Saratoga, he had never been one of the leaders of the movement, if indeed it had genuine leaders, but for reasons never made clear, the groups began to refer to themselves as the "Shays Men."[59] In September, just after the New Hampshire siege, the Shays Men occupied the state supreme court building for three days and forced the court to adjourn.

In Boston, Governor Bowdoin viewed the incipient uprising with growing alarm. He had taken no action at first, certain the demonstrations would peter out on their own when the weather turned colder. When that did not occur, Bowdoin and his fellow merchants, creditors all, decided to bankroll an army as a precaution against outright revolution. As a carrot to the stick, Bowdoin offered amnesty to any rebel who laid down his arms and returned to his farm, many of which remained in danger of foreclosure, a prospect Bowdoin did nothing to mitigate. Not surprisingly, this gesture was not embraced by the farmers.

Bowdoin also asked Congress to, if not supply, at least bankroll an army of four thousand men, but "every state except Virginia rejected the $530,000 requisition and effectively undermined the federal troop plan."[60]

Forced to raise the army and foot the bill themselves, Bowdoin and his fellow creditors approached Massachusetts-born former general Benjamin Lincoln. Lincoln had also been the first United States Secretary of War, though his tenure had lasted only two years. Despite these impressive credentials, Lincoln's war record was uneven—his most notable achievement was allowing his entire army to be captured in South Carolina after an unsuccessful attempt to break the siege of Charleston. Since leaving government, he had turned his attention to land speculation in Maine, then still part of Massachusetts, and was therefore eager to put down a growing insurrection that could threaten his investments. Writing to Washington, Lincoln dismissed the protesting farmers as "indolent and improvident … diverted from their usual industry and economy" seduced by a "luxuriant mode of living," an astounding sentiment from a man whose soldiers had been drawn from this very stock and had volunteered to fight and then not been paid.[61]

Lincoln proved to be just the man the merchants needed. Bowdoin's initial efforts to raise money had been only marginally successful, but Lincoln helped get things moving. He "went immediately to a club of the first characters in Boston, who met that night and … suggested to them the importance of becoming loaners of a part of their property if they wished to secure the remainder."[62] The plea, describe as "very persuasive," garnered more than £6,000 pounds in a week and by the end of January, "129 of the leading coastal merchants had loaned enough money for operations to begin."[63]

Almost all Lincoln's troops were recruited from the Atlantic coast and included a number of the merchants themselves, as well as their sons. The plan was to march to Worcester, in the center of the state, open the courts there, and then continue west until the state was cleared of rebels. That plan changed when the Shays Men, hearing of a well-equipped army on its way to engage them, decided to supplement their meager armaments by raiding a federal arsenal in Springfield before Lincoln could cut them off. But the arsenal was not unguarded. When the raiders approached and refused to disperse, a militia brigade leader, General William Shepard, "ordered Major Stephens, who commanded the Artillery, to fire upon them. He accordingly did. The first two shots, he endeavoured to overshoot them, in hopes they would have taken warning without firing among them, but it had no effect on them. Major Stephens then directed his shot through the center of the column."[64] After two or three volleys, the invaders turned and ran, leaving four dead and twenty wounded behind them. "Had I been disposed to destroy them," Shepard added, he could have pursued with his infantry "and killed the greater part of [Shays's] whole army within twenty-five minutes."

Although Shepard chose to let the Shays Men flee, Lincoln's force was already in pursuit. He ran the rebels down in Petersham, dealt them a near fatal blow, then completed a mop-up operation in Sheffield at the end of February. Some of the rebels were jailed, a few hanged, and rest disarmed and sent home. Shays himself fled to Vermont, which, not yet in the Union, was technically a foreign country.[65]

All in all, Shays's "rebellion" had not amounted to much. The Regulators had been easily routed, order had been restored, and the authority of government reaffirmed, all with no more than temporary disruption. Nothing about this aborted uprising should have instilled fear in government officials. That it did was thanks in good part to Henry Knox.

Knox was perhaps the Revolution's unlikeliest hero. With no formal military training, Knox, a bookseller, was appointed Washington's artillery commander when he was only twenty-five years old. He proved expert in both tactics and logistics, with an instinctive feel for not only how to effectively deploy cannons in battle, but also how to move artillery pieces long distances in minimal time. Knox had been Lincoln's successor as Secretary of War, a position he would also hold during Washington's first term.

In late 1786, Knox heard rumors that the British were planning to incite a counterrevolution and that Tories in western Massachusetts had recruited and armed perhaps 15,000 disaffected farmers and war veterans to seize the arsenal at Springfield and march on Boston. The British were said to be planning to foment an uprising by local Native American tribes as well. Knox, without bothering to confirm the details, wrote a letter to Washington in October 1786, in which he took a dim view of farmers. "Men at a distance … are apt to accuse the rulers and say that taxes have been assessed too high and collected too rigidly. This is a deception equal to any that has been hitherto entertained. It is indeed a farce, that high taxes are the ostensible cause of the commotions, but that they are the real cause is as far remote from truth as light from darkness. The people who are the insurgents have never paid any, or but very little taxes."[66]

Knox went on to present what were at best half-truths, appending some embellishment in case Washington needed additional persuasion. "The numbers of these people may amount in [M]assachusetts to about one fifth part of several populous counties, and to them may be collected, people of similar sentiments, from the States of Rhode Island, Connecticut and New Hampshire so as to constitute a body of 12 or 15,000 desperate and unprincipled men," he wrote, multiplying the eventual number of Regulators by ten.

Knox portrayed the rebels as having what would later have been called radical a socialist agenda. "They see the weakness of government and they feel at once their poverty, compared to the opulent, and their own force, and they are determined to make use of the latter to remedy the former. Their creed is that the property of the U.S. has been protected from the confiscations of Britain by the joint exertions of all, and therefore should be the common property of all."

Knox's letter added anxiety to an already jittery creditor class, which included almost all the delegates to Congress, where the idea of 15,000 determined anarchists mounting an armed revolt that required military force to suppress was terrifying. If it could happen in Massachusetts, it could happen elsewhere—and, to a lesser degree, from Pennsylvania to South Carolina, it was happening elsewhere. The rebels were largely portrayed as Knox had described—seeking to seize the property of others rather than merely wishing to protect their own.

Southerners had the additional fear that one day it might be slaves that would mount an insurrection, or even slaves and poor farmers banding together. Of course, a careful inquiry into the actual events might have dispelled some of the concern, but panic does not usually generate rational thought.

What did seem clear was that states going it alone would increase their risk. A stronger central government capable of marshalling the forces necessary to keep public order—and protect private property—suddenly had increased allure. As one Virginian wrote, "The period seems fast approaching when the people of these United States must determine to establish a permanent capable government or submit to the horrors of anarchy and licentiousness."[67] Before permanent, capable government could be established, however, every state in the Union, including Massachusetts, would be forced to implement some form of debt relief. Thus, the potential that a Shays-type uprising could occur anywhere, in any state, and threaten anyone's property, made the proposed national convention much more difficult to ignore.

Still, necessity does not always correlate with desire, and while the call for a national convention became a more serious consideration for many, it did not mean that they were willing to alter the basic state-based power structure. In fact, before the Shays Men evoked a healthy dose of overwrought fear in the creditor and ruling classes, there had been little appetite for an exercise that many thought a waste of time and others considered a dangerous experiment that would result in decreased authority for state governments.

Even Washington debated for weeks whether to attend a meeting whose aims might be totally and publicly frustrated. According to Madison, who, later in life, penned what was to be a preface to the publication of his convention notes, asserted, "in the interval between the … Comrs. at Annapolis … and the meeting of Deps. at Phila," public sentiment had "continued to develop more & more the necessity & the extent of a Systematic provision for the preservation and Govt. of the Union; among the ripening incidents was the Insurrection of Shays in Massts. against her Govt; which was with difficulty suppressed, notwithstanding the influence on the insurgents of an apprehended interposition of the Fedl. troops."[68] At the end of March 1787, Washington, with some reluctance, committed to Madison that he would attend as well. Once that occurred, every state but Rhode Island agreed to send a delegation to Philadelphia.

Madison had also harbored misgivings, but once the convention had become a reality, he seized the opportunity. Although fully aware that every state delegation would protect its interests before ceding authority to a central government, he gambled that the risk of doing nothing would outweigh parochial considerations and, with proper groundwork, his vision of an actual United States just might be achieved. There were many, mostly landowners and creditors, who feared the nation was on the verge of civil war and Madison, although not an alarmist himself, intended to provide the antidote.

As he had done at the Annapolis conference, Madison arrived in Philadelphia early, on May 6, and set to work. He needed the time because he intended to provoke a much more radical alteration of government than most of the delegates either suspected or would approve of. Madison recognized, as did most of the nationalists, including Washington, that there could be no strengthening of the central government without a weakening of the states. That in turn implied that the central government must have coercive power; to be able issue demands to the states, not merely requests. Since the states had heretofore felt comfortable in ignoring any dictum from Congress with which they disagreed, there was every reason to believe they would resist agreeing to a central government against which they had no recourse. As it was, Rhode Island had refused to send a delegation and New Hampshire, whose treasury was bare, was not expected to.[69]

The Virginia and Pennsylvania delegates were the only ones to arrive before the convention was due to begin. Madison met constantly with both groups to hammer out a plan. He was fortunate that the Pennsylvania delegation, led by Gouverneur Morris, Benjamin Franklin, James Wilson, and Robert Morris, had an especially nationalist bent, and were willing participants in Madison's cabal.

The Pennsylvanians were a potent group. Morris, born into a patrician slave owning family in New York with vast land holdings, was considered one the Convention's loftiest intellects but was often irascible and intolerant of disagreement. He was also an elegant wordsmith and would later be asked to write the final version of the Constitution in which he coined the phrase "We the people of the United States." (The draft going in was "We the people of," followed by a listing of each state. The change turned out to be anything but academic as it grounded legitimacy in the "people" rather than the states.) Wilson was one the nation's most able legal scholars, and Robert Morris, although a good deal more controversial than erudite, was a brilliant, if not always totally upstanding, financier.

By the time the convention convened, almost two weeks late for lack of a quorum, Madison had drawn up a prototype that became known as the Virginia Plan, since only Virginia delegates had put their names to it. But few were fooled. This was Madison start to finish, and even though the document was officially introduced by Virginia's governor, Edmund Randolph—why Madison was so shy is unclear—it would be Madison who would be its prime sponsor over the ensuing four months.

He was not coy about the role he intended to play:

> In pursuance of the task I had assumed, I chose a seat in front of the presiding member with the other members, on my right & left hand. In this favorable position for hearing all that passed, I noted in terms legible & in abbreviations & marks intelligible to myself what was read from the Chair or spoken by the members; and losing not a moment unnecessarily between the adjournment & reassembling of the Convention I was enabled to write out my daily notes during the session or within a few finishing days after its close in the extent and form preserved in my own hand on my files.[70]

When the Convention finally got under way, the Virginia Plan was presented to the delegates. After listing what the plan was meant to accomplish and offering a disingenuous assurance that the "Articles of Confederation [were merely] to be … corrected and enlarged," Madison's offering contained fifteen points, in which the Articles were scrapped.[71]

Madison knew full well that most states would only agree if they perceived sufficient checks on government power. He sought to provide those with a bicameral legislature, one house elected by the "people," although by that Madison meant the wealthy and landholding, and the other appointed by members of the first branch from lists submitted by state legislatures. Many details were left murky, especially how many representatives each state would be granted in the two houses and what standards—the number of white inhabitants or "quotas of contribution"—would be employed for apportionment. Regardless of how the formula was arrived at, Madison seemed to hope that it provided cover for his elevation of the national government.

He was vague on the range of authority the legislature would be granted. All the powers granted Congress under the Articles would remain, but its power would be expanded to include "all cases to which the separate states were incompetent, or in which the harmony of the United States may be interrupted by the exercise of individual legislation." To ensure that the states could not simply implement laws that ran counter to this aim, Congress would have the power to veto state laws at its discretion, a provision certain evoke strong opposition. If a state refused to back down, Congress could "call for the power of the Union," although what power that was remained undefined.

Madison would also create both an executive and judiciary. The powers of the executive were also left extremely vague, that "besides a general authority to execute the national laws, it ought to enjoy the Executive rights vested in Congress by the Confederation." The judiciary was to "consist of one or more supreme tribunals, and of inferior tribunals to be chosen by the National Legislature," with judges serving during "good behaviour," which was not defined, and whose jurisdiction was restricted to "all piracies and felonies on the high seas, captures from an enemy; cases in which foreigners or citizens of other states applying to such jurisdictions may be interested, or which respect the collection of the national revenue; impeachments of any National officers, and questions which may involve the national peace and harmony." The plan also provided for the admission of new states and amendments.

The Virginia Plan was a roll of the dice. Madison was gambling that the need in every state to strengthen the central government would overcome the provincialism and mistrust that had characterized state relations since the nation's founding. Washington, in a letter to Thomas Jefferson shortly after the convention began, framed the dimensions of the problem. "That something is necessary, none will deny; for the situation of the general government, if it can be called a government, is shaken to its foundations, and liable to be overturned by every blast. In a word, it is at an end; and unless a remedy is soon applied, anarchy and confusion will inevitably ensue."[72]

But that remedy would not be easy to come by. Different states and different regions had different needs, and so they would want different powers for the central government and different controls on that power. While the entire South would demand protection for the slave system, South Carolina and Georgia wanted to continue the slave trade while Virginia wanted to end it. The North would not accept any plan that threatened their commercial and shipping interests. Smaller states would veto any proposal that left them at the mercy of larger states, and larger states would likely refuse to abdicate dominance in the new government. While under the Articles, small states could indeed reject any law that they found oppressive, Congress was so toothless that it mattered little. With a stronger central government, the upshot might be different.

For Madison, the task was to convince all parties that they would be better off by giving up some freedom, liberty, and influence than if they stubbornly refused to compromise, which Madison would categorize as petty self-interest. One thing in his favor was that most state delegations included some strong nationalists and many others who would become so if they did not have to give up fundamental rights in the process.

But regardless of where opposition arose—and there were early protests from a number of prestigious delegates, including Connecticut's Oliver Ellsworth, South Carolina's Charles Cotesworth Pinckney, New Jersey's William Paterson, and Elbridge Gerry of Massachusetts that neither the convention itself nor Madison's submission were legitimate—and what conciliation would be necessary, by submitting the Virginia Plan as the convention opened, Madison had succeeded in setting the agenda. Unless anti-nationalist delegates walked out *en masse*, debate would be on the specifics of a strong national government rather than on its mere existence.

Chapter 3

The Early Rounds: Probing for Weakness

"Power without a nation's confidence is nothing."
– Catherine the Great.

"If you don't know where you are going, you'll end up someplace else."
– Yogi Berra.

Ultimately, any meeting such as the Constitutional Convention, be it in government, business, or even a family powwow, is about power—who will get more of it and who will get less. At the Convention, that the states would lose power at the expense of the national government was a given, although by how much would be in great dispute and a threat to the success of the venture. As Forrest McDonald put it, "One absolutely central issue—perhaps the absolutely central issue—was the role, if any, that the states would play in the reorganized and strengthened common authority."[73] But other fault lines existed as well: region to region; state to state; creditor to debtor, although debtors were underrepresented; even person to person. Each of those conflicts would demand compromises, sometimes overlapping, and ensure shifting alliances during the course of the proceedings.

The division of power depended largely on the outcome of two debates—how strong would be the national government and who would get the largest say. Those who emerged on the winning side of the second question would likely be in favor of a more robust federal government, while the losers would attempt to insert as many checks on government authority as they could push through. For each side was the additional question of whether the structure of the new government would allow it to maintain the power it was granted initially or if it would erode as the country grew, handing the reins to their opponents.

Control of the new national legislature was generally assumed to be the key to victory and therefore where the most ferocious battles would be fought. If the delegates failed to come to an agreement on its size, powers, and apportionment, the entire structure would collapse. In addition, unlike the executive or a national judiciary, every delegate in Philadelphia had experience with a state legislature and thus a point of view on how the new Congress should be structured. The carefully thought-out Virginia Plan might have been the only set of specifics available as the Convention came to order, but it was still only one vision of how the nation should be governed. There would be others.

Madison recognized that his plan would be greeted with skepticism and that he would need to entice delegates to his point of view rather than attempt to bully them. When Randolph, ordinarily self-assured and immodest, introduced the Virginia Plan on May 29—what Madison termed "the main business"—his uncharacteristic humility was indicative of how controversial his remarks would be. Randolph "expressed his regret that it should fall to him, rather those who were of longer standing in life and political experience, to open the great subject of their mission. But as the convention had originated from Virginia and his colleagues supposed that some proposition was expected from them, they had imposed the task on him."[74]

Before laying the plan itself before the convention, Randolph spent a good bit of time expounding on the defects of the present system.[75] He took great care to do so without condemnation and emphasized, as his first resolution expressed, that his intention was merely to "correct and enlarge" the Articles, while intending no such thing. He "concluded with an exhortation not to suffer the present opportunity of establishing peace, harmony, happiness, and liberty in the U. S. to pass away unimproved."[76]

James McHenry, a nationalist delegate from Maryland, wrote that Randolph, attempting to rally support from delegates who feared populist rule, lamented that, "None of the [state] constitutions have provided sufficient checks against the democracy … that the powers of government exercised by the people swallow up the other branches."[77] Only a strong central government, he implied, could protect the property and wealth of the landed gentry and mercantilists from the clawing hands of the rabble. Randolph, a patrician from one of Virginia's first families and a descendent of Pocahontas, exhorted the Convention to save the United

States from "democracy" because, he correctly believed, such a sentiment would strike a sympathetic chord.

Other key delegates soon voiced reluctance to entrust government to ordinary citizens. Elbridge Gerry of Massachusetts grumbled, "The evils we experience flow from the excess of democracy," and Connecticut's Roger Sherman insisted, "The people immediately should have as little to do as may be about the Government."[78] In subsequent sessions, a number of nationalist delegates, such as Gouverneur Morris, would endeavor to severely limit the degree of democracy in theoretically democratic institutions. These were among the first indications that "the people" might not be well served by whatever product emerged from the convention.

Despite Randolph's pandering, not everyone found his presentation persuasive. Robert Yates, an anti-nationalist from New York, commenting on what he termed Randolph's "long and elaborate speech," noted that the Virginian did not mean a "federal" government, but rather "a strong consolidated union, in which the idea of states should be nearly annihilated."[79] As if to prove Yates's point, the following day, Randolph made a motion, seconded by Gouverneur Morris, that "a union of the States, merely federal, will not accomplish the objects proposed by the articles of confederation, namely 'common defence, security of liberty, and general welfare.'"[80] The motion was tabled but the first dividing lines were drawn.

The question of whether state governments would be abolished was not an idle one and would be hinted at more than once by some of the delegates. A more pressing issue, however, was whether, if states continued to exist, would they be subordinate to the central government or retain the virtual autonomy they then enjoyed. Gouverneur Morris repeated Yates's contention that a "federal" government was "a mere compact resting on the good faith of the parties," whereas a "national, supreme government [had] a compleat and *compulsive* operation." But he went in the opposite direction from the New Yorker and "contended that in all communities there must be one supreme power, and one only."[81]

(Given this distinction, that the nationalists would be later be called "Federalists," and federalists would become known as "Antifederalists" might be seen as something of an irony. Maryland's Antifederalist attorney general Luther Martin, however, saw it as something else. During the convention, he wrote later, "It was resolved 'that a national government ought to be formed.' Afterwards the word '*national*' was struck out by them, because they thought the *word* might tend to *alarm;* and although, *now*, they who *advocate* the system pretend to call themselves *fœderalists*, in convention the distinction was quite the reverse; those who *opposed* the system were *there* considered and styled the *federal party*, those who advocated it, the *antifederal*.")[82]

Smaller states, such as New Jersey, had thrived under the Articles, at least politically, in that, with voting by state, they had power equal to the larger states, including Madison's Virginia. If the Virginia Plan were adopted, that advantage would disappear. Although Madison had proposed two houses in the legislature, with the first apportioned by population and second chosen by the first, small states would have no real protection against their interests being trampled. While the delegates soon agreed that the new government would contain an executive and a judiciary in addition to a legislature, how the legislature would be defined remained an open question.[83]

With a by-state legislature unacceptable to large states, Madison argued that "an equitable ratio of representation ought to be substituted." Some of the strongest nationalists, included Morris, James Wilson, and George Mason also insisted that a proportionally constituted lower house was a must.[84] By a 6-2 vote, with two states divided, the Convention agreed. Given the anti-democratic sentiments of many of the delegates, however, that did not necessarily mean ordinary citizens would choose who served in it.

The delegates could not settle on any of the particulars of the second house, including the number of members or if it would be chosen by the first house or by state legislatures. (No one suggested the people directly.) Rather than continue to debate the Virginia Plan proposal, this question was also tabled by the delegates. "The clause was disagreed to and a chasm left in this part of the plan," Madison noted unhappily.[85]

Although the delegates had tentatively agreed that "the people" would elect members of the first house, which some still referred to as the House of Commons, just who those "people" might be and who would figure in apportionment remained vague. The key question for any population-based plan of apportionment was whether slaves, who had no legal standing as human beings, would figure in the formula.

As the convention began, the nation's population was approximately

3.75 million, of whom more than 700,000 were slaves, the vast majority in the South. If these slaves were included in the total, the population of slave and free states would be near equal; without them, free states would have a huge advantage. Slave states, therefore, wanted slaves counted for apportionment and free states did not, which put each in an odd position. To achieve their goal, Southerners, who had always insisted that Blacks were property, now had to assert they were people. Northerners, who had denounced the enslavement of human beings, were in the morally challenging position of insisting that they were property.

Madison, whoafter all represented the largest slave state, sought to prevent apportionment from being based only on the number of "free inhabitants," choosing instead to reiterate his more opaque standard of "quotas of contribution," which would likely mean the total slave population would be included. Northerners, led by Rufus King, a Massachusetts merchant and defender of equal rights, knew precisely what Madison was driving at and pointed out that there was no way to accurately determine what those "quotas" were and, however they were computed, that they would be in constant flux. Madison grudgingly agreed that "some better rule ought to be found."[86]

Hamilton then reintroduced "free inhabitants" as the standard, but that was deemed unacceptable as well and, on a motion from Virginians Mason and Randolph, the matter was tabled.

With a basis for apportionment on hold, on June 6, debate renewed on whether the people or state legislatures should elect the members of the lower house. The point was raised by members of the South Carolina delegation, one of the other states, which, like Massachusetts, was acutely divided by class. There as well, the gentry lived along the coast, while small yeoman farmers dominated the state's backcountry. South Carolina's four delegates were all aristocrats, coastal planters who had been educated in England, and they feared the backcountry riffraff as much as Massachusetts' merchant class had feared its own small farmers.

Charles Pinckney, considered by some, especially himself, a young genius, moved that the lower house be chosen by state legislatures, which engendered an extended philosophical discussion on the fundaments of government, to which Madison, Dickinson, Sherman, and James Wilson, some of the best minds present, all contributed.[87] Only Connecticut's Sherman spoke in favor of the motion and, in the end, the South

Carolinians were unsuccessful, with only Connecticut and New Jersey voting aye.[88] In both of those states, their delegations were holding out for voting in Congress to be by-state, as in the Articles, and so, having the state legislature choose members of the national legislature seemed obvious.

To this point, even after days of discussion, no formula for assigning the seats in the Senate had proved acceptable. Although it had been suggested that the second branch be chosen by members of the first branch, the general sentiment was that "the second branch of the national legislature be elected by individual [state] legislatures." A motion to that effect had been passed unanimously on June 7, one for the few occasions where there were no dissenting votes.

In addition to determining how much power each state would be granted in each house, another area of dispute was how large congressional districts would be, or even if there would be districts rather than allowing a state to have its entire delegation elected at-large. Underlying this issue was the need most delegates felt to limit the influence of all but the wealthy and well educated in the new government. Few delegates favored allowing non-property holders to have a say, but they also wanted to prevent small farmers, such as those who joined Shays's Rebellion, from having more than a miniscule role, just enough to allow them the illusion that were participating in the new government without giving them the means to impact it.

There was general agreement that the larger the districts—and the fewer the representatives—the less influence ordinary citizens would wield. A smaller number would leave fewer openings for populist rabble rousers, and larger districts would make it more expensive and more time consuming for would-be legislators to effectively campaign. As James Wilson noted, "There is no danger of improper elections if made by large districts. Bad elections proceed from the smallness of the districts which give an opportunity of bad men to intrigue themselves into office."[89]

Wilson was referring to state legislatures, which tended to have smaller districts and larger assemblies. Many of the delegates saw these state bodies as contributing to the unrest that had occurred in Massachusetts and elsewhere. The Virginia General Assembly, for example, had one delegate for every 5,000 whites. Even if the state's 250,000 slaves were included, the number would increase only to one per

8,000. In the Pennsylvania Assembly, the ratio was also one per 5,000. Many of the delegates favored congressional districts a good deal larger, as would become the case when numbers were discussed.

In those first weeks, delegates debated what for many were deal-making or deal-breaking issues, like apportionment, with remarkable civility. There was no invective, little sarcasm, and no one threatened to walk out. Those who had foreseen encounters marked by intransigence and antipathy seemed to have proven wrong.

The reason was simple. The delegates had quickly become aware that nothing would be decided immediately and so they felt free to engage in the sort of theoretical discourse that prompted one historian to declare it "one of the most brilliant displays of learning in political theory ever shown in a deliberative assembly."[90] In other words, with the Virginia Plan as the only basis, debate was almost entirely devoted to where power *should* reside. When the debates turned from philosophy to pragmatism—where power *would* reside—the tone changed markedly.

The bonhomie began to fray on June 11, when Roger Sherman once more brought up the thorny issue of apportionment.

Until that point, the delegates had tried to avoid practicalities, where consensus would be difficult to achieve, and instead tried to build a base from which the convention could move forward as one. But when Sherman opened the meeting proposing "that the proportion of suffrage in the 1st branch should be according to the respective numbers of free inhabitants; and that in the second branch or Senate, each state should have one vote and no more," the veneer of tentative agreement began to peel away. In addition to attacking the notion of the "slave bonus" in proportional representation head on, Sherman had also brought into question how the Senate would be populated. Staking out the "small state" position, Sherman added, "as the States would retain individual rights, each State ought to be able to protect itself; otherwise, a few large States will rule the rest."[91] Thus "state sovereignty," as Robert Yates wrote in his notes, was now integral to the establishment of a new national legislature. It would soon become more so.

South Carolina's John Rutledge, the Convention's second largest slaveholder—he would have been first except for his losses during the war—immediately struck back. He "proposed that the proportion of suffrage in the 1st branch should be according to the quotas of contribution. The justice of this rule he said could not be contested," although contested it would be. Fellow South Carolinian Pierce Butler, who also owned hundreds of slaves, agreed. He "urged the same idea: adding that money was power; and that the States ought to have weight in the Govt. in proportion to their wealth." Rufus King and James Wilson attempted to diffuse the coming argument by retreating to generalities, moving "that the right of suffrage in the first branch of the national Legislature ought not to be according the rule established in the articles of Confederation, but according to some equitable ratio of representation."

Wilson further diffused the grumbling by taking the floor to read into the record an extremely long, rambling monograph penned by Benjamin Franklin, who was too frail to give long speeches. After Wilson's reading, the exhausted delegates happily voted to suspend discussion on apportionment.

But Rutledge would not let the subject go. He renewed his motion to add "according to quotas of contribution," to the representation clause. Wilson, seconded by Charles Pinckney, moved to postpone Rutledge's motion to instead, "add, after, after the words 'equitable ratio of representation' the words following 'in proportion to the whole number of white & other free Citizens & inhabitants of every age sex & condition including those bound to servitude for a term of years and *three fifths of all other persons not comprehended in the foregoing description*, except Indians not paying taxes, in each State,' this being the rule in the Act of Congress agreed to by eleven States, for apportioning quotas of revenue on the States and requiring a census only every 5-7, or 10 years."[92]

James Wilson, another Northerner who personally abhorred slavery, had thus introduced the most notorious fraction in American history into the constitutional debates. Wilson seems to have chosen that number because, as he pointed out, it had been the formula for apportioning taxes adopted by Congress in 1783, but perhaps he had also discussed the matter privately with Rutledge, who was staying at his home. Whatever the reason, three-fifths had never been applied to legislative apportionment since voting had been by state. Although Elbridge Gerry once again "thought property not the rule of representation. Why then shd. the Blacks, who were property in the South, be in the rule of representation more than the cattle & horses of the North?" His objection was brushed aside, and the Convention voted 9-2 to adopt three-fifths as the South's slave bonus.

New Jersey and Delaware, who objected to any rule except state-equality, were the only dissenters.[93]

On Friday, June 15, New Jersey's William Paterson, to defend state sovereignty, presented a plan of his own. Paterson's objections had been simmering for weeks, and the New Jersey Plan was the definitive announcement that Madison's vision was to be subject to severe scrutiny and necessitate compromise if the meeting were to end with a tangible product.

The New Jersey Plan vested ultimate power in the states rather the national legislature. The unicameral Confederation Congress would be maintained, with each state retaining a single vote, and its members appointed by state legislatures or popularly elected as each state saw fit. The executive would be appointed by Congress, rather than elected, and the judiciary, consisting of only a supreme court, would be appointed by the executive. Congress's power would be expanded with the power of "raising a revenue, by levying a duty or duties on all goods or merchandizes of foreign growth or manufacture, imported into any part of the U. States," as well as "to pass Acts for the regulation of trade & commerce as well with foreign nations as with each other." Lawsuits contesting these powers would continue to be heard in state court, unless appealed to the Supreme Court as a "dernier resort."[94]

Paterson would also allow Congress to "be authorized to make such requisitions [for taxes] in proportion to the whole number of white & other free citizens & inhabitants of every age sex and condition including those bound to servitude for a term of years & three fifths of all other persons not comprehended in the foregoing description, except Indians not paying taxes." And so, a second Northerner who opposed slavery accepted that a Black person was worth only three-fifths of someone white. Congress would also have the right to compel payment with a sufficient number of votes, although the number was left blank.

The New Jersey plan was debated for the next three sessions. It had no chance of adoption, but nor could it be summarily dismissed. The anti-nationalists might lack the power to push their own plan through, but they were quite powerful enough to scuttle Madison's. One of them, John Lansing of New York, opened the Saturday, June 16, session by asking that the first resolution of each plan be read, "which he considered as involving principles directly in contrast." Paterson "sustains the sovereignty of the respective States," while Randolph "destroys it." Lansing added, "He was sure that ... his State. N. York would never have concurred in sending deputies to the convention, if she had supposed the deliberations were to turn on a consolidation of the States, and a National Government."[95]

Lansing did not mince words. After attacking Virginia for end-running both the mandate from Congress and the desire of most Americans merely to reform the current system of government, he added, "It is in vain to adopt a mode of government, which we have reason to believe the people gave us no power to recommend—as they will consider themselves on this ground authorized to reject it ... If we form a government, let us do it on principles which are likely to meet the approbation of the states. Great changes can only be gradually introduced. The states will never sacrifice their essential rights to a national government. New plans, annihilating the rights of the states (unless upon evident necessity) can never be approved."[96]

When Lansing was done, Paterson himself took the floor, observing, "As I had the honor of proposing a new system of government for the union, it will be expected that I should explain its principles." He noted the agreement for unanimity in the Articles that Madison and the nationalists were attempting to annul, and reminded the nationalists, "although it is now asserted that the larger states reluctantly agreed to that part of the confederation which secures an equal suffrage to each, yet let it be remembered that the smaller states were the last who approved the Confederation. On this ground, representation must be drawn from the states to maintain their independency, and not from the people composing those states."

If Paterson's view held, the Convention would be able to do no more than revise the Articles, which the nationalists saw as a disastrous outcome, since this Convention seemed to be the only opportunity they would get to scrap a fatally flawed formula for one far more workable. James Wilson then responded with a thorough, point-by-point comparison of the two plans. He also attacked Paterson personally. "It is said and insisted on, that the Jersey plan accords with our powers. As for himself, he considers his powers to extend to everything or nothing; and therefore, that he has a right and is at liberty to agree to either plan or none. The people expect relief from their present embarrassed situation and look up for it to this national convention; and it follows that they expect a national government, and therefore the plan from Virginia has the preference to the other." Pinckney added that he "supposes that if New-Jersey was indulged with one vote out of 13, she would have no objection to a national government."

Randolph concluded the day's business with an equally harsh attack on Paterson and his plan. "As the state assemblies are constantly encroaching on the powers of congress, the Jersey plan would rather encourage such encroachments than be a check to it; and from the nature of the institution, congress would ever be governed by cabal and intrigue."

What is most noteworthy in the June 16 debates is the change in tone. For the first time, there had been genuine acrimony as the nationalists and anti-nationalists staked out what seemed to be incompatible positions on the most essential question the Convention would need to resolve. It had certainly become clear to Madison and his supporters that states' rights would require deeper concessions than they had anticipated; and to Lansing, Paterson, and the anti-nationalists that to retain small states' power in government would require returning to a confederation that had proved itself untenable.

When negotiations reach such a stalemate, resolution is only possible when each side abandons fringe issues and focuses on the core, where compromise must be fashioned. The Convention did not meet on Sunday, so the delegates had a respite after the bruising Saturday debate. Still, there was likely a good bit of private intrigue. In addition to slave-owner John Rutledge being a guest at abolitionist James Wilson's home, many of the other delegates had clumped together in various rooming houses in the city. Madison stayed at Mary House's Boarding House, as did Edmund Randolph. George Mason stayed at the nearby Indian Queen, which was also owned by Mary House. Washington had planned to stay there as well but became financier Robert Morris's houseguest instead. Hamilton, Gouverneur Morris, and Elbridge Gerry stayed at Mrs. Dailey's, one of the best accommodations in the city and, with those three outsized egos in residence, likely one of the sprightliest. Connecticut's Roger Sherman and Oliver Ellsworth stayed at Mrs. Marshall's, a bit out of the way but, in true Yankee spirit, far less costly. In addition, the City Tavern had become an unofficial after-hours meeting place and for the entirety of the convention hosted any number of strategy sessions between like-minded conspirators.

Although most of the delegates arrived for Monday's session prepared to renew the battle over apportionment, they would all be surprised when Alexander Hamilton asked for the floor to present his own views. Hamilton, ordinarily arrogant, opinionated, and intolerant of disagreement, had been uncharacteristically silent during the proceedings. He made up for it here. He would speak for six hours.

While Hamilton clearly had many problems with the Virginia Plan, the presentation of the New Jersey Plan seemed to push him over the edge. Not only did he summarily reject both, but he took aim at democracy as well. His plan was so radical that there can be little doubt many of his fellow delegates were aghast. After noting, as recorded in Yates's notes, that his "own ideas are so materially dissimilar to the plans now before the committee," Hamilton, combining humility and arrogance, continued, "My situation is disagreeable, but it would be criminal not to come forward on a question of such magnitude. I have well considered the subject and am convinced that no amendment of the confederation can answer the purpose of a good government, so long as state sovereignties do, in any shape, exist." Madison's notes have Hamilton "fully convinced, that no amendment to the confederation, leaving the states in possession of their sovereignty could possibly answer the purpose."[97]

While others had hinted about abolishing the states as political entities, no one had suggested it seriously. Here, however, was a genuine proposal from one of the nation's leading political thinkers, a man who was also Washington's favorite. But Hamilton was not nearly done. In his bicameral legislature, his lower house, the Assembly, would be manned by representatives elected by "the people"—although he meant very few of the people—for three-year terms. In the upper house, "Let one branch of the Legislature hold their places for life or at least during good-behaviour … their election to be made by electors chosen for that purpose by the people."[98] Yates also remembered Hamilton proposing, "Let one body of the legislature be constituted during good behaviour or life."

Hamilton was no fan of popular sovereignty. Under his plan, as he would subsequently make clear, voting would be extremely restrictive, limited to citizens he considered among the elite. "In order to do this the States to be divided into election districts. On the death, removal or resignation of any Senator his place to be filled out of the district from which he came."

Hamilton's legislature had the power to pass all laws with a powerful executive to enforce them. "The supreme Executive authority of the United States to be vested in a Governour to be elected to serve during good behaviour—the election to be made by Electors chosen by the people in the Election Districts aforesaid." Like the executive, judges would also be chosen by electors and serve during good behavior.

The remainder of the plan, like these main points, made clear that not only would the national government be all powerful but, as long as they behaved themselves, everyone but members of the lower house could potentially serve without the periodic approval of the people. To justify this rather extreme position, Hamilton cited the government of the recently defeated Great Britain. "The English model was the only good one on this subject. The Hereditary interest of the King was so interwoven with that of the Nation, and his personal emoluments so great, that he was placed above the danger of being corrupted from abroad." There was vast disagreement on how the executive department should be defined, but no one else favored a warmed-over monarchy.

At the conclusion of Hamilton's marathon, the delegates gratefully adjourned for the day. William Samuel Johnson, Hamilton's friend and admirer, later observed, "A gentleman from New York, with boldness and decision, proposed a system totally different from both [other plans]; and though he has been praised by everybody, he has been supported by none."[99]

Although Hamilton was a divisive figure, he was usually too powerful an intellect to be ignored. But here he presented a plan so radical, such a departure from what any other delegate had in mind, that the Virginia Plan appeared moderate by comparison and may well have prompted some reconsideration among his fellow delegates. As Jack Rakove noted, "If there was one evening on which a historian would have liked to eavesdrop on the delegates' conversation, it was that of June 18."[100]

Whatever discussions had taken place the night before, the following day, the delegates gave Hamilton little consideration. Even nationalist James Wilson was dismissive, noting "that by a Natl. Govt. he did not mean one that would swallow up the State Govts. as seemed to be wished by some gentlemen. He was tenacious of the idea of preserving the latter. He thought, contrary to the opinion of (Col. Hamilton) that they might not only subsist but subsist on friendly terms with the former." Finding no support at all, Hamilton was forced walk back his previous remarks, claiming, "He had not been understood yesterday. By an abolition of the States, he meant that no boundary could be drawn between the National & State Legislatures; that the former must therefore have indefinite authority." In Yates's notes, Hamilton added, "Even with corporate rights the states will be dangerous to the national government, and ought to be extinguished, new modified, or reduced to a smaller scale."[101]

But Hamilton's participation in drawing up a plan for the government was at an end. Little more than a week later, he would leave the Convention, writing to Washington en route from New Jersey that he would return to Philadelphia only if it would not be a "mere waste of time."[102] Except for one brief visit, he kept his word and did not return until September, so that New York would have at least one signatory on the new constitution.[103]

Although there is some miniscule possibility that Hamilton, who would be a lion in working for ratification, had intentionally presented his ice water proposal to propel the more reasonable nationalists and anti-nationalists to compromise, more likely is that he achieved that result by accident. But when the delegates returned the next day, practicalities had replaced fancy. "Hamilton's plan forever tarred him in the view of some as a monarchist, but it had the effect of moving the Virginia Plan to the center of the spectrum."[104]

In fact, the next day, the delegates voted to make the Virginia Plan alone the basis for discussion, dismissing the New Jersey plan and ignoring Hamilton's. That did not mean that Paterson's demands had been abandoned, but anti-nationalists would now be forced to push for alterations to the Virginia Plan rather than fighting for their own. The alteration they would want most was by-state representative in the second house.

For the next week, the delegates debated peripheral issues, unwilling to take on the overriding question of who would control the government. By June 30, with Hamilton gone, the convention seemed doomed. The two main divisions over apportionment, population based or by-state and whether slaves would be counted in whole or in part remained unresolved.

Although both sides had dug in, Madison realized that the two divisions were actually only one. Georgia, a sparsely populated backwoods wilderness, consistently voted with the large state bloc, principally with its fellow slave states, while New York voted with small states. “The States,” he wrote, “were divided into different interests not by their difference of size, but by other circumstances; the most material of which resulted partly from climate, but principally from the effects of their having or not having slaves. These two causes concurred in forming the great division of interests in the U. States. It did not lie between the large & small States: It lay between the Northern & Southern, and if any defensive power were necessary, it ought to be mutually given to these two interests.”[105]

His solution was “instead of proportioning the votes of the States in both branches, to their respective numbers of inhabitants computing the slaves in the ratio of 5 to 3, they should be represented in one branch according to the number of free inhabitants only; and in the other according to the whole no. counting the slaves as if free. By this arrangement the Southern Scale would have the advantage in one House, and the Northern in the other.” But, while he had identified the problem, his solution, as had Hamilton’s, pleased no one. The debate continued without the delegates even voting on the idea.

After Charles Pinckney also agreed that principal division was sectional—“There is a real distinction between the Northern & South”—it became clear that if all the southern states would vote with the large state bloc, by-state apportionment in the second house would never be agreed to. “We are now at full stop,” lamented Roger Sherman.

In a last-ditch effort to save the convention, the delegates voted 9-2 to appoint a “Grand Committee” of eleven, one from each state, to come up with a proposal. The Committee contained a surprising number of delegates who favored a weaker central government: Paterson, Gerry (who would be chairman), Maryland’s Luther Martin, Yates of New York (Hamilton had left), and Ellsworth. With Franklin, who wanted to promote compromise, representing Pennsylvania, the split was effectively 5-5. As Yates wrote in his journal, “By the proceedings in the convention they were so equally divided on the important question of representation in the two branches, that the idea of a conciliatory adjustment must have been in contemplation of the house in the appointment of this committee.”[106]

On July 5, after the delegates suspended the proceedings for what would become known as Independence Day, the Committee delivered its report.

It was at this point that the real political struggle began.

Chapter 4

New Math: Apportionment and the Census

"Partisan interest in the census is simply nothing new."
– Kenneth Prewitt, former Director of the United States Census Bureau.

"If there is a 50-50 chance that something can go wrong, then 9 times out of 10 it will."
– Paul Harvey.

Although few would question that representative government is the cornerstone of democracy, it is also axiomatic that the democratic process is necessarily adversarial, which engenders either healthy or unhealthy competition to assert control of whatever institutions control the process. Competition is healthy when the parties involved attempt to gain that control by force of argument and advocating policies that meet with the approval of the majority of the governed; it is unhealthy when the parties attempt to create advantage by either manipulating the system or suppressing the voice of those in the citizenry who oppose their ideas.

While ideally, healthy competition should predominate, real-world politics makes at least some unhealthy competition inevitable. The key is to keep the balance on the positive side, and thus prevent a democratic structure in theory from descending to an undemocratic structure in practice. Since it is naïve to expect a competing party to police itself, adequate and appropriate checks need to be built into the system. Even then, an additional layer of controls will be necessary to prevent what has been termed "tyranny of the majority" or, even worse, allowing an unscrupulous minority from gaining and then holding on to power. Tyranny of the majority might be a threat to democracy, but tyranny of the minority is no democracy at all.

The potential for tyranny is generally the concern only of those denied a sufficient say in government to protect their interests, as was the case in Philadelphia. Because the political system that the delegates were attempting to create was as yet unformed, fear of a new constitution that left one at the mercy of one's enemies was widespread. To prevent such domination, the various factions maneuvered furiously protect their interests. The risk was that the bargains that were entered into and compromises that were fashioned would leave the final product either too weak to deal with the grave problems facing the nation as well as future crises that were certain to arise, or too strong to guarantee sufficient liberty to individuals or states.

"Weakness" and "strength," however, would be subjective terms, applied by delegates whose needs were either met or unmet. At the farthest extreme was if the plan promised to become so weak—or so strong—that delegates would choose to pack up and leave, ending the effort to create a new government and returning the United States to rule under the Articles. Although some delegates did leave, Yates and Lansing of New York in July, Luther Martin and John Francis Mercer of Maryland in August, and Hamilton, of course, for almost all of July and August, most were willing to stick it out and try to get the best deal they could.

Those delegates who did stay needed to determine the minimum guarantees or minimum restrictions they could accept in order to support the plan. Hammering out the compromises required to achieve a product might result in threats to walk out—and there would be many—but threats are not action. In the end, the decisions to be made would be about what must be included in the new plan—or what must be left out.

Although Yates indicated that Franklin had been the instigator, the Grand Committee's report contained what became known as the Connecticut Compromise. The first house would be apportioned by population, with one representative for every 40,000 residents—a much larger electoral district than in any of the thirteen states—and the second house would be by-state.

The July 5 session, in which the Committee's report was first discussed, was one of the most contentious to that point.[107] Gerry began by announcing that the members "agreed to the Report merely in order that some ground of accommodation might be proposed. Those opposed to the equality of votes have only assented conditionally; and if the other side do not generally agree will not be under any obligation to support the Report," hardly an auspicious beginning. Wilson immediately accused the committee of exceeding its powers. When Martin attempted to have the entire report considered and voted on, Wilson, unwilling to take "a leap in the dark," insisted that it be debated in parts, which would hardly reduce the acrimony.

Madison homed in on another of the report's recommendations, a sop to the large states, that money bills originate in the lower house, with the upper house unable to alter or amend them. Madison gave any number of reasons that it "could not therefore be deemed any concession on the present and left in force all the objections which had prevailed agst. allowing each State an equal voice." Going to the heart of the matter, he added, "It was in vain to purchase concord in the Convention on terms which would perpetuate discord among their Constituents."

Although he couched it in philosophical terms, Madison had essentially called the small states bluff. "He was not apprehensive that the people of the small States would obstinately refuse to accede to a Govt. founded on just principles and promising them substantial protection. He could not suspect that Delaware would brave the consequences of seeking her fortunes apart from the other States, rather than submit to such a Govt: much less could he suspect that she would pursue the rash policy of courting foreign support, which the warmth of one of her representatives (Mr. Bedford) had suggested, or if she shd. that any foreign nation wd. be so rash as to hearken to the overture."

Butler agreed. "He could not let down his idea of the people of America so far as to believe they would from mere respect to the Convention adopt a plan evidently unjust. He did not consider the privilege concerning money bills as of any consequence. He urged that the 2d. branch ought to represent the States according to their property."

Other delegates took the floor, none having anything good to say about a report that was supposed to be a compromise. Paterson went so far as to "complain of the manner in which Mr. Madison & Mr. Govr. Morris had treated the small States." Even Elbridge Gerry, the committee's chairman complained of having "serious objections."

If the convention was at "full stop" before, it had not moved a good deal since. Mason tried to smooth the waters, insisting the report was merely a starting point and accommodations on all sides must be made. Mason added, "He would bury his bones in this city rather than expose his Country to the Consequences of a dissolution of the Convention without any thing being done."

Soon afterward, the Convention adjourned for the day. Gouverneur Morris, opting for a strategic retreat, opened the next day's session by proposing that apportionment in lower house be given to yet another committee.[108]

This one, however, would be different—it included five men: Rutledge, Randolph, Gouverneur Morris, Rufus King, and another Massachusetts merchant, Nathaniel Gorham, all strong nationalists. Gorham, who had made a good deal of money privateering during the war, but had fallen on hard times after it, wanted any new constitution to protect the free flow of commerce so he could rebuild his fortune in shipping. King, a shopkeeper's son, had married well and arrived as a major stockholder in the Bank of New York. Both were outspoken in their revulsion of slavery, but sufficiently pragmatic not to make too big an issue of it. Conspicuously bypassed was Madison, a telling omission that would become more significant later in the proceedings.

Their task was to come up with a formula that would fit the proposed 1/40,000 guideline suggested by the Grand Committee and would also distribute power, if not equally, then at least acceptably.

On July 7, while the committee of five was off trying to come up with a workable formula for the lower house, the convention had its first tentative breakthrough. By a 6-3 vote with two states divided, the Convention agreed "That in the second Branch of the Legislature each State shall have an equal vote." Large states were none too pleased. Voting against were Pennsylvania, Virginia, and South Carolina, with Massachusetts divided. (New York, with only Yates and Lansing present, had once again voted with the small states.) Gerry explained why the proposal had his grudging support. "He had rather agree to it than have no accommodation. A Governt. short of a proper national plan if generally acceptable, would be preferable to a proper one which if it could be carried at all, would operate on discontented States."[109]

However it had been achieved, the small states had won one.

Two days later, the committee of five delivered its report, a state-by-state plan of apportionment for the lower house. It proposed "that in the 1st. meeting of the Legislature the 1st. branch thereof consist of 56. members of which Number N. Hamshire shall have 2. Massts. 7. R.Id.1. Cont. 4. N. Y. 5. N. J. 3. Pa. 8. Del. 1. Md. 4. Va. 9. N. C. 5, S. C. 5. Geo. 2."[110]

The skew toward slave states was apparent. They had been allocated twenty-five of the fifty-six seats, just three less than half, although they had little more than one-third of the free population. The math worked better when three-fifths of the slaves were added in, meaning the theoretical fraction that Wilson had mentioned earlier had now become the guideline. Still, there had yet to be agreement to count slaves at all and Roger Sherman immediately protested that the calculations "did not appear to correspond to any rule of numbers."

Gorham, who had been a party to creating the formula, attempted to dodge the question. "The number of blacks & whites with some regard to supposed wealth was the general guide," which made little or no sense. He also raised another potentially incendiary issue, "that the Westn. States who may have a different interest, might if admitted on that principal by degrees, out-vote the Atlantic." The committee's solution was hardly democratic. "The Atlantic States having ye. Govt. in their own hands, may take care of their own interest, by dealing out the right of Representation in safe proportions to the Western States."

If Madison were correct and the main division was slave state and free, then these initial numbers represented a capitulation to slavery, an odd result given that abolitionist delegates outnumbered slave owners on the committee three to two. Although there is no record of their deliberations, it is likely the Randolph and Rutledge made it clear to the Northerners that without slaves counted for apportionment, there would be no agreement. If true, it was one of the first major concessions delegates would make to practicalities. There would be many more.

When other northern delegates protested the numbers, Morris backed off and said they "little more than a guess … The Committee meant little more than to bring the matter to a point for the consideration of the House," ensuring the convention would wrangle further. But William Paterson soon ripped the veneer off the equivocation. "He could regard negro slaves in no light but as property." He noted that slave owners got no advantage in state legislatures, "And if Negroes are not represented in the States to which they belong, why should they be represented in the Genl. Govt?"

There was no legitimate response to Paterson's assertion that slave states were asking for bonus representation in the new Congress that they had refused to grant in their own state legislatures, nor did any delegate offer one. In addition to demonstrating that Madison's slave/free state division was key, it also showed that in order to succeed in creating a stronger central government, state prerogative would have to be respected to a much greater degree than Madison or Hamilton had anticipated. Once again, the limits on what could be accomplished in Philadelphia had narrowed if the main objective were to be achieved.

With neither North nor South willing to sign on to the committee of five's plan, the convention attempted to break the impasse by appointing another committee of eleven.

That committee's report, delivered the next day, increased the number of representatives to 65, but left the slave states four short of half, rather than three, and so the convention returned to bickering over how many representatives each state would be allotted.[111] Charles Pinckney moved that New Hampshire's allocation be decreased by one. Gouverneur Morris lamented that he "regretted the turn of the debate ... the Southern States have by the report more than their share of representation. Property ought to have its weight, but not all the weight." After a series of votes in which motions to decrease the apportionment of northern states or increase southern were defeated, the second apportionment was tentatively, and grudgingly, agreed to.

Counting slaves as three-fifths of a human being had thus been officially accepted in the first working model of the House of Representatives.

Although Rutledge and his fellow South Carolinians would later attempt to have the slaves counted in full, to deter them, Gouverneur Morris suggested linking apportionment to direct taxation, which was how most delegates assumed the nation would raise money. Northerners thought that an excellent idea. Gaining extra representatives by counting slaves was one thing, paying taxes on them quite another. Virginia in particular would have found an assessment based on the full number of its estimated 280,000 slaves daunting. Many of the planters were already in debt and the proposed tax would only make them more so. So, after a bit more wrangling, three-fifths was accepted without further rancor.

While for the slave states, three-fifths was better than nothing—a good deal better, as it turned out, since the slave-bonus electors would allow Thomas Jefferson to defeat John Adams in 1800—it left them short of control of the House of Representatives.[112] Although slave states feared leaving their fortunes in the hands of a northern majority, their minority position seemed certain to be temporary. Population, nearly everyone believed, would trend south and west, and as soon as this drift manifested slave states would control the House of Representatives. In addition, the Northwest Ordinance, which was debated and formalized as the Convention was meeting, sometimes by the same people, would restrict new free states to five, while the Southwest would potentially add as many as ten slave states to the Union.[113]

And so, while the three-fifths compromise would help slave states fatten their representation in the short run, it would leave them short of control, a shortfall that could only be overcome if they could find some way to incorporate the anticipated population shift into legislative apportionment. The obvious solution was a periodic census in which the results would form the new basis for representation.

Immediately after apportionment was agreed to, Edmund Randolph proposed one periodic census. "In order to ascertain the alterations in the population & wealth of the several States the Legislature should be required to cause a census, and estimate to be taken within one year after its first meeting; and every _ years thereafter — and that the Legislre. arrange the Representation accordingly."

Although Randolph left the number of years blank, the battle lines were clear. Southerners wanted reapportionment early and often, while the North wanted to perpetuate the status quo as long as possible. That left Northerners with the unenviable task of trying to persuade the convention to not count the number of people in the country, or at worst, leave the matter for Congress to decide while the North was in the majority. The first alternative seemed out of the question, and Charles Pinckney joined his fellow slaveowners in finding the second unacceptable. He foresaw that if the "revision of the census was left to the discretion of the Legislature, it would never be carried into execution. The rule must be fixed, and the execution of it enforced by the Constitution."

That the North had the more difficult task was demonstrated by Gouverneur Morris, who told his fellow delegates that he opposed a census entirely because it would "fetter the legislature too much," a statement that it is hard believe that the wily and astute Morris did not deliver with some embarrassment. Morris was never forced to elaborate because, as with slave apportionment, it was clear that the nation would have a census, the only questions being how frequently and under what ground rules.

On July 13, the same day the three-fifths rule was finally accepted, squabbling over the census reached its zenith.[114] Oliver Ellsworth asserted that the North would accept three-fifths only if the rules for a census were left to Congress. Randolph, like Pinckney, would not agree. "The danger will be revived that the ingenuity of the Legislature may evade or pervert the rule so as to perpetuate the power where it shall be lodged in the first instance." He would accept the three-fifths formula only if a census were taken within two years of the first meeting of the legislature and each year thereafter.

Ellsworth indicated he might accept such a formula, but Massachusetts's Rufus King would not. "He must be shortsighted indeed who does not foresee that whenever the Southern States shall be numerous than the Northern, they can and will hold a language that will awe them into justice." King then asked the slaves states to accept on trust that the North would agree at some future date to "periodical readjustment." South Carolina countered by resurrecting its demand that slaves be counted in full for apportionment without mentioning taxes.

Northern delegates recognized that they could not win this one. Without a compromise on the census, the agreement on apportionment might collapse and the entire plan along with it. They proposed a twenty-year interval, which was defeated, but agreed to settle for ten years. South Carolina's half-hearted motion to have all slaves counted for apportionment was also defeated, and the three-fifths/ten-year-census compromise was written into Article I.

Having achieved a workable solution and unwilling to risk further contentiousness, the delegates left the specifics of census taking to Congress. The final wording was simply, "The actual Enumeration shall be made within three Years after the first Meeting of the Congress of the United States, and within every subsequent Term of ten Years, in such Manner as they shall by Law direct." With the census pivotal in determining who would control the House of Representatives, and perhaps the presidency as well, avoiding a delineation of methods and standards for conducting the census risked abuse of the process.

It was crucial to determine just who would be counted and what would be the rules for doing so. With the delegates happy just to have reached agreement on the overall question, neither of these had been spelled out. While voting was certain to be restricted to citizens, apportionment and thus the census could not be since "three fifths of all other persons," as slaves were euphemized, had to be included as well.[115]

But what did "all other persons" actually mean? With the framers unwilling to offend the sensibilities of slave state delegates by including the words "slave" or "slavery" in the Constitution, the answer was murky. If taken textually, as it has been since the first census in 1790, the phrase seems to indicate that apportionment was to include all residents with no distinction between citizens and non-citizens. After slavery was abolished and fractions abandoned, that reading was reinforced in Section 2 of Fourteenth Amendment, which stated, "Representatives shall be apportioned among the several States according to their respective numbers, counting the whole number of persons in each State, excluding Indians not taxed."

In the past, the lack of demarcation between citizens and non-citizens has been used by unscrupulous politicians, such as William Magear "Boss" Tweed, to artificially and often fraudulently increase the population of key electoral districts to favor one political party or another.[116] More recently, it raised the question of whether immigrant non-citizens, even those in the country illegally, would be part of the determination of how many congressional seats a state would be assigned.

In anticipation of the 2020 census, the Trump administration made a well-publicized effort to include a citizenship question, which would, critics claimed, "either benefit the Republican Party and red states or advance the Trump administration's anti-immigration agenda."[117] In either case, "The widespread expectation was that the question would stoke fear among unauthorized immigrants and their family members, scaring off millions of mostly Latino residents from responding, and meaning states where those residents are concentrated will be undercounted. (Those states, which mostly favor Democrats, would then get smaller House of Representatives delegations and less federal funding because of the undercount.)."[118] Census data is also used to determine the distribution of federal funding, which could exceed $1.5 trillion, enough of an incentive to invite chicanery.

When asked by the Supreme Court to justify adding the citizenship question, Commerce Secretary Wilbur Ross, to the snickers of many, insisted the new data was aimed at helping the Department of Justice enforce the Voting Rights Act and thus safeguard equal access to the ballot box for minority voters. Although Chief Justice Roberts accepted the constitutionality of adding the question, speaking for a 5-4 majority, he joined the Court's liberal wing to rule against the Trump administration because he deemed Ross's reasoning "contrived."[119] Trump subsequently abandoned the attempt, although, with Roberts and the other conservative justices seeming to approve of the idea in principle, it is likely to arise again in the runup to the 2030 census.

For the 2020 census, the upshot of counting non-citizens was significant. According to the Pew Research Center, "If unauthorized immigrants were excluded from the apportionment count, California, Florida and Texas would each end up with one less congressional seat than they would have been awarded based on population change alone."[120] Gaining those seats would be Alabama, Minnesota, and Ohio.

But gaining or losing seats by state did not tell the entire story. Amanda Frost, writing in the *Atlantic* noted, "As the late Republican strategist Thomas Hofeller put it in a 2015 report, excluding noncitizens 'would be advantageous to Republicans and Non-Hispanic whites.' Urban areas tend to lean Democratic and have a younger, more diverse population, including more immigrants, than rural areas. Those older, whiter rural areas, then, tend to have fewer immigrants and vote Republican. Excluding noncitizens from being counted in redistricting would shift political power—and the state tax dollars and resources that come with it—to Republicans representing these less populated, less diverse rural regions."[121]

Although not directly the result of the lack of sufficient constitutional controls over the process, census data has been the source of other abuses, the most egregious of which was its use by Franklin D. Roosevelt's administration to facilitate the internment of more than 120,000 innocent Japanese-Americans, more than two-thirds of them citizens, after the attack on Pearl Harbor. Although "Federal law explicitly requires data collected by the census be kept private and not used by the government to identify individuals ... Within months of the Japanese attack on Pearl Harbor in 1941, tens of thousands of Japanese Americans living on the West Coast were rounded up and forced into internment camps. It later became clear that the speed of the detentions was possible in large part because of information shared by top Census Bureau officials. Those officials had access to up-to-date data from the 1940 census."[122]

After the 1920 census, a period of rabid nativism, showed not only a major shift of population from rural to urban areas but also that a large number of urban residents were recent immigrants, "representatives elected from rural districts worked to derail the process, fearful of losing political power to the cities. Reapportionment legislation was repeatedly delayed as rural interests tried to come up with mechanisms that would blunt the impact of the population shift."[123] As a result, for the only time in American history, a reapportionment was not carried out. As a consequence, in 1929, a law was passed that fixed the number of House members at 435 and triggered an automatic reapportionment after every census.

The census, as much of American democracy, remains fragile. And while, for the present, the census will include everyone, regardless of citizenship, the question is headed for a renewed political and judicial battle. If non-citizens continue to be counted, states with larger populations of what are either termed "undocumented aliens" or "illegal immigrants" will receive a bonus similar to that which slave states received in the antebellum South. It is not impossible therefore, that, like Thomas Jefferson, a president may eventually be elected because those in the country illegally have provided him or her with extra electoral college votes to determine the result. If non-citizens are eliminated from the tally, states with smaller populations of those here illegally will a receive a boost in apportionment instead.

With control of the House of Representatives, vast federal allocations, and the presidency all potentially at stake, the census bureau will be ripe for partisan appointments and pressure to count or not count certain residents in battleground states and localities will beget new conflict, if it has not already.

Chapter 5

A Few Good (White) Men: Voting...

"Governments are instituted among Men,
deriving their just powers from the consent of the governed."
– Thomas Jefferson, the Declaration of Independence.

"Remarkably, this new Constitution, born in celebration of 'republican government,' did not grant anyone the right to vote."
– Alexander Keyssar, "The Right to Vote: The Contested History of Democracy in the United States.

Among the most vital decisions any nation that wishes to perpetuate a successful democracy must make is who will be granted the right to vote, for what offices, and how to ensure that the process is fair and equitable. If the right to vote is skewed to favor one group or another, not only will minority rule likely become inevitable, but the stability, even the survival, of the underlying system will come under threat. The United States has wrestled with those questions since before the nation was officially founded, and after more than two centuries, the answers remain frighteningly uncertain. There is a legitimate argument that the lack of voting rights has been the single greatest impediment to the United States becoming the democracy it claims to be. But when Americans look to the Constitution for guidance, many are surprised that there is little or none to be found, and what there is leaves far too much to interpretation or even to chance.

To a great degree that outcome was inevitable.

As the delegates arrived in Philadelphia, eligibility to vote or hold public office was a muddle. Each state had its own restrictions based on religion, gender, race, residency, or wealth. Some charged a fee to vote, while most but not all excluded immigrants, and every state denied the franchise to slaves and Native Americans. Some states specifically banned servants, while others targeted paupers. However, the most common restriction was financial, based on property holding or the payment of taxes.

In the early 1780s, with the convention not yet in view, only male landowners—freeholders with title to at least 50 acres could vote in Virginia, Delaware, Maryland, South Carolina, and North Carolina. In the same period, Connecticut, Georgia, New Jersey, New York, Rhode Island, and Massachusetts also restricted voting to freeholders, but qualification was based on the value of the land, rather than acreage.[124] In each of these states, however, a movement was under foot to supplement the property requirement by including those with a record of paying taxes, as was already the case in Pennsylvania. Eight had already done so by the time the convention met. New Hampshire had no landowning requirement, men needing only to pay a poll tax in order to vote.

Religious restrictions abounded. "Nine out of thirteen states had some sort of religious test requirement for officeholders in their constitutions. At the time, many believed religious oaths were supposed to guarantee honorable public service for fear of incurring the wrath of God. Public officials who violated their oaths might escape punishment here on earth but could not avoid punishment in the hereafter."[125]

Five states prohibited Catholics from voting, and four banned Jews. In Massachusetts, only Protestants or Catholics who renounced papal authority were allowed to hold public office. New York barred Catholics from holding office, and Delaware demanded officeholders sign an oath avowing the Trinity. Other states, including Massachusetts and South Carolina, had official, state-supported Protestant churches. South Carolina, Georgia, and New Hampshire limited officeholding to men "professing a belief in the faith of any Protestant sect." Pennsylvania, which prided itself on tolerance, only granted voting rights to those who accepted Jesus as their savior. Jews were allowed to settle in the commonwealth and become citizens but not to vote.

While no state allowed slaves to vote, including New York, which had 20,000 of them, voting rights for free men of color who met a state's property requirement were surprisingly widespread. Black men could vote by law in Maryland, Massachusetts, Pennsylvania, and New Hampshire, and were not specifically restricted from voting in Connecticut, New York, New Jersey, Delaware, Rhode Island, and, surprisingly, North Carolina. The only states legally barring free Blacks from voting were Virginia,

South Carolina, and sparsely populated Georgia. (That would change drastically in the ensuing decades, when almost every state restricted the vote to white men.)

Because each state was free to make its own rules, a number of quirks worked their way into the system. One of the oddest was in New Jersey, where the 1776 state constitution granted all "persons" who met the property requirement the right to vote. As a result, to the horror of many men, widows and other women who owned property regularly cast ballots. Some New Jersey men disparagingly called women voting "government in petticoats."[126] (In 1807, they would rectify their error and specifically bar women from the franchise.)

Elections differed as well, but votes were generally cast in public. In many areas, they became community social outings, with food and drink provided. In six states, voters signified their choices by standing, raising their hands, or calling out the name of their chosen candidate.

In Virginia, voting was public theater. "As each freeholder came before the sheriff, his name was called out in a loud voice, and the sheriff inquired how he would vote. The freeholder replied by giving the name of his preference. The appropriate clerk then wrote down the voter's name, the sheriff announced it as enrolled, and often the candidate for whom he had voted arose, bowed, and publicly thanked him."[127]

Although paper ballots were employed in some states, they were not secret. In some locations, lists were posted in the town square with each voter's choice available for public view. Secret ballots did not begin to become standard until the 1890s, when what was known as the "Australian ballot" came into fashion. Ironically, secret ballots were favored by perpetrators of election fraud, especially in the pre-Jim Crow South, since boxes of genuine ballots could be conveniently disposed of, or false ones deposited with vote counters.

As a result of this hodgepodge, convention delegates were left to wrestle with what government by the "consent of the governed" actually meant. While it was a simple matter to identify the governed, who among them would be called upon to give their consent was not at all clear.

There was no model on which to base requirements and restrictions for voting in national elections, and many delegates were uncertain whether there should be any. There were, however, some broadly accepted principles to give them a starting point. Prevailing wisdom held that the franchise should be limited to citizens "with a stake" in the government they were choosing. But even that notion had a hazy first derivative. Large property owners certainly qualified—thus the 50-acre requirement—but did small farmers eking out a subsistence existence on tiny plots of land? Or tenant farmers? What about those whose wealth did not include real property? Then there were professionals—lawyers and doctors—servants and other service workers, all the way down to common laborers. What was their "stake" in the government?

The other accepted norm was that a vote should be given freely and intelligently. Fear was widespread that a voter who was not sufficiently independent or sufficiently learned would cast a ballot either for someone he was told to or someone not in the best interest of the government. And a voter should certainly be a resident of the state in which he lived, but for how long and under what circumstances was another open question. In any event, the vast majority of the nation's leaders favored stringent limitations on voting and almost no one favored universal suffrage, or anything close to it.

Alexander Hamilton, ever the elitist, insisted that only freeholders could be trusted to vote responsibly. In a 1775 pamphlet, "The Farmer Refuted," Hamilton cited the great British legal philosopher, William Blackstone, who, in his classic *Commentaries on the Laws of England*, wrote that those "under the immediate dominion of others"—workers—or "persons of indigent fortunes"—the poor—could not be trusted to "give his vote freely, and without influence of any kind, then, upon the true theory and genuine principles of liberty."[128] Blackstone, widely read throughout the colonies, emphasized the rights of the individual and protection of property, which created the legal justification for the American Revolution. After the war, he became the theorist of choice for Federalists, and to this day, largely due to his defence of property rights, remains an icon of conservative judges.

Hamilton's views did not moderate over time. At the convention, during his six-hour oration on June 18, he observed, "All communities divide themselves into the few and the many. The first are rich and well born; the other, the mass of the people. The voice of the people has been said to be the voice of God, however it is not true in fact. The people are turbulent and changing; they seldom judge or determine right. Give therefore to the first class a distinct, permanent share in the government."[129] It is uncertain if Hamilton was also indicating that only those in the "first class" could be citizens, or if the nation should have two classes of citizenship, one that chose leaders and one that did not. Given the stunned reception by his fellow delegates, no one thought to ask.

John Adams, then the nation's chief diplomat in London, was not present in Philadelphia, but had previously made his views known. In a letter written only six weeks before he would sign the Declaration of Independence, Adams expressed a firm conviction that those without property should be not allowed to vote. "Such is the frailty of the human heart, that very few men who have no property have any judgment of their own," he wrote. "They talk and vote as they are directed by Some Man of Property, who has attached their Minds to his Interest."[130]

Lest there be confusion, Adams, as much of an elitist as was Hamilton, added, "Depend upon it, Sir, it is dangerous to open so fruitful a source of controversy … there will be no end to it. New claims will arise; women will demand the vote; lads from 12 to 21 will think their rights not enough attended to; and every man who has not a farthing, will demand an equal voice with any other, in all acts of state."

Denying ordinary Americans the vote in national elections, however, promised to be difficult. Those who fought and died in the Revolution had done so to attain what the English philosopher John Locke had termed "natural rights," and what right could be more natural than choosing the people who would make the laws under which one must live?[131]Nonetheless, granting the vote to those that many of the nation's leaders considered little more than rabble seemed to guarantee the descent into the anarchy that Shays's Rebellion had foretold.

The most prominent among those few at the convention who did favor an expansion of voting rights was Benjamin Franklin. Franklin was eighty-one and gout-ridden in 1787, and often had to be carried into the proceedings in a chair borne by servants, but almost sixty years earlier he had penned a short anecdote, still famous as "Franklin's Jackass," which jabbed at those who thought property owners were the only qualified voters.

"Today a man owns a jackass worth 50 dollars and he is entitled to vote; but before the next election the jackass dies. The man in the meantime has become more experienced, his knowledge of the principles of government, and his acquaintance with mankind, are more extensive, and he is therefore better qualified to make a proper selection of rulers—but the jackass is dead and the man cannot vote. Now gentlemen, pray inform me, in whom is the right of suffrage? In the man or in the jackass?"[132]

The other prominent American who favored liberalized voting rights—at least among adult white males—was Thomas Jefferson, who in 1787 was representing the United States in Paris, and, like Adams, did not attend the convention. Jefferson had written in a 1776 letter, "I was for extending the rights of suffrage (or in other words the rights of a citizen) to all who had a permanent intention of living in the country. Take what circumstances you please as evidence for this, either the having resided a certain time, or having a family, or having property, any or all of them."[133] In a 1789 letter, he would add, "Whenever the people are well-informed, they can be trusted with their own government; whenever things get so far wrong as to attract their notice, they may be relied on to set them to rights."[134]

It was perhaps a coincidence that Jefferson's power base was among small farmers and others of limited means. Perhaps not.

Franklin was too feeble to influence the proceedings, and Jefferson was across the Atlantic. Given the extreme reluctance to grant the "people" too large a voice, the delegates were left to figure out how to guarantee them a modicum of participation without intruding excessively on what the states considered one of their most inviolable entitlements. That led to the question of whether the new national government should—or even could—impose a common or minimum standard on all existing and future states. If not, would the United States have a true national government with states totally free to devise their own voting standards?

These issues would come to the fore in early August. After the squabbling in June and July had produced at least tentative agreement on many key issues, in late July, the delegates selected a five-person "Committee of Detail," to produce a draft constitution. That decision was the most significant of the entire four months. These five men would produce a document that set the boundaries for the remainder of the debate. The Convention could, and would, alter provisions that the committee reported out, but any extreme departure would put the delegates back to square one, which, after more than two hot, contentious months, was an extremely uninviting prospect.

The members were selected by secret ballot, and makeup of the committee was telling. Chosen to head the group was not James Madison—who once again was not chosen at all—but South Carolina's Rutledge. Although Madison did not express it publicly, being left off the committee that would produce the Constitution's prototype must have been galling, especially since he had no way of knowing who had chosen to bypass him. But as the Convention moved past philosophy and on to practicalities, Madison lost a good deal of influence.

Rutledge, on the other hand, was not a political theorist, but rather a hard-nosed trial lawyer, one of the best in the nation. He was reputed to have gone years without losing a case, and as South Carolina's governor had been dubbed "The Old Dictator." As such, Rutledge was more likely to get the job done and move the Convention past the theoretical discussions of which all but Madison and a few of the other delegates had grown weary.

But Rutledge was also an unapologetic slave owner whose defence of slavery on both economic and moral grounds was unyielding and ferocious. With him in the lead, the committee's product was certain to be friendly to slave state interests, a fact with which the other delegates could not have helped but be aware. (Rutledge's attitude toward slaves would have an ironic twist. In 1795, he was nominated by George Washington to be Chief Justice of the Supreme Court, a position he had desperately sought, but the Senate rejected the nomination amidst rumors Rutledge had gone mad, although the real reason was that he had turned on Washington. The rumors might have had some basis after all, however, as, after the Senate vote, Rutledge threw himself into Charleston Bay but was saved from drowning by two slaves who jumped in to rescue him.[135] Rutledge likely did not welcome the gesture, as he became a recluse, living in isolation until his death in 1800.)

The other committee members, all of whom favored strengthening the national government, were Connecticut judge Oliver Ellsworth, Massachusetts merchant Nathaniel Gorham, Pennsylvania lawyer James Wilson, and Virginia's patrician governor, Edmund Randolph. All except Randolph were powerful personalities and able dealmakers. Rutledge's committee mates were determined to make the process work, even if it meant setting aside moral qualms. Wilson had demonstrated a willingness to compromise his personal antipathy to slavery to achieve consensus, as had Ellsworth. Gorham, with Shays's Rebellion a recent memory, needed a stronger national government to protect the merchant class and Randolph, of course, was a slave owner himself.

In addition, the committee had the flavor of a cabal. Not only was Rutledge James Wilson's houseguest during his stay in Philadelphia, where the two pragmatists could plot strategy every night over drinks and dinner, but it was no secret that Ellsworth and Rutledge had been meeting privately for weeks, sometimes with Roger Sherman. Ellsworth and Gorham had been on the same side of almost every debate. The committee needed a representative from the nation's most populous state and the delegates had chosen the malleable Randolph instead of Madison or the more powerful but often intransigent George Mason.

After eleven days of meeting in secret, often at the Indian Queen tavern or Wilson's home, during which Washington went fishing (not while the Convention was in session as is sometimes claimed), the delegates reconvened on August 6. Each of the members present received a printed copy of the committee's report, which they were to read overnight. The report was prefaced by a note from Randolph that informed the delegates that the committee had dealt in "essential principles only." They were unwilling, he said, to let "the operations of government ... be clogged," by trying to make Constitutional "provisions permanent and unalterable" but the new Constitution should be "accommodated to times and events."[136]

In addition to providing a convenient framework for further horse trading, the committee was thus advocating a "living constitution," one which not only anticipated needed changes and alterations as the nation grew in size and complexity, but also allowed for a certain flexibility of interpretation based on current conditions. (Whether the Constitution is indeed "living," as most liberal Supreme Court justices profess, or "dead" as textualists and originalists insist, is at the center of many contemporary controversies, including abortion, gun rights, voting rights, and environmental legislation.)[137]

Eschewing specifics also seemed an effective method to avoid rekindling the hostility and deadlock that had characterized the earlier debates. But hostility and deadlock would not be banished that easily. When the August 7 session got underway, the delegates moved quickly to suffrage and two days of bitter debate would follow.

Article IV, Section 1 of the report proposed that access to the national ballot would remain under state control, the only caveat being, "The qualifications of the electors shall be the same … as those of … the most numerous branch of [a state's] own legislature." This rule would have great appeal to a number of state delegations, none more than South Carolina's. There, the state legislature was controlled by the coastal planter class, to which all its delegates belonged, at the expense of yeomen farmers from upcountry with whom they were in constant conflict. So long as state legislatures determined who had a right to the ballot, South Carolina's congressional delegation could be contorted to give planters the same outsized representation in the new Congress that they enjoyed at home. Class struggle in other states, such as Massachusetts and New York, was similarly fraught.

The lack of a hard and fast rule, however, disturbed Gouverneur Morris, who immediately objected, moving to "restrain the right of suffrage to freeholders." For a man who would write "We, the people," Morris did not have a good deal of faith in ordinary citizens, and he saw the committee's proposal as creating a dangerous precedent. Ten of the thirteen states had extended suffrage to unlanded taxpayers, which included tenant farmers, workers, artisans, professionals, and even some poorer merchants, all of whom Morris would prohibit from voting nationally. "The time is not distant," he would say later in the debate, "when this Country will abound with mechanics & manufacturers who will receive their bread from their employers. Will such men be the secure & faithful Guardians of liberty? Will they be the impregnable barrier agst. aristocracy? … The man who does not give his vote freely is not represented. It is the man who dictates the vote."[138]

Committee member James Wilson saw trouble in attempting to disenfranchise state voters, however. He acknowledged the challenge in devising "a uniform rule of qualifications for all the States," but called it "disagreeable" for "the same persons, at the same time, to vote for representatives in the State Legislature and to be excluded from a vote for those in the Natl. Legislature." Morris countered that voting for the national legislature should not "depend on the will of the States."

Here was the crux of the problem, one that would bear greatly on the future success of American democracy. Who, if anyone, would guarantee the right to vote, both for those made eligible by the new government and those allowed into the electoral system in the years to come? If left to the states, restrictions could be as loose, extreme, or arbitrary as their state legislatures desired. If, on the other hand, voting qualifications were national, the same in every state, individual states and the ruling parties within them would lose the ability to deny the vote to specific unfavored classes inside their own borders.

Without the support of those state ruling parties, there would be no ratification, as committee member Oliver Ellsworth pointed out. "The right of suffrage was a tender point, and strongly guarded by most of the (State) Constitutions. The people will not readily subscribe to the Natl. Constitution, if it should subject them to be disfranchised. The States are the best Judges of the circumstances and temper of their own people."

George Mason agreed. "What will the people there say, if they should be disfranchised... A power to alter the qualifications would be a dangerous power in the hands of the [national] Legislature."

Dangerous power indeed. Mason was not speaking theoretically. He, like the delegates from other slaveholding states, had two reasons for opposing national voting rights. First, Virginia, like South Carolina, had a large population of backcountry farmers whose support for a state government dominated by coastal planters was tenuous at best. Keeping as many of them as possible from being guaranteed the vote would ensure that the balance of power would remain in the planters' favor. Of equal if not more importance, voting standards set by a national government that would have northern majorities in each house of the legislature presented a threat to slaveholders who lived in fear that the North was always seeking some means to move to abolition.

And protecting slavery was always foremost on Mason's mind. He was perhaps the Convention's most misunderstood member. Mason owned more than 300 slaves, the most of any delegate, yet after the Convention, acquired an anti-slavery reputation from an August speech denouncing the "nefarious institution." But Mason was referring not to slavery, which was the source of his fortune, but the continuation of the slave trade, which robbed him of his market for excess slaves in the Lower South. His embrace of slavery as an institution never wavered.

Pierce Butler, a South Carolina planter, whose fear of Northern dominance matched Mason's, agreed. "There is no right of which the people are more jealous than that of suffrage," he added coyly.

But those who wanted the new Constitution to set the parameters for voting were not ready to give up. John Dickinson "considered [freeholders] as the best guardians of liberty; And the restriction of the right to them as a necessary defence agst. the dangerous influence of those multitudes without property & without principle, with which our Country like all others, will in time abound."

But were freeholders the only repository of principle? Ellsworth thought not. "Ought not every man who pays a tax [be allowed] to vote for the representative who is to levy & dispose of his money? Shall the wealthy merchants and manufacturers, who will bear a full share of the public burdens be not allowed a voice in the imposition of them."

Morris saw his motion heading for defeat and his short temper got the better of him. In a strange twist of logic for man proposing limiting the vote to men of means, he denounced the committee's report as threatening the United States with "aristocracy." He insisted that granting "the vote to people who have no property" will allow them "to sell them to the rich who will be able to buy them." Although Morris perhaps missed the irony that in rejecting one aristocracy, he was advocating another, his warning about the pitfalls of allowing the monied classes to exert undue influence on the electoral process has been anything but hollow.

The most interesting comments came from the man who had been determined to be the father of the Constitution, James Madison. A few weeks prior, on July 26, shortly after he learned he would not be on the Committee of Detail, he had asserted, "Landed possessions were no certain evidence of real wealth. Many enjoyed them to a great extent who were more in debt than they were worth. The unjust laws of the States had proceeded more from this class of men, than any others."[139] Furthering his distrust of limiting the vote to freeholders, he had added "It was politic as well as just that the interests & rights of every class should be duly represented & understood in the public Councils" and that "he wished if it were possible that some other criterion than the mere possession of land should be devised."

But when it came time to debate a report he had no hand in fashioning, Madison suddenly reversed his position. Speaking in support of Morris, he observed, "Viewing the subject in its merits alone, the freeholders [that is, landowners] of the country would be the safest depositories of republican liberty."[140] That Madison hopped from one side of the fence to the other without explanation was not the last time he would abruptly abandon one set of values for another. He would later forsake the Federalists entirely to become Jefferson's most valued convert, and would again support expansion of voting rights.

In any event, his support for Morris's motion did not help. It was defeated, gaining only one "aye" vote, oddly, from Delaware, meaning that Morris could not even persuade his own Pennsylvania delegation to back him. And so, the first sentence of Article I, Section 2 would read, "The House of Representatives shall be composed of members chosen every second year by the people of the several states, and the electors in each state shall have the qualifications requisite for electors of the most numerous branch of the state legislature." There would, therefore, be no national standards for voting eligibility … or voting rights. States would be free to create rules as they saw fit, which would often mean disenfranchisement for any group of Americans that a state found inconvenient to allow access to the ballot box. The only caveat was that however unfair and undemocratic were a state's voting standards for national elections, they must be equally so in the state itself.

Still, an unwillingness to protect citizens' right to vote was not something delegates wanted to publicize during ratification. Since the proceedings had been secret, with no record published until long afterward, those campaigning for ratification could say anything they pleased about what had transpired in Philadelphia. (Slave owners, for example, would portray Northerners as far more amenable to slavery as an institution than they had been during the debates.)

The following year, in Federalist 52, Madison wrote, "The definition of the right of suffrage is very justly regarded as a fundamental article of republican government. It was incumbent on the Convention, therefore, to define and establish this right in the Constitution." He added, "To have left it open for the occasional regulation of the Congress would have been improper … To have submitted it to the legislative discretion of the States, would have been improper for the same reason; and for the additional reason that it would have rendered too dependent on the State governments that branch of the federal government which ought to be dependent on the people alone."[141]

Almost none of this was true. The Convention did almost nothing to define the right to vote, leaving it almost entirely "to the legislative discretion of the States." States could and did exercise that power as they saw fit until after the Civil War, when the right to vote began to come under the authority of the Constitution with the enactment of the Fourteenth and Fifteenth Amendments. Until then, since there were no national standards, there were no grounds for appealing voting restrictions to the federal judiciary.

But even amendments drafted specifically to ensure equal access to the ballot were undermined by state governments determined to maintain control at any cost and a Supreme Court that too often allowed them to do so.

The Fifteenth Amendment, which stipulated that the right to vote "shall not be denied or abridged by the United States or by any State on account of race, color, or previous condition of servitude," seems clear in its intent. Some in Congress, such as Charles Sumner and John Bingham, wanted stronger language, but because the drafters of the amendment had been forced to word the amendment narrowly, in the negative, in order to gain a two-thirds vote in Congress, voting rights for people of color were anything but assured. Eric Foner writes, "Republicans had to choose between …an amendment establishing a uniform national standard that enfranchised virtually all adult male citizens, or a 'negative' one barring the use of race or other criteria to limit the right to vote but otherwise leaving qualifications in the hands of the states. The first possibility represents a road not taken that would have barred the methods used by southern states … to disenfranchise their Black populations."[142]

The negative construction did not take long to have a negative effect. In 1874, in a circuit court opinion in *United States v. Cruikshank*, Associate Supreme Court Justice Joseph P. Bradley wrote, "The Fifteenth Amendment confers no right to vote. That is the exclusive prerogative of the states. It does confer a right not to be excluded from voting by reason of race, color or previous condition of servitude, and this is all the right that Congress can enforce."[143]

Bradley's linguistic tap dance was precisely what equal rights advocates had feared, and it totally changed both the amendment's meaning and its potential as a tool for the federal government to protect Black voters. Under Bradley's definition, if an African-American was threatened, beaten, and his house burned to the ground in order to terrorize him into not voting, and the state refused to prosecute the offenders, the federal government could do nothing unless the victim could prove that the actions were motivated *only* by race.

Bradley had therefore transferred the burden of proof from the state to demonstrate it had not discriminated to the individual whose right to vote had been denied. That task was difficult enough, but it had the potential, which was realized, to become virtually impossible depending on the standard of proof the Court would require. Bradley's opinion and a number of others, most notably Oliver Wendell Holmes's in *Giles v. Harris* in 1903, ushered in decades of almost total voter suppression and the horrors of Jim Crow.[144] Not for another six decades, until the Voting Rights Act of 1965, did Congress try to right the wrong the Supreme Court had perpetuated. (The Nineteenth and Twenty-sixth Amendments, granting the right to vote to women and to those eighteen and over, were also worded in the negative but, unlike with Americans of color, gender, and age were much more difficult to make subjective, as Bradley had with race.)

Threats to voting rights today are the source of a major democratic crisis. While the courts should be the check on a minority grasping and then holding on to power by undemocratic means, they have, as in *Shelby County v. Holder* in 2013 and *Brnovich v. DNC* in 2021, more often acted as supporters rather than adversaries to anti-democratic forces.

Certainly, even if voting rights had been defined in the original Constitution, anti-democratic forces could have initiated legal challenges based on the wording, hoping for a Joseph Bradley to issue an opinion denying the obvious. But if the Constitution had mandated that the standards for voting in national elections were to be the same in each state, it would take either an act of Congress or a Constitutional amendment to implement voter suppression initiatives, such as today's state rules demanding exact match signatures, enhanced identification requirements, or denying the vote to former felons who had re-entered society as law-abiding citizens. It is unlikely that any of those would have had sufficient national support to be enacted.

The effect of the lack of national standards in these and other areas has been telling. Until 2018, Florida, for example, had been one of four states to permanently deny voting rights to former felons. That year, however, two-thirds of Florida voters, including many conservative Republicans who voted for Ron DeSantis for governor, ratified an amendment to the state constitution that restored the right to vote to felons who had completed their sentences and were off parole and probation. Only murderers and sex offenders were excepted. More than 1.5 million Florida citizens thus became eligible to vote, almost ten percent of the state's entire voting age population. Of these, as many as a half million were African American.

But Florida's legislature, overwhelmingly white and conservative, was not about to let these new potential voters shift the balance of power in the state. In 2019, with DeSantis's support, Florida enacted a law that required all former felons seeking to register to have paid off any fines, court costs, restitution, or interest, or face arrest. Some of these financial obligations were so obscure as to be unknown to the registrant. In the absence of federal standards, this law, a transparent attempt to suppress Black voting through the threat of rearrest, has succeeded in reducing the number of former felons trying to cast legal ballots to a trickle.

And so, despite a raft of laws and even Constitutional amendments designed to prevent the disenfranchisement of vulnerable members of American society, lack of a more specific guarantee in both Article I and the Fifteenth Amendment has meant that voting rights for many remain ephemeral to this day.

Chapter 6

...and Citizenship

"The distinctions between Virginians, Pennsylvanians, New Yorkers and New Englanders are no more. I am not a Virginian, but an American."
Patrick Henry at the First Continental Congress, 1774.

Nowhere does the Constitution define who or what a citizen might be; nowhere does it explicitly assign the privileges and duties of a citizen; nowhere does it clearly delineate the relationship of state citizenship to national citizenship; nowhere does it clarify who should settle fights between the states and the nation.
Douglas Bradburn, *The Citizenship Revolution: Politics and the Creation of the American Union, 1774-1804.*

Among the key precepts of American democracy are the "privileges and immunities" of citizenship. American citizenship guarantees a variety of political rights, including (supposedly) the right to vote, to apply for a passport, to work for the federal government, to run for elected office, and not to be denied re-entry into the United States. There is also a plethora of legal and civil rights associated with citizenship, although some may be granted to non-citizens as well. These include First Amendment freedoms of speech, religion, assembly, the press, and petitioning the government. Then, following interpretive laws and court rulings, there is the right to an attorney, to a fair trial, and not to be discriminated against on the basis of race, religion, and, in some cases, gender or sexual orientation. Some rights are controversial, such as the Second Amendment's right to bear arms.

Although there have been and continue to be disputes as to the reach of some of these rights and the breadth of their application, most Americans believe they understand quite well, at least in a general sense, what rights United States citizenship grants them. But if that notion seems clear now, it certainly did not in 1787. In fact, as the Convention got under way, national citizenship in a strict sense did not exist.

After the Declaration of Independence, Americans' allegiance had transferred not to the "United States," which had yet to be defined as a political entity, but rather to the states in which they lived. "In the king's place, there now stood thirteen independent states, each claiming the fidelity of the inhabitants remaining within its bounds."[145]

To cement that relationship, each of the former colonies drafted a constitution to codify how independence had altered the relationship of its inhabitants to what was now a state government. In each of these constitutions, jurisdiction was established, as were definitions of state citizenship. Although most Americans also felt some degree of allegiance to the new nation, most considered that to mean as opposed to being subjects of the crown. Few, if any, believed allegiance to the nation superseded their allegiance to their home state. "As the colonies redefined themselves as independent states, the legal rights and privileges remained unequal and uncertain. Like the ambiguity of nationality in the new United States, the stresses between the ideal and the reality of equal citizenship in America remained complex and potentially destabilizing."[146]

There was the additional question of the status of those who arrived after independence had been won. Many of the nation's leaders were already looking west to inevitable expansion, at least to the Mississippi and likely beyond, a vast wilderness that would need to be cultivated both economically and politically. Gaining a sufficient number of new settlers had been problematic because the British government had tried to limit immigration to the colonies, if not choke it off entirely, and to limit settlement beyond the frontier. Thomas Jefferson made just that point in the Declaration of Independence, in which he said of King George III, "He has endeavoured to prevent the population of these States; for that purpose obstructing the Laws for Naturalization of Foreigners; refusing to pass others to encourage their migrations hither, and raising the conditions of new Appropriations of Lands."[147]

As a result, each of the thirteen states, even those without claims to western lands, sought to bolster its population with new settlers seeking the freedoms and republican form of government that the new nation promised, especially if they brought needed skills, wealth, or both. To encourage "desirable" immigrants, states attempted to set liberal rules for naturalization, although widespread fear that newcomers might not share the values of "natives" often resulted in waiting periods or other conditions for the granting of state citizenship. The dilemma in virtually all of the new states was how to attract the maximum number of desirables without also opening the gates to those who, in one way or another, they saw as threats to the government or their way of life.

Pennsylvania, for example, allowed foreign settlers of "good character" who took "an oath or affirmation of allegiance" to acquire "land or other real estate," and then after one year's residence to be "deemed a free citizen." New York had no waiting period but gave the state legislature jurisdiction over naturalization, requiring applicants for citizenship "to abjure and renounce all allegiance and subjection to all and every foreign king, prince, potentate and state, in all matters ecclesiastical as well as civil." Maryland, Virginia, South Carolina, and Georgia also assigned naturalization authority to the state legislatures. Maryland required that an applicant declare "belief in the Christian religion," with a seven-year waiting period to hold public office, while Virginia granted citizenship to all white persons who had sworn fidelity and resided in the state for two years.[148] Residence requirements varied in the other states, sometimes in conjunction with property holding requirements, wealth, or religious or civic affirmations, and political rights were often granted only after an additional period of residence. While each state set its own standards for naturalization, none indicated that citizenship in the new nation came along with it or in fact even existed. Nor, however, did they declare citizens of other states "aliens," as had been the case earlier in the colonial period.

Some states, as in Pennsylvania, established classes of citizenship, wherein, for example, a first-class citizen had both political and civil rights, but a second-class citizen could not vote or hold office. In most cases, a man, almost always a white man, based on a term of residence or payment of taxes, could petition either the state legislature or local officials to move up in class. Other states, such as Massachusetts and Georgia, required testaments from third parties, sometimes a magistrate, that a potential citizen was committed to a republican form of government. In any case, "The states' preoccupation with the qualifications for citizenship obscured the ill-defined nature of the status itself."[149]

The Articles of Confederation provided little clarity. The term "perpetual union" used in the preamble merely indicated that the states were "binding themselves to assist each other, against all force offered to, or attacks made upon them, or any of them, on account of religion, sovereignty, trade, or any other pretense whatever," not creating a sovereign nation with a controlling central government.[150]

Article IV added to the confusion. It stated that "to better secure and perpetuate mutual friendship and intercourse among the people of the different states in this union, the free inhabitants of each of these states, paupers, vagabonds and fugitives from Justice excepted, shall be entitled to all privileges and immunities of free citizens in the several states." Unclear was what the differentiation of "people," "inhabitant," and "citizen" might be.

In January 1788, Madison, in Federalist 42, would expound on this "fault" in the Articles. "There is a confusion of language here, which is remarkable. Why the terms *free inhabitants* are used in one part of the article, *free citizens* in another, and *people* in another … cannot easily be determined." The polyglot citizenship laws did not escape his notice. "In one State, residence for a short term confirms all the rights of citizenship: in another, qualifications of greater importance are required. An alien, therefore, legally incapacitated for certain rights in the latter, may, by previous residence only in the former, elude his incapacity; and thus the law of one State be preposterously rendered paramount to the law of another, within the jurisdiction of the other."[151]

Article IV further stipulated that "the people of each state shall have free ingress and regress to and from any other state, and shall enjoy therein all the privileges of trade and commerce, subject to the same duties, impositions and restrictions as the inhabitants thereof respectively, provided that such restrictions shall not extend so far as to prevent the removal of property imported into any state, to any other State of which the Owner is an inhabitant; provided also that no imposition, duties or restriction shall be laid by any state, on the property of the united states, or either of them."[152] These guarantees could just as easily have been given in a treaty among sovereign nations as to states in the same nation. Although "individual states were obliged to confer the privileges and immunities of free citizens on free citizens of the other states of the Confederation," a definition of national citizenship was lacking.[153]

The explanation might be found in the middle-ground approach favored by John Dickinson, the main author of the Articles. Dickinson's moderation had caused him to refuse to sign the Declaration of Independence because he had not given up hope for a reconciliation with Britain.

Dickinson never specifically addressed why he had created three classes of American in Article IV, but the use of different terms was clearly intentional. Although he had been a major force in getting the convention called, his initial goal had been to try to reform the Articles—his creation—to strike a more effective balance between the states and national government. There is no way to be certain, but the jumble in Article IV could well have been an effort to strike a similar balance.

Whatever his reasoning, Dickinson had done little to resolve the inherent conflict between national and state citizenship, and when the Convention took up citizenship, the contradictions remained. What was clear was that states were unlikely to look favorably on any constitution that denied them the right to delineate naturalization as they saw fit. Nor would any attempt to fashion a single definition of citizenship find an easy road.

These questions were first broached on July 26, the last day of debate before the Convention recessed to allow the Committee of Detail to prepare its report. The committee's membership had been determined on July 24, and there is no indication how much, if at all, some of the more prominent delegates, such as Gouverneur Morris, George Mason, and of course James Madison, were miffed at being passed over.[154]

Regardless, Mason was determined to influence the outcome. He opened the July 26 session with a long speech criticizing every proposal for selecting the executive, including direct election, use of electors, state legislatures, state executives, and even a lottery. He then moved that the committee simply report that the executive "be appointed for seven years, & be ineligible a 2d. time," which the Convention approved 7-3.[155]

Mason surely wanted the committee to heed that vote, but he was not done. He later made a motion "that the Committee of detail be instructed to receive a clause requiring certain qualifications of landed property & citizenship of the U. States in members of the Legislature, and disqualifying persons having unsettled Accts. with or being indebted to the U. S. from being members of the Natl. Legislature."

After Charles Pickney seconded, Gouverneur Morris objected to such requirements, preferring "them in the electors rather than the elected." He then asserted that debtors in the nation "were few," a statement that was blatantly false, unless he was referring only to the wealthy, but acknowledged that there were many "with unsettled accounts." He observed, "The delay of settlemt. had been more the fault of the public than of the individuals. What will be done with those patriotic Citizens who have lent money, or services or property to their Country, without having been yet able to obtain a liquidation of their claims? Are they to be excluded?"

Mason and Madison argued for some provision to exclude debtors from Congress, but Morris had a potent response, evoking one of the few men in the hall who engendered almost universal respect—the Convention's president, George Washington. Morris "mentioned the case of the Commander in chief's presenting his account for secret services, which he said was so moderate that everyone was astonished at it; and so simple that no doubt could arise on it. Yet had the Auditor been disposed to delay the settlement, how easily might he have affected it, and how cruel wd. it be in such a case to keep a distinguished & meritorious Citizen under a temporary disability & disfranchisement."[156]

The word "landed" was subsequently removed from Mason's motion, as was "unsettled accounts," and eventually, references to debtors as well. The Committee of Detail was therefore sent off to do its work with none of the questions regarding either citizenship or qualifications to serve in Congress or the presidency in the least bit settled.

The Committee would not do much better. In its report, it merely required that "Every Member of the House of Representatives shall be of the age of twenty-five years at least; shall have been a citizen in the United States for at least three years before his election; and shall be, at the time of his election, a resident of the State in which he shall be chosen." For the Senate, the minimum age was raised to thirty, the citizenship requirement to four years, while residency remained the same. For the president, there were no requirements. The clause read, as Mason had suggested, "He shall be elected by ballot by the Legislature. He shall hold his office during the term of seven years; but shall not be elected a second time."[157]

Key here is the phrase "citizen *in* the United States," rather than "citizen *of* the United States." The committee might have felt "of" could not have been included since there was no existing definition of when citizenship in the nation might have begun. Was it 1776, when independence was declared, 1781, when the Articles were adopted, or 1783, when the Treaty of Paris was signed? A starting date for the United States had been conveniently omitted from any of the committee's proposals. From a technical standpoint, the United States did not exist until the Articles were adopted, meaning that, if national citizenship were the standard, no one in the nation was eligible to be a senator. (Despite the difficulty, the phrase was quickly amended to "citizen *of* the United States" although the record gives no indication of at whose behest the change was made.)

But regardless of the wording, the delegates still viewed state citizenship as of equal and possibly greater weight with whatever definition of national citizenship, if any, would later be agreed on. That engendered problems of its own, since, as each state had its own set of citizenship requirements, residents of some states would be eligible to be elected to national office while residents of different states with exactly the same set of circumstances would not. The difference in requirements might prompt potential officeholders who did not qualify to run in their home states to move to states where the requirements were less stringent, as both Rutledge and Charles Pinckney would soon point out.

Pinckney noted, "At present the citizens of one State, are entitled to the privileges of citizens in every State. Hence it follows, that a foreigner, as soon as he is admitted to the rights of citizenship in one, becomes entitled to them in all."[158] Nonetheless, rights that went across state lines were not the same as uniform rules for all states, which left the question of whether a genuine national government could be fashioned without a corresponding national standard on who could hold office.

This uncertainty led right into naturalization, in which the ease of becoming a citizen varied greatly among the states and could result in new arrivals being eligible for national office sooner than some would prefer. On August 8, Mason stated that while he was "for opening a wide door for emigrants, did not chuse to let foreigners and adventurers make laws for us & govern us." Citizens of only three years, he feared, might encourage a conspiracy. "It might also happen that a rich foreign Nation, for example Great Britain, might send over her tools who might bribe their way into the Legislature for insidious purposes." He moved to increase the citizenship requirement to seven years for service in the House, which Gouverneur Morris seconded, and which passed with only Connecticut voting no.[159]

When Sherman proposed substituting "inhabitant" for "resident," Madison noted that both terms were vague and that "Great disputes had been raised in Virga. concerning the meaning of residence as a qualification of Representatives which were determined more according to the affection or dislike to the man in question, than to any fixt interpretation of the word."

When Rutledge agreed that seven years residence "shd. be required in the State Wherein the Member shd. be elected" because "an emigrant from N. England to S. C. or Georgia would know little of its affairs and could not be supposed to acquire a thorough knowledge in less time," George Read of Delaware aptly "reminded him that we were now forming a *Natil* Govt and such a regulation would correspond little with the idea that we were one people."

But, Rutledge might have asked, could "one people" be said to live under "one government" if the states retained the autonomy they enjoyed under the Articles?

After Wilson "enforced the same consideration," Maryland's John Francis Mercer pointed out the pitfalls of imposing national standards on the states. "Such a regulation," he noted, "would present a greater alienship among the States than existed under the old federal system. It would interweave local prejudices & State distinctions in the very Constitution which is meant to cure them. He mentioned instances of violent disputes raised in Maryland concerning the term 'residence.'" Mercer, only twenty-eight, was the second youngest delegate after New Jersey's Jonathan Dayton at twenty-six, but he was unyielding in his distrust of centralized power.[160] While in the minority among the Convention delegates, his views had a substantial following in the nation at large.

Although many agreed that without common standards among the states, the goal of a single nation would be difficult to achieve, they were faced with the prospect that with them there might be no nation at all. Ellsworth, who proposed a one-year residency requirement, Mercer, Dickinson, and Madison all weighed in until Mason once again raised the specter of manipulated government. "If residence be not required, Rich men of neighbouring States, may employ with success the means of corruption in some particular district and thereby get into the public

Councils after having failed in their own State."

In the end, other than agreeing to change "resident" to "inhabitant" and extending the residency requirement for election to the House of Representatives to seven years, the Convention provided no further definition of national citizenship, including fixing a term before an immigrant could attain United States citizenship.

The following day, August 9, when Article V, Section 3 of the Committee of Detail's report came up for debate, the requirements to be a senator, the hesitancy to open Congress or the presidency to immigrants came fully to the fore.[161]

Gouverneur Morris immediately proposed extending the four-year citizen requirement for senators to fourteen, because of "the danger of admitting strangers into our public Councils." Charles Pinckney seconded the motion. Ellsworth quickly opposed it "as discouraging meritorious aliens from emigrating to this Country."[162]

Pinckney countered that since the Senate would "have the power of making treaties & managing our foreign affairs," there was a "peculiar danger and impropriety in opening its door to those who have foreign attachments." Mason agreed and if not for the immigrants who had "acquired great merit during the revolution," he would favor restricting the Senate to the native born.

Madison rose to present a long rebuttal. He was "not averse to some restrictions," although he would have favored none at all, but he found Morris's proposal excessive. Since Congress would be entrusted to set rules for naturalization, they could easily "fix different periods of residence as conditions of enjoying different privileges of Citizenship," a new version of Hamilton's proposal to create classes of citizenship with regard to voting. He also disapproved of embedding such a lengthy term in the Constitution "because it will put it out of the power of the Natl Legislature even by special acts of naturalization to confer the full rank of Citizens on meritorious strangers & because it will discourage the most desirable class of people from emigrating to the U. S."

Madison left no doubt about who was included in that desirable class. "Should the proposed Constitution have the intended effect of giving stability & reputation to our Govts. great numbers of respectable Europeans; men who love liberty and wish to partake its blessings, will be ready to transfer their fortunes hither." And so, Madison, in addition to favoring classes of citizenship, would allow Congress to cherry-pick among "respectable Europeans" for those who would benefit the nation while dismissing those who would not.[163]

Pierce Butler did not agree. He was "decidedly opposed to the admission of foreigners without a long residence in the Country. They bring with them, not only attachments to other Countries; but ideas of Govt. so distinct from ours that in every point of view they are dangerous." He was, ironically, forced to acknowledge that he himself was an immigrant, in fact, the son of a British aristocrat and former officer in the British army, whose unit had fired on civilians during the Boston Massacre.

Franklin, as he often did, tried to avoid extreme solutions, also pointing out how many potential national assets could be had from Europe. Randolph then reminded the delegates of the many immigrants who had fought in the revolution because of the promise of liberty, a promise that would be undermined if the Constitution would "disable them for 14 years to participate in the public honours." Halving the distance, he proposed seven years as a citizen rather than fourteen, although, as with the others, did not indicate when citizenship would begin or if it would be state or national citizenship.

Wilson, another delegate who had been born abroad, noted the "possibility, if the ideas of some gentlemen should be pursued, of his being incapacitated from holding a place under the very Constitution which he had shared in the trust of making."

Morris, again caustic when his ideas were questioned, argued "that we should not be polite at the expense of prudence." He denounced what he called "Citizens of the World," adding, "he did not wish to see any of them in our public Councils. He would not trust them. The men who can shake off their attachments to their own Country can never love any other."

But Morris had little backing. Fourteen years was defeated 7-4, as was Morris's next motion for thirteen years, and Pinckney's for ten. Finally, the Convention voted 6-4 to settle for nine years.

On August 13, Wilson asked the Convention to reconsider their decision and "The debate showed a continued division of opinion on the propriety of granting political rights to the foreign born."[164] Elbridge Gerry "wished that in future the eligibility might be confined to Natives. Foreign powers will intermeddle in our affairs, and spare no expence to influence them." North Carolina's Hugh Williamson wanted to extend the seven-year requirement to election to the House to nine. His reason was quite different than Gerry's. "Wealthy emigrants do more harm by their luxurious examples, than good, by the money, they bring with them." Pierce Butler was also "strenuous agst. admitting foreigners into our public Councils."

Madison, Hamilton, and Wilson, on the other hand, were against extending the time requirement, citing the benefits, both economic and political, of making the United States as attractive as possible to Europeans that could help in the nation's growth. But the delegates declined to further tinker with the formula. Both Hamilton's motion to require only citizenship to serve in national office and Williamson's to extend seven years to nine were defeated, as was Wilson's to shorten it to four years.[165]

The dilemma was obvious. As all agreed, a growing nation would need a continued influx of new arrivals, but many, perhaps most, "natives" were loath to share power in the new government. In addition, southern states, where barriers to state citizenship tended to be higher than in the North, were, as Pinckney had implied, leery of immigrants gaining citizenship in a northern state and then traveling to the South. Once there, because the Articles promised that "the free inhabitants" of each state "shall be entitled to all privileges and immunities of free citizens in the several states," they would be free to seek public office, a precursor to what would be called "carpetbagging" almost a century later. This fear was likely compounded by the need to protect a fragile, slave-based economic and social structure in which only a small slice of the wealthy elite benefited from owning slaves while the majority of poorer, backcountry farmers struggled.

The means to solve the problem, of course, was that illusive national standard for naturalization so that there would be no advantage for an immigrant to settle in any state except the one in which he intended to live. The Virginia Plan had made no mention of naturalization, although Randolph later indicated he thought it implicit in a "provision for harmony among the states."[166] James Paterson's New Jersey Plan was more specific, stipulating that the "rule for naturalization ought to be the same in every State."[167] But neither Randolph nor Paterson elaborated as to what that rule might be, nor did anyone else.

Eventually, the Committee of Detail was left to decide whether to include naturalization in its report and in what level of detail. The committee chose to bypass details entirely. Included in the powers of the legislature in Article VII was "To establish a uniform rule of naturalization throughout the United States." Also once more, there would be a price for vagueness. "The Convention did not explore the implications of the clause, nor did the delegates indicate whether the actual power to naturalize was to be exclusive or concurrent. These questions would be open to debate into the nineteenth century."[168] There was also no discussion on whether citizenship conferred political rights as well as legal rights, and to whether there would be classes of citizen.[169]

During the remaining weeks of the Convention, the wording changed very little, and in final version, in Article I, Section 8, Congress was given the power to "To establish a uniform Rule of Naturalization, and uniform Laws on the subject of Bankruptcies throughout the United States."

The First Congress soon took up the task. As at the Convention, most in Congress agreed that immigration was to be enthusiastically encouraged. John Lawrence of New York observed in the debates over naturalization in February 1790, "The reason of admitting foreigners to the rights of citizenship among us is the encouragement of emigration, as we have a large tract of country to people."[170]

There also remained general agreement that the country did not want just anybody. When discussing a residency requirement, James Madison, by then a Virginia representative, warned, "When we are considering the advantages that may result from an easy mode of naturalization, we ought also to consider the cautions necessary to guard against abuses; it is no doubt very desirable, that we should hold out as many inducements as possible, for the worthy part of mankind to come and settle amongst us, and throw their fortunes into a common lot with ours…" but, "those who acquire the rights of citizenship without adding to the strength or wealth of the community are not people we are in want of." Madison concluded, "I should be exceeding sorry, sir, that our rule of naturalization excluded a single person of good fame, that really meant to incorporate himself into our society; on the other hand, I do not wish that any man should acquire the privilege, but who, in fact, is a real addition to the wealth or strength of the United States."[171]

In the end, Madison's hesitation worked itself into the final bill. On March 26, 1790, President George Washington signed "An Act to establish a uniform Rule of Naturalization" into law. It stipulated: "That any alien, being a free white person, who shall have resided within the limits and under the jurisdiction of the United States for the term of two years, may be admitted to become a citizen thereof ... in any one of the states wherein he shall have resided for the term of one year at least ... that he is a person of good character, and taking the oath or affirmation prescribed by law, to support the constitution of the United States."[172]

Although naturalization was limited to free whites, just how to determine race was left unspecified and would cause a good bit of controversy in the decades to come, especially when Asians and East Asians began to arrive in the West.[173] In addition, the use of "he," as it had been with representation, was not an accident. In practice, few women could become naturalized citizens, except by application with her husband, or sometimes her son. Most significant was that the national standard for naturalization was not really national at all. Deciding who among their new arrivals met the criteria and qualified for United States citizenship was left to state agencies who could—and often did—manipulate the rules for political advantage.[174]

Although almost every member of Congress, as well as President Washington, favored the limitation of "whites of good character," there were dissenting voices. Senator William Maclay of Pennsylvania, who served only one two-year term and kept a lacerating and often hilarious account of the experience, wrote, "The truth of the matter is that it is a Vile bill, illiberal. Void of philanthropy and needed mending much."[175]

Maclay left Congress in disgust with no mending of the 1790 law to be had. In the end, the only part of the legislation that caused widespread controversy was the residency requirement, which was directly related to the understanding that over time it would become easier (for men) to vote, with the property holding prerequisite likely to eventually disappear. Residency was raised from two years to five in 1795, and then, in 1798, with Thomas Jefferson's populists threatening to displace John Adams's stodgier Federalists, to fourteen years. (It wouldn't help Adams, who, as noted, would lose to Jefferson in 1800, not because landless whites were counted for electoral votes, but because 3/5 of the slaves were.) In 1802, with Jefferson in the President's House—it wasn't officially called the White House until 1901—the requirement was again put at five years, where it has remained since.

But whether or not the law was vile, it was certainly not sufficiently defined, as revealed during the aborted senatorial career of Pennsylvania's Albert Gallatin in 1793. Gallatin was born in Switzerland, but settled in the United States in 1780, and "had taken oaths of allegiance and purchased lands in Virginia and Massachusetts between 1783 and 1785, and had fought for the American cause during the War of Independence."[176] Gallatin was a good deal more than an ordinary patriotic immigrant. One of the keenest financial minds in America, he helped formulate and implement financial policy for decades and, under Jefferson and Madison, would become Secretary of the Treasury before being appointed minister to France and then to Great Britain. Gallatin would be instrumental in helping Jefferson gain the presidency over Aaron Burr, and, after Lewis and Clark trekked through Montana, in 1804 became one the three American statesmen, along with Jefferson and Madison, to have counties named for them.

But despite his dedicated service and lofty reputation, when Gallatin was elected to the Senate by the Pennsylvania legislature in 1793, nineteen state residents—who happened to be Federalists, political opponents—petitioned the Senate to deny him his seat because he had arrived after independence had been declared and, as an immigrant, had not been a citizen of any state for the required nine years. Gallatin, on the Senate floor, recited his bona fides and claimed the accusation was ludicrous. But, although obviously an American to everyone in the chamber, it was revealed that Gallatin had not technically fulfilled the requirements for citizenship in any of the thirteen states. He had, for example, taken only one rather than the two required oaths in Virginia.

Although Gallatin, an avowed Jeffersonian, once again spoke for himself on the Senate floor and made an impassioned plea for fairness, the Senate, dominated by Federalists rejected him.

Lack of specifics on national citizenship would cause further problems, not the least of which arose in 1857 when the Supreme Court, under Chief Justice Roger Brooke Taney, ruled in *Dred Scott v. Sandford* that not only could slaves not be United States citizens, but also "A free negro of the African race, whose ancestors were brought to this country and sold as slaves, is not a 'citizen' within the meaning of the Constitution of the United States."[177] Taney's ruling, meant to clarify the status of Blacks in the United States and thus prevent a war, instead helped start one.

Soon after the end of that war, in 1868, to wipe Taney's judgment from the books, the Fourteenth Amendment was ratified, declaring "All persons born or naturalized in the United States, and subject to the jurisdiction thereof, are citizens of the United States and of the State wherein they reside." This was the Constitution's first definitive mention of national citizenship and also the first time in American history that people who were not "white" were officially allowed to become citizens of the United States.[178]

But, while the amendment further stated, "No State shall make or enforce any law which shall abridge the privileges or immunities of citizens of the United States," there was no constitutional definition of what those "privileges and immunities" might be. Since the delegates in Philadelphia had avoided a discussion of national citizenship, it would once again be left to the legislature and the courts to determine the limits of state prerogative, which would prove a fatal delegation of authority.

That began to become clear just four years later when the Supreme Court heard what became known as the Slaughter-House Cases.[179]

In 1869, New Orleans, after years of public outcry, finally addressed the unspeakable quality of the city's water supply. Among the most prominent culprits were the local butchers, most with slaughtering facilities upriver from the city, who persisted in sweeping the bones, organs, body parts, dung, and urine of cows, sheep, and pigs into the Mississippi, such that occasionally bits of these products would flow out of water taps. Periodic epidemics of cholera and yellow fever had become regular occurrences.

A new state law required the butchers to slaughter, gut, and carve up animals in a single facility downriver from the water mains and under the supervision of trained inspectors. This central slaughterhouse would be run by a private corporation licensed by the state. Butchers, almost all of whom were white, would pay a small fee for every animal they acquired but would no longer be required either to purchase or lease facilities of their own.

Although this was in no way a bad deal for the butchers, they were a cantankerous bunch who bristled at being told what to do. They sued on the grounds that the Fourteenth Amendment guaranteed them "privileges and immunities" of citizenship, in this case the right to conduct business how and where they wished. The butchers were represented by John A. Campbell, a brilliant legal theorist who had himself been on the Supreme

Court until he left in 1861 to become the Confederacy's Assistant Secretary of War. After Lincoln's assassination, Campbell had been arrested and held in jail for six months as a potential conspirator.

Campbell set a trap for his former colleagues. Although the amendment had been drafted to apply federal citizenship rights to newly freed slaves, race was never mentioned. After the privileges and immunities clause, the text read "nor shall any State deprive any person of life, liberty, or property, without due process of law; nor deny to any person within its jurisdiction the equal protection of the laws." The use of "person" allowed Campbell to argue that the amendment covered white citizens as well as black.

If true, Louisiana had no right to herd butchers into a common facility and force them to pay fees to ply their trade. Unless, of course, state citizenship was different than national citizenship, with different "privileges and immunities." In that case, state governments could do things the federal government could not. Although Campbell carefully avoided saying so, if there were two categories of citizenship, states could other pass laws that fit their own definition covering such subjects as voting rights.

The justices, therefore, could either use the Fourteenth Amendment to protect a group of white butchers who were poisoning New Orleans's drinking water, or they could limit the amendment's reach by narrowing when its guarantees could be applied. Although Campbell almost certainly did not inform his clients, his personal agenda of undermining Reconstruction would be much better served if he lost the case.

Which he did.

The Court ruled, in a 5-4 decision, that "the Fourteenth Amendment only banned the states from depriving blacks of equal rights; it did not guarantee that all citizens, regardless of race, should receive equal economic privileges by the state." Having ruled that the amendment was not color blind, the Court narrowed its reach still further. "Any rights guaranteed by the Privileges or Immunities Clause were limited to areas controlled by the federal government, such as access to ports and waterways, the right to run for federal office, and certain rights affecting safety on the seas."

In a ruling motivated by the desire to protect the rights of Black Americans, the Court thus succeeded in undermining them. "In the

Slaughter-House Cases the Supreme Court could have ruled that the Fourteenth Amendment's privileges or immunities clause meant that the federal government had the power to protect, from infringement by state governments, citizens' basic rights-both those enumerated in the Bill of Rights and other fundamental rights such as the right to pursue an occupation. By declining to do so, the Court left to southern state governments the responsibility of protecting the rights of African Americans."[180]

As decades of Jim Crow would attest, southern state governments would do no such thing.

The lack of specifics with respect to national citizenship has been at the root of a number of other controversies, the most recent of which has arisen over the Fourteenth Amendment's guarantee of what has been termed "birthright citizenship." Although the meaning of "All persons born or naturalized in the United States, and subject to the jurisdiction thereof, are citizens of the United States and of the State wherein they reside," in Section 1 seems clear, some have questioned whether the term has blanket application, including, for example, children born in the United States to parents who have entered the country illegally.

For years, a small group of conservative legal scholars have argued that such children are not constitutionally protected, but their protests gained little traction until Donald Trump, in his campaign for the presidency in 2016, promised, if he won, to deport this group of native-born citizens.[181] Two years later, Trump tried to keep that promise and announced that he could end birthright citizenship by executive order, a position that had little or no support even among conservatives. House Speaker Paul Ryan, for example, categorically denied that the president had such a power.[182]

But the battle is not over. "Left-leaning" constitutional law scholar Rogers Smith, "has argued that the Constitution doesn't require that birthright citizenship be extended to undocumented individuals, and that Congress could pass a law denying it to them."[183]

To test that theory, in January 2021, Texas Republican Brian Babin introduced the "Birthright Citizenship Act," which "limits birthright citizenship by redefining what it means to be *subject to the jurisdiction* of the United States. Under the bill, a person is subject to U.S. jurisdiction if he or she is born to a parent who is (1) a U.S. citizen or national, (2) a lawful permanent resident residing in the United States, or (3) an alien performing active service in the Armed Forces."[184] The bill was referred to a subcommittee, where it languished in the Democrat controlled House. If Republicans take control of Congress and the presidency, the result might be different, especially if a Supreme Court that has shown little hesitance in promoting a conservative agenda approved.

Such a law would have far-reaching and destabilizing impact. Michael Fix, a senior fellow at the Migration Policy Institute, wrote in 2016, "Repealing birthright citizenship would create a self-perpetuating class that would be excluded from social membership for generations … Ending birthright citizenship for U.S. babies with two unauthorized immigrant parents would increase the existing unauthorized population by 4.7 million people by 2050 … 1 million would be the children of two parents who themselves had been born in the United States. Under a scenario denying U.S. citizenship to babies with one parent who is unauthorized … would balloon … the unauthorized population to 24 million in 2050 from the 11 million today."[185]

Thus, as with voting rights, the unwillingness of the delegates in Philadelphia to risk rejection by the states by addressing controversial issues created opportunities for those who would use the omissions as springboards to power.

Chapter 7

Contorting the Truth: Gerrymandering

"By gerrymandering the State, seven hundred Democratic votes were equal to one thousand Republican votes."
Gustave Koerner, former governor of Illinois, referring to the 1858 election which Lincoln lost to Democrat Stephen Douglas for Illinois Senator.

"All animals are equal, but some are more equal than others."
George Orwell, *Animal Farm*

The right to vote is fundamental to democratic rule, but casting ballots alone does not guarantee that democracy will function fairly and effectively. Votes must also be cast so that a minority of the electorate cannot skew the course of government to usurp the will of the majority.

In contemporary American politics, absence of majority rule has become a source of unending debate. At issue is whether the House of Representatives and, through the Electoral College, the presidency, genuinely represent the will of the American people, or whether the system has been manipulated to favor groups employing undemocratic means to seize and hold power. In addition to voter suppression, if electoral districts are unfairly drawn, a partisan minority can claim a greater share of influence in the House than that to which it is entitled. (The Senate, in which Wyoming with its population of 600,000 has the same presence as California's almost forty million, has been minority-ruled since the founding.)[186]

Unfairly drawn electoral districts were not unknown to the delegates in Philadelphia. All were aware of the presence in Great Britain of what would later be called "rotten boroughs," once-highly populated districts that had lost most or sometimes nearly all of its residents but still retained a seat in parliament. Many of these ghost districts evolved in the eighteenth century, when industrialization spurred a vast population shift to urban areas, leaving the countryside often denuded. Sparsely settled and lacking diversity, these districts often came under the control of one or two powerful families and thus functioned as private fiefdoms.

Allusions to rotten boroughs were sprinkled throughout the debates on representation. In the June 18 session, James Wilson, who had already spoken against the dangers of small electoral districts, noted, "An inequality in [representation] has ever been a poison contaminating every branch of Govt. In G. Britain ... this poison has had a full operation ... The political liberty of that Nation, owing to the inequality of representation is at the mercy of its rulers ... It is a lesson we ought not to disregard, that the smallest bodies in G. B. are notoriously the most corrupt."[187]

Later in the proceedings, New York's John Lansing added, "The point of Representation could receive no elucidation from the case of England. The corruption of the boroughs did not proceed from their comparative smallness: but from the actual fewness of the inhabitants, some of them not having more than one or two. A great inequality existed in the Counties of England."[188]

Mason and Gorham were among other delegates who commented on the corruption in the British system, and so it is fair to conclude that the need for electoral districts to be fairly drawn was not lost on the delegates. Here again, however, any attempt to impose national standards on what had been strictly a state prerogative was bound to be an impediment to ratification.

The Committee of Detail sought to navigate between the extremes. On August 9, the Convention took up Article VI, Section 1 of the committee's report, which read, "The times and places and the manner of holding the elections of the members of each House shall be prescribed by the Legislature of each State; but their provisions concerning them may at any time be altered by the Legislature of the United States."[189]

Pinckney and Rutledge immediately "moved to strike out the ... provisions [that elections] may at any time be altered by the Legislature of the United States. The States they contended could & must be relied on in such cases." Rutledge had chaired the committee, and so the provision granting oversight to national legislature must have been forced on him. Gorham, his fellow committee member, countered, "It would be as improper take this power from the Natl. Legislature, as to Restrain the British Parliament from regulating the circumstances of elections, leaving this business to the Counties themselves."

Madison, as Gorham had been, was prescient in his fear of leaving these questions only to the states, recognizing a greater threat from state legislatures abusing their power than the national government:

> Legislatures of the States ought not to have the uncontrolled right of regulating the times places & manner of holding elections. It was impossible to foresee all the abuses that might be made of the [states'] discretionary power. Whether the electors should vote by ballot or viva voce, should assemble at this place or that place; should be divided into districts or all meet at one place, shd all vote for all the representatives; or all in a district vote for a number allotted to the district; these & many other points would depend on the Legislatures and might materially affect the appointments. Whenever the State Legislatures had a favorite measure to carry, they would take care so to mould their regulations as to favor the candidates they wished to succeed. Besides, the inequality of the Representation in the Legislatures of particular States, would produce a like inequality in their representation in the Natl. Legislature.

Rufus King agreed. "If this power be not given to the Natl. Legislature, their right of judging of the returns of their members may be frustrated. No probability has been suggested of its being abused by them." Referring to impotence engendered by the Articles, King added, "Although this scheme of erecting the Genl. Govt. on the authority of the State Legislatures has been fatal to the federal establishment, it would seem as if many gentlemen, still foster the dangerous idea." Gouverneur Morris feared "that the States might make false returns and then make no provisions for new elections."

Pinckney's and Rutledge's motion was dismissed out of hand but neither did the delegates choose to include in the new Constitution standards under which electoral districts must be drawn. Once again, the delegates avoided a potentially divisive issue by passing it off to Congress.

Although on its face, the clause as written would seem to grant final authority to the national legislature, this was not as big a concession to the central government as it might appear. As Congress was to be dominated by the very states whose laws would come under scrutiny, the chances that they would be forced to adhere to some yet formulated standards were slim. States would thus retain maximum flexibility because of the perceived need to allow ruling parties to design specific procedures to keep them in power and the rabble out. In addition, legislation could, and would, be subject to review by the judiciary, which, although not considered a serious impediment at the time, has most certainly become one.

But because the oversight clause, however weak, had been included, during state ratification conventions, former delegates who favored the plan scrambled to reassure their fellows that the national government had not usurped their power.

In the Massachusetts convention, Rufus King "rose to pursue the inquiry, why the place and manner of holding elections were omitted in the section under debate. It was to be observed, he said, that in the Constitution of Massachusetts, and other States, the manner and place of elections were provided for; the manner was by ballot, and the places towns; for, said he, we happened to settle originally in townships. But it was different in the southern States." Alluding to England's rotten boroughs, he added "A district that may now be fully settled, may in time be scarcely inhabited; and the back country, now scarcely inhabited, may be fully settled. Suppose this State thrown into eight districts, and a member apportioned to each: if the numbers increase, the representatives and districts will be increased. The matter, therefore, must be left subject to the regulation of the State legislature."[190]

William Davie, in the North Carolina ratifying convention, also insisted the clause was favorable to the states:

> A consolidation of the states is said by some gentlemen to have been intended. They insinuate that this was the cause of their giving this power of elections. If there were any seeds in this Constitution which might, one day, produce a consolidation, it would, sir, with me, be an insuperable objection, I am so perfectly convinced that so extensive a country as this can never be managed by one consolidated government. The Federal Convention were as well convinced as the members of this house, that the state governments were absolutely necessary to the existence of the federal government.[191]

Those who opposed the Constitution had a different interpretation. On November 29, 1787, Maryland's Luther Martin, his state's attorney general and one of the Constitution's fiercest opponents, delivered a long, point-by-point—110 of them—refutation of the proposed Constitution to the Maryland legislature. It was called "Genuine Information" and in point 35, he wrote, "In the fourth section of the first article, it is *expressly provided*, that the *Congress* shall have a power to *make and alter* all regulations concerning the *time* and manner of *holding elections for senators;* a provision *expressly looking forward to*, and, *I have no doubt designed* for, the *utter extinction* and *abolition of all State governments*."[192]

Despite Martin's predictions, state governments were not abolished. On the contrary, states soon recognized that in the absence of genuine federal regulation or redistricting rules that were standard across the nation, they could artificially increase their supporters' influence the legislature or in some cases prevent political opponents from winning elections.

One of the first victims was James Madison, the man who warned that leaving districting to the states was ripe for abuse.

One June 2, 1788, the Virginia ratifying convention met in Richmond to decide whether to endorse the new Constitution. The outcome was very much in doubt. Sentiment against ceding power to a national government that would, at least at first, be controlled by northern states was strong. "A substantial portion of the delegates were concerned about the concentration of power in the new government, and they demanded that before ratification, a second federal convention be called to enact various amendments for the protection of both state sovereignty and individual rights."[193]

Leading the opposition was the brilliant and ruthless Patrick Henry, "the spellbinder from Prince Edward County," considered the finest trial lawyer in the United States.[194] Leading the pro-Constitution forces was Madison. Other larger-than-life Virginians, including George Mason and John Marshall, were arrayed on either side of the question but for more than three weeks, this was largely a head-to-head battle.

> "Henry dominated the Convention. For the first time in his life, however, he was overmatched in public debate. The Convention lasted twenty-two days, and Henry took the floor on all but five, speaking as many as eight times at one meeting, with one diatribe lasting seven hours. In contrast, Madison spoke chiefly in rebuttal, and oftentimes his voice was so low that he could not be heard

throughout the meeting hall on Shockoe Hill."[195]

But Madison "knew he was strongest where Henry was weakest—he had his facts straight and could rely on a logic that was unassailable." He "deflated Henry's position by exposing his faulty logic, inaccurate reading of history, and misconstruction of the language of the document." After Henry's last-ditch effort to attach a string of conditional amendments was defeated, Virginia, the most populous and important state in the nation, voted narrowly to ratify the Constitution.

Henry, furious in defeat, vowed revenge. When the Virginia General Assembly met in October 1788, one its first orders of business was choosing the state's two new senators and setting the conditions for the election of members of the House of Representatives. "As he had not in the 1788 convention, in that year's state legislature Patrick Henry commanded a large majority of the delegates."[196] Aware that Madison wanted very much to be in the new Congress, Henry successfully connived to prevent the General Assembly from appointing him to the Senate, the seats going to Antifederalists William Grayson and Richard Henry Lee.

Henry then set his sights on keeping Madison out of the House of Representatives. State law required a candidate to reside in the district in which he would run. Henry prevailed on state officials drawing the district lines to create the Madison's district to skew heavily Antifederalist.[197] An early Madison biographer observed, "In laying off the State into districts for the election of representatives, ingenious and artificial combinations were resorted to for the purpose of insuring [Madison's] defeat. The county in which he resided [Orange] was thrown into association with seven others, five of which, through their delegates in [Virginia's ratifying] convention, had given an undivided vote against the acceptance of the Constitution."[198]

Madison, in New York, sitting in the last Confederation Congress, received a warning in a letter from Washington. "The Accts. from Richmond are indeed, very unpropitious to fœderal measures. The whole proceedings of the Assembly, *it is said* may be summed up in one word—to wit—that the Edicts of Mr. H—are enregistered with less opposition by the Majority of that body, than those of the Grand Monarch are in the Parliaments of France. He has only to say let this be Law—and it is Law."[199]

Henry then helped persuade James Monroe, a young and popular war hero, to seek the seat. The election was set for early 1789. Madison, who could be shut out of the new government entirely, left New York and rode home quickly through freezing weather. After he arrived, he was forced to campaign through cold and snow while ill from the journey.

One of the main issues in the election was Madison's resistance to amending the new Constitution with a Bill of Rights. Madison, once more, was not about to let ideology get in the way of practicalities, and he quickly pivoted and became a champion of the very amendments he had opposed. He tried to explain his reversal by claiming after ratification he was "free to espouse such amendments as will, in the most satisfactory manner, guard essential rights, and will render certain vexatious abuses of power impossible," as if his previous opposition was not totally heartfelt.[200]

In the end, Madison, armed with his newly adopted support for a series of amendments, bested Henry for a second time, beating Monroe handily. Eventually, he would create their first draft and submit twelve to Congress, ten of which would be adopted.

Madison's views had begun to change and in 1792 he abandoned the Federalists and, with Thomas Jefferson, founded what was soon called the Democratic Republican Party. That Madison had been forced to compete so desperately for a seat in a district whose boundaries had been jiggled to stop him could only have occurred because the delegates ignored his warning and included neither standards nor prohibitions on the electoral process.

Another member of Jefferson's new party was the Convention's quixotic gadfly, Elbridge Gerry, and in 1812, Gerry used the lack of constitutional restrictions to help create one of American politics' most famous portmanteaus.

Gerry, one of three delegates present at the Constitution's signing who refused to put his name to the document, had been profiled by Georgia delegate William Pierce. "Mr. Gerry … is a hesitating and laborious speaker; possesses a great degree of confidence and goes extensively into all subjects that he speaks on, without respect to elegance or flower of diction."[201] In a letter to Jefferson by an unknown correspondent, almost certainly a fellow delegate, Gerry was described as, "from New England, a man of sense, but a Grumbletonian. He was of service by objecting to everything he did not propose."[202] His good friend John Adams lamented to Gerry that he had an "obstinacy that will risk great things to secure small ones."[203]

For all his quirky behavior, Gerry was thought by most to have great personal integrity and always held true to his distrust of centralized power. Without Shays's Rebellion as incentive, he might well have refused to attend the Constitutional Convention at all. Although wary of Federalists' embrace of a powerful national government, he served as an elector for Adams in the 1796 presidential election. But he soon decided the Federalists were growing too dictatorial and, like Madison, abandoned the party. He ran for governor of Massachusetts as a Democratic-Republican in 1800 and again in 1803, losing to fellow delegate and Constitution signer, Caleb Strong. In 1810, he was finally successful, winning a narrow victory.

Gerry ran for re-election in 1812 in state elections that promised to be especially bitter. Political affiliation was almost evenly divided between Federalists, who had ruled the nation for the first dozen years, and Democratic-Republicans, who had done so for the second dozen. Democratic-Republicans controlled the Massachusetts legislature and decided to redraw the state's senate districts to increase their majority. Electoral districts had traditionally followed county lines, but the new map contorted the state into a series of odd shapes that Federalists called "carvings and manglings."[204]

Gerry, albeit reluctantly, signed the bill into law on February 11, 1812, and shortly after it was signed, Benjamin Russell, a Federalist newspaper editor, hung a map of the new districts over his desk. Gerry's home district in Essex County was so tortuously drawn that it seemed to be in the shape of a dragon. It is said that the painter Gilbert Stuart, best known for his portrait of George Washington, visited Russell's office one day, saw the creature and added a head, wings, and claws. Rather than a dragon, however, he said, "That will do for a salamander." Russell replied, "Better say a Gerry-mander!"[205]

Within a month, the image, with its newly coined name, appeared as a cartoon-map in the *Boston Gazette.* Below it, a fanciful satire joked that the beast had been born in the extreme heat of partisan anger—the "many fiery ebullitions of party spirit, many explosions of democratic wrath and fulminations of gubernatorial vengeance within the year past."[206]

Although the tale of its origin may be apocryphal, there is no doubting the result. Republicans won 29 seats with 50,164 votes, while the

Federalists' 51,766 votes secured only 11 seats. But it couldn't help Gerry, who lost the statewide popular vote for governor to his old nemesis, Caleb Strong.

For a time, another favored gambit to win overrepresentation of a party in power was switching back and forth between single member districts and general ticket representation. With the latter, each voter could cast as many votes as there were congressional seats but could only vote once for a candidate. Thus, "If your party garners 55 percent of the vote statewide, moving all House races to general ticket at-large elections means your party can win the entire slate." States were not shy about changing the rule to whichever rule favor them at any one time. "At any time between 1789 to 1840, roughly one-quarter of all congressional seats were allocated statewide, but which quarter was in constant flux."[207]

Although the lack of specifics in the elections clause made this back and forth totally permissible, the resulting chaos was too much, even for congressmen. In 1839, for example, "New Jersey, which at the time used general-ticket voting, sent rival delegations of Democrats and Whigs to the House, each claiming to have been duly elected. The confusion ended in March of 1840 when a ruling from the Committee on Elections put to rest the months-long controversy and gave control of the chamber to Democrats."[208]

To end such shenanigans, after rancorous debate, Congress passed and President John Tyler signed the Apportionment Act of 1842, which effectively eliminated general ticket voting and mandated single member districts for all Congressional seats.

With the demise of general ticket voting, gerrymandering remained an all too-standard method of gaining power in both state and national legislatures and remains so today.[209] The judiciary, which has become the default arbiter of redistricting complaints, has an uneven record in enforcing prohibitions against even blatant cheating by parties in power. In many cases, the courts refused to intervene because they claimed that "political questions" were beyond their purview and drawing district boundaries was a political act.

In 1961, however, the Supreme Court heard an appeal by Charles Baker, a Republican who lived in a small city in Shelby County, Tennessee, and who claimed that the Democrat-dominated Tennessee legislature had denied him his Fourteenth Amendment guarantee of equal protection of the law by refusing to redistrict every ten years, as required by state law. The last redistricting had been1901, based on the 1900 census. Since then, in true rotten borough fashion, although many rural districts had lost large percentages of their residents, they maintained control of the state legislature at the expense of urban districts whose populations had soared.

Tennessee countered by citing *Colegrove v. Green*, a 1946 decision in which Justice Felix Frankfurter, writing for a 4-3 majority, ruled that since the elections clause, Article I, section IV, entitled state legislatures of each state, in this case Illinois, the authority to establish "the time, place, and manner of holding elections for Congressional Representatives," unless overruled by Congress, that the federal courts could therefore play no role in the process.[210]Illinois, like Tennessee, had also refused to redistrict since the 1900 census, despite an enormous shift in population from rural to urban areas.

Frankfurter was still on the Court in 1961, and his views had not changed. Hugo Black and William O. Douglas, who had dissented in *Colegrove* were still serving as well. Black's dissent in *Colegrove* went to the heart of the omission in Philadelphia. Noting that "The Constitution contains no express provision requiring that congressional election districts established by the States must contain approximately equal populations," he nonetheless insisted that, "the constitutionally guaranteed right to vote, and the right to have one's vote counted clearly imply the policy that state election systems, no matter what their form, should be designed to give approximately equal weight to each vote cast."

Although Black's commitment to equal rights was admirable, his reasoning was a stretch. The delegates in Philadelphia had specifically avoided including the necessity of having votes count for equal weight and left it to the states to do pretty much as they pleased and nothing in the ratifying conventions would indicate differently.

But the Fourteenth Amendment was a powerful tool when the Court chose to use it, and in *Baker v. Carr* it did. In a rancorous 6-2 decision, Frankfurter one of the dissenters, the Court ruled that Baker's "allegations of a denial of equal protection presented a justiciable constitutional cause of action upon which appellants are entitled to a trial and a decision."[211] Frankfurter, joined by Justice John Marshall Harlan, vitriolically disagreed, seeing the Court as issuing "a massive repudiation of the experience of our whole past in asserting destructively novel judicial power."

Frankfurter went on to issue a warning that has a distinctly contemporary ring. "The Court's authority—possessed of neither the purse nor the sword—ultimately rests on sustained public confidence in its moral sanction. Such feeling must be nourished by the Court's complete detachment, in fact and in appearance, from political entanglements and by abstention from injecting itself into the clash of political forces in political settlements."

Although he was one the Court's great legal scholars, Frankfurter here was naïve. Not only is "complete detachment in fact" a likely unattainable goal, "in appearance" it is impossible. With the Constitution and the laws that flow from it subject to interpretation that generally supports the political view of the beholder, any decision by the Court can be seen as biased or politically motivated by a substantial segment of the citizenry.

Although the Court did not rule directly in *Baker*, returning the case to district court, it had introduced the principle of "one man, one vote" into American jurisprudence, affirmed two years later in *Reynolds v. Sims*, which mandated that electoral districts for state legislatures must be population based.[212]

But for all the progress, gerrymandering did not go away. Although "gerrymandering in the 1970s and 1980s and even into the 1990s was primarily an incumbent-protection racket, with both parties complicit," it has evolved into bitter partisan warfare.[213] With the nation at ideological loggerheads, many states, especially those with Republican-dominated legislatures, have openly embraced redistricting on both the state and national level to either perpetuate their control or enhance it.

As a result, gerrymandering falls unevenly on the states. Those such as New York and California, which have mandated either non-partisan commissions or judicial oversight of their redistricting processes, are helpless to counter states with blatantly partisan redistricting, such as Alabama or Texas. As a result, control of the House of Representatives may go to the party that behaves in the most undemocratic manner, which would also increase its influence in the Electoral College.

Recently, another threat to fairly drawn electoral districts emerged, this one from the long discredited "independent state legislature theory," which postulated that since the Constitution authorizes only a state's legislature to regulate federal elections within that state, neither the governor nor state courts can intervene.

This construct gained traction in the wake of *Bush v. Gore*, when the Supreme Court seemed to indicate that "a state legislature directing the manner of appointing electors pursuant to Article II operates with independence from its own state constitution."[214]

Proponents of this notion insist the Article I phrase, "The Times, Places and Manner of holding Elections for Senators and Representatives, shall be prescribed in each State by the Legislature thereof," and the Article II direction that "each state shall appoint [presidential electors] in a manner the legislature thereof may direct," prohibits oversight by the other branches of state government.

If adopted, the independent state legislature theory would mean that if a gerrymandered state legislature created gerrymandered congressional districts without interference from the state's executive or judiciary, and if the United States Supreme Court refused to intervene in "political questions," a minority party could rule in perpetuity. In effect, the rotten borough doctrine would have been adopted nationwide, and all semblance of genuine democratic rule would vanish.

The theory is textualism run wild and, in this case, to the surprise of many Court watchers, the Supreme Court agreed. By a 6-3 in *Moore v. Harper*, Chief Justice Roberts, writing for the majority, ruled that the elections clause "does not insulate state legislatures from the ordinary exercise of state judicial review."

Although the nation dodged this very real threat to the fundaments of democracy, the danger remains. Without specific guidelines in the Constitution, state ruling parties can resort to whatever gamesmanship will work to remain in power. That this manifestation was too extreme, even for three conservative justices, does not mean that slightly less egregious ploys will not achieve greater success.

Chapter 8

Judicial Review: Nature...and Chief Justice Marshall...Abhor a Vacuum

"Liberty may be endangered by the abuse of liberty, but also by the abuse of power."
James Madison.

"By ensuring that no one in government has too much power, the Constitution helps protect ordinary Americans every day against abuse of power by those in authority."
Chief Justice John Roberts

On June 25, 2013, in the halls of the Supreme Court, a building whose motto reads, "Equal Justice Under Law," Chief Justice John Roberts delivered the opinion for a 5-4 majority in the most important voting rights case to come before the Court in more than half a century, *Shelby County, Alabama v. Holder*.

Shelby County was spawned by the 1965 Voting Rights Act, passage of which had followed "Bloody Sunday," March 7, 1965, when a voting rights march in Selma, Alabama, led by Hosea Williams and the twenty-five-year-old future Congressman John Lewis, resulted in six hundred peaceful protestors being tear gassed, run down by horses, and clubbed unmercifully by Dallas County sheriff Jim Clark, his deputies, and Alabama state troopers. Many of the victims were spat on as they lay injured on the ground. Lewis suffered a fractured skull.

What made the incident noteworthy was that, unlike the many other occasions in which voting rights advocates had been attacked and sometimes murdered by Southern whites, this entire episode was filmed by national news organizations and televised across the country that same night—ABC television interrupted the premier broadcast of *Judgment at Nuremberg*, a film about the trial of Nazi war criminals, to air the entire horrifying spectacle.

Within days, demonstrations against Southern racism were held in more than eighty United States cities, and finally, after decades of looking the other way, the government in Washington was forced to act. On March 15, President Lyndon Johnson appeared before a special joint session of Congress and told the assembled senators and representatives, "What happened in Selma is part of a far larger movement which reaches into every section and State of America. It is the effort of American Negroes to secure for themselves the full blessings of American life. Their cause must be our cause too. Because it is not just Negroes, but really it is all of us, who must overcome the crippling legacy of bigotry and injustice. And we *shall* overcome."[215]

Two days later, Senate majority leader Mike Mansfield and minority leader Everett Dirksen together introduced a bill to guarantee voting rights to African Americans. A similar bill was introduced in House of Representatives. Over the fervent opposition of southern Congressmen, the bill passed in both houses and, on August 6, 1965, President Johnson signed into law the Voting Rights Act, "To enforce the fifteenth amendment to the Constitution of the United States."[216]

The opening passage was an enhanced rewording of the amendment itself, stating, "No voting qualification or prerequisite to voting, or standard, practice, or procedure shall be imposed or applied by any State or political subdivision to deny or abridge the right of any citizen of the United States to vote on account of race or color." As such, the law effectively banned literacy tests and many other of the Jim Crow contrivances that had been employed by southern states since 1890 to deny the ballot to men and women of color.

The law allowed the federal government to send election supervisors to any state or county where discriminatory practices existed as of the 1964 presidential election or where voter turnout or registration for that election had fallen below fifty percent of the voting age population. These became known as "special coverage areas," and in these locations, local and state governments would be required to gain permission from the Justice Department or a federal district court in Washington, D. C. before making any change to their election laws or voting procedures.

The Voting Rights Act was an enormous and immediate success. In Selma, eight days after its enactment, federal officials helped 381 African Americans register to vote, more than had been able to sign up in Dallas

County for sixty-five years. By Election Day 1965, eight thousand new Black voters helped turn Sheriff Clark out of office and into a mobile home salesman. After Black voter registration exploded in every state that had been a part of the old Confederacy, the Voting Rights Act was characterized as "the single most effective piece of civil rights legislation ever passed by Congress."[217]

In April 2010, however, Shelby County, Alabama, filed suit to declare Section 4b, which delineated the formula for preclearance, and Section 5, which mandated preclearance, unconstitutional. As the *New York Times* reported, "In its suit, Shelby County argued that the widespread discrimination of the Jim Crow era had ended, and that 'it is no longer constitutionally justifiable for Congress to arbitrarily impose' on the county and other covered jurisdictions the 'disfavored treatment' of having to obtain preclearance from Washington. The county said that Congress 'lacked the evidence of intentional discrimination' to justify the extension. The suit also said parts of the act violated the principle of equal state sovereignty."[218]

In September 2011, District Court Judge John D. Bates, appointed by George W. Bush, disagreed. Voter discrimination had not ended, he wrote, and he cited several examples, one from Shelby County itself, where potential violations has been deterred by federal oversight. Judge Bates dismissed the lawsuit and upheld the constitutionality of Sections 4b and 5.[219]

Shelby County appealed in circuit court with the same result. In a 2-1 decision, David Tatel, who had been appointed to the court of appeals for the District of Columbia by Bill Clinton to replace Ruth Bader Ginsburg, ruled that although the Constitutional questions were serious, "voting rights discrimination is heavily concentrated in covered jurisdictions, and that overt discrimination persists in those places despite decades of Section 5 preclearance."[220] In fact, to most observers there was little question that without the Voting Rights Act, many of the gains made by Black Americans would likely evaporate.

Despite ample evidence for the need of such legislation, Shelby County appealed to the Supreme Court hoping to find a more receptive audience with the five conservative justices.

They got one.

Chief Justice Roberts in his majority opinion, which was joined by

Justices Scalia, Thomas, Kennedy, and Alito, declared it a violation of the rights of states and localities to require them get permission before they could change their election laws and therefore ruled that Sections 4b and 5 of the Voting Rights were an unconstitutional encroachment on Tenth Amendment guarantees.[221]

Roberts' reasoning was simple—after almost fifty years, conditions in the South and other "special coverage areas" had improved sufficiently that the formula no longer represented reality. "Our country has changed," he wrote. "While any racial discrimination in voting is too much, Congress must ensure that the legislation it passes to remedy that problem speaks to current conditions." Ignoring both the examples Judge Bates had cited in his district court opinion and many others submitted by voting rights advocates, Roberts claimed that "current conditions" no longer dictated draconian control over matters ordinarily left to the states.[222]

Justice Ginsburg wrote a strong dissent, in which she was joined by Justices Breyer, Kagan, and Sotomayor. She agreed that racial discrimination in the states that still required pre-clearance had decreased, but that was precisely because the law had remained in place. "Throwing out pre-clearance when it has worked and is continuing to work to stop discriminatory changes," she argued "is like throwing away your umbrella in a rainstorm because you are not getting wet."

If the requirement were eliminated, the dissenters predicted, discrimination might well begin again. And so it did. According to the Brennan Center for Justice, "The decision in *Shelby County* opened the floodgates to laws restricting voting throughout the United States. The effects were immediate. Within 24 hours of the ruling, Texas announced that it would implement a strict photo ID law. Two other states, Mississippi and Alabama, also began to enforce photo ID laws that had previously been barred because of federal preclearance."[223]

Other states followed suit. In Georgia, for example, in July 2017, 600,000 people, eight percent of the state's registered voters, were purged from the rolls and required to re-register; an estimated 107,000 of them simply because they had not voted in recent elections. In 2018, the state blocked the registration of 53,000 state residents, seventy percent of whom were black. In other states, voter identification requirements were tightened, polling locations closed, early voting restricted, and registration rules made stricter, all, critics insisted, to suppress the vote of certain classes and races.

Not surprising, then, that voting rights advocates consider *Shelby County* a travesty, some even comparing the ruling to *Dred Scott*. Many constitutional law scholars have been highly critical of the Court's reasoning as well.

Still, the most serious criticism is never brought—the Constitution did not grant nor intend to grant the Supreme Court the authority to rule on cases such as *Shelby County* nor to be the final arbiter of the constitutionality of laws passed by Congress and signed by the president. That power, known as "judicial review," is not included in Article III, nor, by design, does it appear anywhere else in Constitution. It was instead claimed for the Court in 1803 with a brilliant piece of political legerdemain by Chief Justice John Marshall, who, in *Marbury v. Madison*, the lead entry in virtually every Constitutional law textbook, wrote, "It is emphatically the province and duty of the judicial department to say what the law is."[224]

Most scholars and almost every judge agree with Marshall, insisting that the delegates to the Constitutional Convention need not have included a specific clause because judicial review is an obvious responsibility of the courts and was so understood by those who drafted the document. Even textualists, such as Justice Antonin Scalia, thought a declarative statement unnecessary.

"The Constitution of the United States nowhere says that the Supreme Court shall be the last word on what the Constitution means," he admitted in a 1996 speech. "Or that the Supreme Court shall have the authority to disregard statutes enacted by the Congress of the United States on the ground that in its view they do not comport with the Constitution. It doesn't say that anywhere. We made it up."

"We made it up very sensibly," Justice Scalia went on, "because what we said was, 'Look, a constitution is a law, it's a sort of super-law … and what the law means is the job of the courts."[225]

Not necessarily. The most persuasive evidence is that judicial review was in no way an accepted function of the Supreme Court and had it been proposed, the Convention would have rejected it.[226] As Larry Kramer, former dean of Stanford Law School wrote, "The Founding generation did not solve the problem of constitutional interpretation and enforcement by delegating it to judges … They were too steeped in republicanism to think that the solution to problem of republican politics was to chop it off at the knees."[227]

Kramer is correct. While some of the delegates to the Philadelphia Convention did arrive envisioning some role for the judiciary in enforcing a separation of powers, its exact function in providing a check on the legislature was by no means clear. Those who believe to the contrary often cite Virginia and Massachusetts, where, they claim, judicial review was already an integral part of state government and could therefore be logically expected to be extended to any national system.

In the Virginia Declaration of Rights, for example, Article V stated, "The legislative and executive powers of the State should be separate and distinct from the judiciary; and that the members of the two first may be restrained from oppression."[228] But in Article VII, "All power of suspending laws, or the execution of laws, by any authority, without consent of the representatives of the people, is injurious to their rights, and ought not to be exercised."

Hardly an endorsement, as Madison in Federalist 41 pointed out. He cited Virginia's Article V, not as a justification for judicial oversight, but to demonstrate that the legislature can provide a check on the judiciary. "The chief magistrate," he wrote, "with his executive council, are appointable by the legislature; that two members of the latter are triennially displaced at the pleasure of the legislature; and that all the principal offices, both executive and judiciary, are filled by the same department. The executive prerogative of pardon, also, is in one case vested in the legislative department."[229]

In Massachusetts, Article XXX of the state constitution read, "In the government of this commonwealth, the legislative department shall never exercise the executive and judicial powers, or either of them: the executive shall never exercise the legislative and judicial powers, or either of them: the judicial shall never exercise the legislative and executive powers, or either of them: to the end it may be a government of laws and not of men."[230] But Article XX also explicitly stated, "The power of suspending the laws, or the execution of the laws, ought never to be exercised but by the legislature, or by authority derived from it, to be exercised in such particular cases only as the legislature shall expressly provide for." Thus in these two states, judicial review seems more likely to have been prohibited than endorsed.

In addition, many of the delegates in Philadelphia were well familiar with the work of the two most prominent and respected legal philosophers of the day, William Blackstone and Baron de Montesquieu, neither of whom supported judicial oversight.

Blackstone, whom Hamilton had cited in *A Farmer Refuted*, was an avowed enemy of judicial activism and specifically rejected the notion of granting the judiciary final say in legislative matters. "If parliament will positively enact an unreasonable thing," he wrote in *Commentaries on the Laws of England*, "there is no power in the ordinary forms of the constitution vested with authority to control it. The judges are not at liberty to reject it, for that were to set the judicial power above that of the legislature, which would be subversive to all government."[231] Thus, to Blackstone, separation of powers, the ultimate guarantor of liberty, *demanded* that the courts have no power to overturn legislative acts.

To Federalists, including future chief justice John Marshall, who revered him, Blackstone was the ultimate authority on legal theory and his views on limiting the power of the judiciary were unambiguous.[232] Antifederalists and Jeffersonians favored Montesquieu, who also rejected both judicial review and an activist judiciary while nevertheless advocating a separation of powers. "National judges are no more than the mouth that pronounces the words of the law," he wrote in *The Spirit of Laws*, "mere passive beings, incapable of moderating either its force or rigor." As had Blackstone, Montesquieu insisted that the legislature must act as a check on itself. "That part, therefore, of the legislative body, which we have just now observed to be a necessary tribunal on another occasion, is also a necessary tribunal in this; it belongs to its supreme authority to moderate the law in favor of the law itself, by mitigating the sentence."[233]

At the Convention, the power of the judiciary to overturn an act of the legislature that it considered in violation of the Constitution was raised almost exclusively with respect to a "council of revision," in which the Supreme Court, with the executive, would essentially either sign off on or veto every congressional act.

Such a body was one of James Madison's pet ideas, enunciated in Section 8 of the Virginia Plan, which proposed that the executive and "a convenient number of the National Judiciary," comprise a council of revision "with authority to examine every act of the National Legislature before it shall [become law]." But granting the Court a say in whether to approve a law passed by Congress is not at all the same thing as ceding it final authority to "say what the Constitution means." Vetoes can be overridden by the same body that passed the law, whereas once declared unconstitutional, a law can only be reinstated by amendment, as Madison understood. In his proposal, if the council rejected the law, and it could do so on any grounds it chose, the legislation would indeed be returned to Congress.[234]

Madison's council of revision, then, would have the same power as is currently enjoyed exclusively by the President. In addition, the Virginia Plan provision did not limit the veto to laws that ran counter to the Constitution, but proposed a much broader application, likely including any law the council deemed "unjust."

The council of revision first came to the floor on June 4. Elbridge Gerry opened the debate by questioning whether the judiciary should be part of such a council. The national courts, he asserted "will have a sufficient check agst. encroachments on their own department by their exposition of the laws, which involved a power of deciding on their Constitutionality."[235]

Although Gerry might here be interpreted as advocating judicial oversight, subsequent statements, as will be seen, make clear that he was not but rather merely trying to get the courts, which he distrusted, out of the process.[236] In any case, Gerry, of course, would later refuse to sign the Constitution.

Gerry's motion was seconded by Rufus King, whose intent was also unclear. In his notes, Madison maintained that King claimed, "the Judges ought to be able to expound the law as it should come before them, free from the bias of having participated in its formation." Robert Yates, however, reported in his journal that "Mr. King was against the interference of the judicial [as] they may be biased in the interpretation," which has a different meaning entirely, although remarkably prescient. King, according to Yates, "therefore [proposed] to give the executive a complete negative."[237] King, then, was voicing opposition to the council of revision, not advocating final authority on the law be given the judiciary.

The real issue in these debates was not whether the judiciary should have the sole power to annul a law, but whether the executive, be it one person or three, should have that power alone.[238] Along with King, Mason,

Franklin, Wilson, and Gunning Bedford of Delaware expressed that fear. Madison had included the judiciary as a counterbalance to unfettered executive power and would equally have opposed granting such authority to the courts.

To many of the delegates, separation of powers was necessary to avoid tyranny or despotism, but there was little agreement on how much to give one branch at the expense of the other two. Wilson, for example, proposed a veto with recourse over the legislature by the other two branches by "varying the proposition in such a manner as to give the Executive & Judiciary jointly an absolute negative." (By jointly, he meant "each" rather than "together," and a veto from either could not be overridden.)

Franklin was leery of absolute power and noted that in Pennsylvania, "the negative of the Governor was constantly made use of to extort money. No good law whatever could be passed without a private bargain with him. An increase of his salary, or some donation, was always made a condition; till at last it became the regular practice, to have orders in his favor on the Treasury, presented along with the bills to be signed, so that he might actually receive the former before he should sign the latter." He favored including the judiciary in the oversight function, since "if the Executive was to have a Council, such a power would be less objectionable."

Roger Sherman agreed, announcing he "was agst. enabling any one man to stop the will of the whole. No one man could be found so far above all the rest in wisdom. He thought we ought to avail ourselves of his wisdom in revising the laws, but not permit him to overrule the decided and cool opinions of the Legislature."

Gunning Bedford opposed any check on the legislature at all. He thought it "sufficient to mark out in the Constitution the boundaries to the Legislative Authority, which would give all the requisite security to the rights of the other departments. The Representatives of the People were the best judges of what was for their interest, and ought to be under no external control whatever." George Mason presented an impassioned denunciation of granting a power without check, insisting "he never could agree to give up all the rights of the people to a single Magistrate."[239]

The motion to grant an absolute veto was defeated 10 states to 0. There would no power of nullification without recourse in the Constitution. The notion that this debate demonstrates that judicial review was an understood part of the judicial function, as is sometimes claimed, is clearly false. The delegates' embrace of separation of powers indicates the opposite, that no one branch should be able to act with impunity against the other two.

After the insertion of a clause providing for an override to a veto if two-thirds of each house approved, Gerry's second motion to provide a veto power to the executive alone passed 8-2, only Connecticut and Maryland against.[240] Although proponents tried again the following day to reconsider the decision to exclude the judiciary from the veto process, in which Madison gave a long, impassioned speech defending his council of revision, the measure failed, 8-3.

The issue was not dead, however. On July 21, Wilson tried again, proposing once more "that the supreme Natl Judiciary should be associated with the Executive in the Revisionary power." Wilson added that although "this proposition had been before made, and failed," he was so certain of its worth that he "thought it incumbent on him to make another effort."[241]

But Wilson was not proposing judicial review, but rather an ability to strike down laws on a completely subjective basis *even if they conform to the Constitution.* "The Judiciary ought to have an opportunity of remonstrating agst. projected encroachments on the people as well as on themselves," he went on. "It had been said that the Judges, as expositors of the Laws would have an opportunity of defending their constitutional rights … but this power of the Judges did not go far enough. Laws may be unjust, may be unwise, may be dangerous, may be destructive; and yet may not be so unconstitutional as to justify the Judges in refusing to give them effect." Give the judiciary a share in the "reversionary power," Wilson exclaimed, and they will "counteract … by the weight of their opinions the improper views of the Legislature." Madison, desperate to save his council of revision, seconded Wilson's motion.

Nathaniel Gorham, who, like his fellow delegates from Massachusetts, opposed the council, "did not see the advantage of employing the Judges in this way." They "are not to be presumed to possess any peculiar knowledge of the mere policy of public measures." He thought "it would be best to let the Executive alone be responsible, and at most to authorize him to call on Judges for their opinions." Oliver Ellsworth, a judge himself, spoke next and felt that with their "systematic and accurate knowledge of the Laws … the aid of the Judges will give more wisdom & firmness to the Executive."

Madison continued to press for the council of revision as "useful to the Community at large as an additional check agst. a pursuit of those unwise & unjust measures which constituted so great a portion of our calamities," and Mason continued to voice his support of a council that "would give a confidence to the Executive, which he would not otherwise have, and without which the Revisionary power would be of little avail."

Wilson's proposal blurred the distinction of the courts deciding on the constitutional fitness of a law with giving judges a kind of executive power over the legislature. Gerry once again protested that the veto was a balancing mechanism in which judges should play no part. He "conceived of the Revisionary power as merely to secure the Executive department agst. legislative encroachment. The Executive therefore who will best know and be ready to defend his rights ought alone to have the defence of them." Judges should not be given veto power because it would be "making Statesmen of the Judges and setting them up as the guardians of the Rights of the people. He relied for his part on the Representatives of the people as the guardians of their Rights & interests." These are hardly the sentiments of a man who wanted the judicial branch to become the ultimate arbiter on constitutionality.

Caleb Strong, another Massachusetts delegate against whom Gerry would repeatedly run for governor, agreed that "the power of making ought to be kept distinct from that of expounding the laws" and added that, "judges in exercising the function of expositors might be influenced by the part they had taken in framing the laws."

Important to note is Strong's use of "expound." Expound means to explain, to give an opinion, not to overturn. Wilson, Gorham, and Ellsworth had expressed the same sentiments earlier in this debate. That distinction would be made again, thus indicating that while the delegates may have expected the judiciary to give an opinion on the fitness of a law, they would not be empowered to annul it.

Gouverneur Morris thought so as well. Although "the public liberty was in greater danger from Legislative usurpations than from any other source," and it was necessary to provide a check on the legislature, "the question is in what hands it should be lodged." The executive, Morris asserted, "appointed for 6 years, and impeachable whilst in office" would not alone "be a very effectual check." The alternative, however, which Morris preferred, was not to leave the power in the hands of the courts, but merely that the executive "be reinforced by the Judiciary department."

Here again, Morris is choosing "expound" rather than "annul." To support his argument he turned to England, where "Judges had a great share in ye Legislation. They are consulted in difficult & doubtful cases. They may be & some of them are members of the Legislature. They are or may be members of the privy Council, and can there advise the Executive as they will do with us if the motion succeeds." But the risk of legislative tyranny was so great, that even the weight of the other two departments might not be enough to prevent it. A council of revision "is indeed a great means of diminishing the evil, yet it is found to be unable to prevent it altogether."

Throughout this debate, the delegates were casting about for the proper role of the executive and the judiciary in preventing the legislature from usurping power but transferring unchecked authority to the Supreme Court to interpret the Constitution did not seem to be on anyone's mind. Among those who agree was John Marshall's biographer, Albert Beveridge. "No words in the Constitution gave the Judiciary the power to annul legislation. The subject had been discussed ... but the brief and scattering debate had arisen upon the proposition to make the President and Justices of the Supreme Court members of a Council of revision with power to negative acts of Congress. No direct resolution was ever offered to the effect that the Judiciary should be given power to declare acts of Congress unconstitutional."[242]

Two delegates did put forth the idea, however, but both were non-signers. Luther Martin of Maryland, ever the opponent of centralized authority, considered "the association of the Judges with the Executive as a dangerous innovation; as well as one which could not produce the particular advantage expected from it." He added, "As to the Constitutionality of laws, that point will come before the Judges in their proper official character. In this character they have a negative on the laws." But Martin's aim was to prevent a council of revision, not to create judicial oversight without recourse. In the same speech, he also exclaimed, "A knowledge of mankind, and of Legislative affairs, cannot be presumed to belong in a higher degree to the Judges than to the Legislature."[243] Almost certainly, Martin, who opposed the entire notion of a strong central government, was simply trying any argument he could to weaken the nationalists' proposal.

Madison replied simply that combining the executive and judiciary in a council of revision was in no way a "violation of the maxim which requires the great departments of power to be kept separate & distinct." In fact, Madison asserted, a council of revision would strengthen separation of powers. "Instead therefore of contenting ourselves with laying down the Theory in the Constitution that each department ought to be separate & distinct, it was proposed to add a defensive power to each which should maintain the Theory in practice." Madison concluded that creating a council of revision with the executive and judiciary, "did not blend the departments together." He would later state that giving the courts final say over constitutionality, "makes the Judiciary Dept paramount in fact to the Legislature, which was never intended and can never be proper."[244]

George Mason, a fervent supporter of Madison's council, also raised the specter of legislative despotism. "Notwithstanding the precautions taken in the Constitution, it would still so much resemble that of the individual States, that it must be expected frequently to pass unjust and pernicious laws," and "a restraining power was therefore necessary." As part of the council of revision, judges "could impede in one case only, the operation of laws. They could declare an unconstitutional law void." He only feared that if an "oppressive or pernicious law" was not unconstitutional, judges would be forced "to give it a free course." Mason lamented this limitation on judicial oversight and hoped "further use to be made of the Judges, of giving aid in preventing every improper law."

Again, this was not a plea for judicial review, but only for judges to be included in the veto process. Mason, after all, was the man who "never could agree to give up all the rights of the people to a single Magistrate."

After James Wilson once more defended the council of revision, Elbridge Gerry struck back. He would "rather give the Executive an absolute negative for its own defence than thus to blend together the Judiciary & Executive departments. It will bind them together in an offensive and defensive alliance agst. the Legislature, and render the latter unwilling to enter into a contest with them."

Gouverneur Morris who, unlike Gerry, Mason, and Luther Martin, endorsed the Constitution and wrote the final draft, was surprised that any provision securing the effectual separation of the branches of government should be considered an improper mixture of them. "Suppose that the three powers, were to be vested in three persons, by compact among themselves;

that one was to have the power of making, another of executing, and a third of judging, the laws." Morris asserted that nothing could be more natural than two parties in a tri-partite agreement acting together to prevent domination by a third. "If three neighbours," he noted, "had three distinct farms, a right in each to defend his farm agst. his neighbours, tended to blend the farms together."

Wilson's motion for a revisionary council failed, although by an extremely close vote, 4-3, with Massachusetts, one of the two states generally cited as having incorporated judicial review into its own government, providing the margin of defeat. Immediately afterward, the vote to establish a qualified executive veto, requiring two-thirds of each house of the legislature to override, passed unanimously. If the delegates wished to discuss a judicial role in the voiding of a law, this was the place to do it, but no one raised the issue.

In the end, there were too many delegates who feared allocating excessive power to any one branch and distrust of a national judiciary was too great to assume they would have made an exception for the Supreme Court. In fact, far more delegates expressly opposed allowing the judiciary a role in legislative nullification than those who favored it. As Leonard Levy put it, "the Framers did not mean for the Supreme Court to have the authority to void acts of Congress."[245]

But nor did the delegates forbid it.

It was not for lack of awareness—there was more than sufficient discussion about the potential for judicial despotism in general and judicial nullification in particular for that to have been the case. The unwillingness to include specific limitations on the judiciary's activities, the choice to simply avoid the issue, regardless of the reason, was exactly what a savvy politician like Chief Justice John Marshall needed. He both recognized the vacuum and knew how to fill it.

And fill it he did. From that omission, John Marshall invented an authority for the Supreme Court that the Constitution did not postulate and that the two most respected legal theorists of the day rejected. And he did so through a contrivance, a rather mundane lawsuit that had nothing at all to do with constitutionality.

Marshall's 1803 opinion in *Marbury v. Madison*, delivered for a unanimous Court, not only established the right of the judiciary, without recourse, to be the final arbiter on the fitness of a law, but also drastically redefined the notion of separation of powers with which the delegates had wrestled so intently for so long. In recasting the Supreme Court's role in American government, Marshall threw open the door for expansion of judicial authority into other areas neither anticipated nor intended by the men drafted the Constitution and the nation has wrestled with the consequences of that expansion ever since.

Marbury arose out of a bitter feud between John Adams' Federalists and Thomas Jefferson's Democratic Republicans.[246] In the election of 1800, after a brutal campaign, Adams, the incumbent, lost the presidency and Federalists lost control of Congress as well. These dual defeats were all the more indigestible since the new Republican majority had only been made possible by the slave bonus southern states had wrung out of northerners in the Convention, without which Adams would have been re-elected.

But Adams's Federalists had no intention of melting quietly away. Instead, they took aim at the one branch of government over which voters had no control. In their last weeks in the lame-duck Congress, Federalist legislators voted to create seven new federal circuit courts to be manned by nineteen new judges. Hundreds of administrative officers and minor judgeships were also added to the federal court system. Among these were forty-two justices of the peace for the new national capital in the District of Columbia, each of whom would serve a five-year term. Jefferson grumbled that the Federalists "have retired into the judiciary as a stronghold. There the remains of federalism are to be preserved and fed from the Treasury; and from that battery all the works of republicanism are to be beaten down and erased."[247]

Adams also filled the nation's most important judicial vacancy. To replace Oliver Ellsworth, who had resigned as chief justice while on a diplomatic mission to Paris, he appointed John Marshall, his Secretary of State, to become Chief Justice only after former chief justice John Jay unexpectedly declined the post.[248] Marshall was confirmed immediately, although he remained Secretary of State as well.

Adams, as it turned out, could not have made a better choice to lead the Federalists' last stand. Although Marshall was a Virginian like Jefferson—they were, in fact, cousins—Marshall was an ardent Federalist who loathed Jefferson personally. (The sentiment was heartily reciprocated.) Marshall could thus be counted on to use the Court wherever possible to curb the new president's power.

When Jefferson took office in March 1801, his secretary of state, former Federalist James Madison, discovered a stack of commissions for the new judgeships, which, although signed and sealed, had yet to be delivered—by Secretary of State John Marshall. When Madison refused to hand them over, one of the appointees, a minor Federalist functionary named William Marbury, sued to have his commission delivered to him, seeking a writ of *mandamus* (literally "we order"), which directs a public agency or governmental body to perform an act required by law when it has neglected or refused to do so.

Instead of opting for the recently empaneled federal circuit court in the District of Columbia, Marbury and three fellow claimants chose to take their suit directly to the Supreme Court, doubtless assuming that by placing the case before a political ally, their petition would receive a sympathetic hearing.

Marshall was in a bind. If he sided with his fellow Federalists and ordered the commissions delivered, Madison would simply ignore him and the Court's authority would be weakened, perhaps fatally. If he denied Marbury's claim, he would be using a Federalist bastion to strengthen Jefferson's power to make arbitrary rulings, an equally unpalatable alternative.

Marshall, a preternaturally talented politician, was up to the task. With inspired misdirection, he began his opinion with a complete validation of Marbury's claim. Yes, Marbury was properly appointed; yes, he was entitled to receive his commission; yes, Secretary of State Madison was obligated to deliver that commission; and no, neither the president nor his secretary of state had the right to void the appointment.

Alas, Marshall went on, Marbury had originated his suit before the Supreme Court. Section 13 of the Judiciary Act of 1789, enacted by the First Congress to flesh out what was a skeletal Article III, seemed to allow the Supreme Court only appellate jurisdiction in issuing writs of *mandamus*, although the wording was ambiguous:

> The Supreme Court shall also have appellate jurisdiction from the circuit courts and courts of the several states, in the cases herein after specially provided for; and shall have power to issue writs of prohibition to the district courts, when proceeding as courts of admiralty and maritime jurisdiction, and writs of mandamus, in

> cases warranted by the principles and usages of law, to any courts appointed, or persons holding office, under the authority of the United States.[249]

From here, the proper course was to refer the case to the appropriate lower court. (In fact, he should have declined even to sit on the case as he had been a party to it.)[250] But if he did, he would have no control over the outcome. Instead, Marshall chose to interpret Section 13 as granting the Court original jurisdiction, thus allowing him to hear *Marbury* and shift the argument from the validity of Marbury's suit to the validity of Section 13. Then, conveniently, Marshall was able to rule that Section 13 was in contradiction to Article III of the Constitution, which had not expressly granted original jurisdiction to the Supreme Court in such cases and was null and void.

He therefore dismissed Marbury's suit, because although Marbury was in the right, he no longer had a valid statute to support his petition. Marshall had thus succeeded in denouncing Jefferson for violating Marbury's civil rights without being forced to issue a writ of *mandamus*, which Jefferson would certainly have ignored.

Now Jefferson was in a bind. If he did nothing, he was tacitly granting power to the Federalist Supreme Court to oversee the constitutionality of legislative acts, a repugnant alternative. The only way to avoid setting such a precedent was to deliver commissions to Marbury and the others and thereby undermine his authority throughout the Union.

Jefferson chose to continue to refuse the commissions and the power of judicial review was born. With his ruling, John Marshall forever expanded the role of the federal judiciary in American life. He went on to serve for thirty-two more years, going down in history as "the second father of the Constitution—the man who made the Court supreme."[251]

The irony was that even if Section 13 *had* granted original jurisdiction, it was not in conflict with the Constitution. Marshall, in his ten-thousand-word opinion, conveniently avoided citing the last section of Article III, Section 2, which stated, "In all the other Cases before mentioned, the supreme Court shall have appellate Jurisdiction, both as to Law and Fact, with *such Exceptions, and under such Regulations as the Congress shall make.*"

Judicial review has since evolved into the most powerful weapon in the Supreme Court's arsenal, although for more than half a century, the justices did not choose to utilize such a formidable tool. The next occasion on which the Court declared a law unconstitutional was in 1857, when Chief Justice Taney invalidated the Missouri Compromise in *Dred Scott v. Sandford*.

Since then, the Court has not been shy about inserting itself in the legislative process. In cases such as *Shelby County* and *Citizens United v. Federal Election Commission*, the Court has wielded sufficient power to determine policy, sometimes to a greater degree than could Congress or the president.

Although many of the cases in which the Court has taken an axe to legislation have favored conservative interests, on other occasions, such as *Miranda v. Arizona* and *Obergefell v. Hodges*, the Court ruled to protect civil liberties. The question then is not so much whether the Supreme Court favors one political philosophy or one political party over another—although those are legitimate concerns in other contexts—but whether a branch of government that is supposed to be above politics should wield such arbitrary political power. That it does is due not to a decision by those who founded the nation to grant it but rather a decision to bypass the question.

Chapter 9

In Judgment Before Foreigners: The Question of a National Judiciary

"We must remember that we have to make judges out of men, and that by being made judges their prejudices are not diminished and their intelligence is not increased."
Robert Green Ingersoll, former attorney general of Illinois

"Judges are the weakest link in our system of justice, and they are also the most protected."
Alan Dershowitz

The lack of specifics as to whether the Supreme Court would be empowered to act as a check on the legislature was not the only omission in Article III that encouraged a betrayal of democratic principles. In fact, the entire article was left ripe for abuse, potential that has been more than realized.

The fear that federal judges would act despotically toward individual state governments was widespread among both the delegates and the citizenry. South Carolinians or Virginians justifiably wondered whether a supreme court would undercut the rights of slave holders, while New Englanders feared an active judiciary limiting free flow of commerce. Add to that the projected cost of a federal court system to a virtually bankrupt nation and it is not difficult to understand why the delegates in Philadelphia were inclined to tread lightly in empowering the national judiciary.

As a result, after the delegates agreed on a national tribunal—a "supreme court"—vast disagreement remained over whether the new government should include a national court system at all. An alternative was to empower state courts to expand their jurisdictions and hear federal cases, with the Supreme Court exercising appellate power over their decisions. Yet in some cases, such as maritime claims or those involving ambassadors or other foreign officials, few were willing to entrust jurisdiction to a state court. Because of this uncertainty, providing a structure of the federal court system seemed far less urgent—and less advisable—than detailing that of the legislature or the executive.

The question of a national judiciary first arose on June 5, the day after the council of revision was first rejected. The debate began, as did they all in those early days, with Madison's Virginia Plan, Section 9 of which read "that a National Judiciary be established to consist of one or more supreme tribunals, and of inferior tribunals to be chosen by the National Legislature, to hold their offices during good behaviour; and to receive punctually at stated times fixed compensation for their services, in which no increase or diminution shall be made so as to affect the persons actually in office at the time of such increase or diminution."[252]

The discussion began with agreement to delete "one or more," after which Wilson opposed Congress appointing federal judges. "Experience shewed the impropriety of such appointmts, by numerous bodies. Intrigue, partiality, and concealment were the necessary consequences."[253] He favored appointment by the executive. The previous day, the Convention had voted against Mason's proposal of a three-person executive in favor of one, about which Mason, used to getting his way, was still grumbling. Sure to irritate Mason further, Wilson added, "A principal reason for unity in the Executive was that officers might be appointed by a single, responsible person."

Rutledge, speaking for his fellow South Carolinians, disagreed. He "was by no means disposed to grant so great a power to any single person. The people will think we are leaning too much towards Monarchy." But Rutledge was not done. He wanted no national court system at all. He "was against establishing any national tribunal except a single supreme one. The State Tribunals (are most proper) to decide in all cases in the first instance."

Franklin, showing that he had not totally lost his wit, countered. He was uncertain of either proposed alternative and wished to explore other possibilities. According to Madison's notes, Franklin, "in a brief and entertaining manner, related a Scotch mode, in which the nomination proceeded from the Lawyers, who always selected the ablest of the profession in order to get rid of him, and share his practice (among themselves). It was here, he said, the interest of the electors to make the best choice, which should always be made the case if possible."[254]

Franklin's humor did not translate into serious discussion, however. Madison, seeming to contradict his own plan, expressed reluctance to grant appointment power to the legislature or, as Wilson had put it, "any numerous body." He then expressed similar misgivings about the executive. Finally, he got to the point. "He rather inclined to give it to the Senatorial branch, as numerous eno' to be confided in but not so numerous as to be governed by the motives of the other branch; and as being sufficiently stable and independent to follow their deliberate judgments." Recognizing that a formal motion was likely to be rejected, "He hinted this only and moved that the appointment by the Legislature might be struck out, & and a blank left to be hereafter filled on maturer reflection."

Wilson seconded his motion, which passed 9-2, with only South Carolina and Connecticut opposed. The delegates were back where they started. Charles Pinckney "gave notice" that he would seek to restore judicial appointments by the legislature, as did Wilson with respect to "inferior tribunals."

This thrashing about continued when the Convention also voted to table the clause that covered compensation and serving during good behavior. Later in the session, Rutledge again stated that he wanted a supreme court only, with no "inferior tribunals." State courts, he insisted, "might and ought to be left in all cases to decide in the first instance the right of appeal to the supreme national tribunal being sufficient to secure the national rights & uniformity of Judgmts: that it was making an unnecessary encroachment on the jurisdiction (of the States,) and creating unnecessary obstacles to their adoption of the new system."

Sherman seconded Rutledge's motion, and here was the crux of the delegates' dilemma. Many states would certainly view a national court system as an "unnecessary encroachment," which would indeed create "obstacles to their adoption of the new system." But leaving jurisdiction to state courts risked state judges interpreting federal law as they saw fit, which would likely differ from state to state with the same statute.

Madison countered that unless "inferior tribunals were dispersed throughout the Republic with final jurisdiction in many cases, appeals would be multiplied to a most oppressive degree," trying to make the federal courts a convenience rather than an impediment. He attempted to paint a frightening picture of a nation with only a supreme court and no "inferior tribunals" to handle the mass of cases.

"What was to be done after improper Verdicts in State tribunals obtained under the biased directions of a dependent Judge, or the local prejudices of an undirected jury? To remand the cause for a new trial would answer no purpose. To order a new trial at the supreme bar would oblige the parties to bring up their witnesses, tho' ever so distant from the seat of the Court." Madison thus saw risk precisely where Rutledge saw virtue—state courts contorting federal law to suit their own purposes.

Madison concluded, "An effective Judiciary establishment commensurate to the legislative authority, was essential. A Government without a proper Executive & judiciary would be the mere trunk of a body without arms or legs to act or move."

Wilson agreed with Madison and added that the national courts should have sole jurisdiction in maritime law, which would favor northern shippers. Sherman opposed lower courts, citing the excessive cost when "State courts would answer the same purpose." Dickinson then "contended strongly that if there was to be a National Legislature, there ought to be a national Judiciary, and that the former ought to have authority to institute the latter."

But despite the entreaties of three of the most prestigious delegates, Rutledge's motion narrowly passed and establishment of lower federal courts was stricken from the proposal.

Madison and Dickinson tried again, using Dickinson's idea that Congress could "institute" the court system, which they said would be discretionary, rather than "establish" it, thereby making the system mandatory. Pierce Butler seemed to find that absurd. "The people will not bear such innovations. The States will revolt at such encroachments."

But Madison's semantic ploy succeeded. The Convention voted to give Congress the discretionary power to establish a national judiciary if it saw fit.

On June 13, the Convention was presented with what had become the modified Virginia Plan, which the nationalists wished to debate. The next day, William Paterson asked for an adjournment so that he could present his own series of proposals. Abetted by delegates from New York, Connecticut, Delaware, and perhaps Luther Martin, who found Madison's proposal extreme, Paterson's New Jersey Plan was a clear counterattack on the nationalists. In a footnote, Madison gave a sense of the gulf between them.

Members of small states, he wrote, "would sooner submit to a foreign power, than submit to be deprived of an equality of suffrage, in both branches of the legislature, and thereby be thrown under the domination of the large States." Their eagerness, according to Madison "began now to produce serious anxiety for the result of the Convention." Madison went so far as say that Dickinson chided him, "You see the consequence of pushing things too far."[255]

In Paterson's plan, there was no provision for lower courts; state courts would handle all federal cases, which, in these instances, would be required to adhere to federal law, with the Supreme Court being final arbiter. Paterson also proposed that judges be appointed by the executive, without the necessity of ratification by Congress.

Both plans provided the Supreme Court with final authority over "all piracies & felonies on the high seas," "captures from an enemy," and "the collection of the National revenue." Paterson granted the Supreme Court original jurisdiction over impeachments of "National officers," while Madison kept original jurisdiction in the "inferior tribunals." Whereas Paterson gave the Supreme Court jurisdiction over "acts for regulation of trade," Madison proposed a sweeping power under which the Supreme Court could rule over "questions which may involve the national peace and harmony." Neither plan specified the size or composition of the Supreme Court, nor did either address or anticipate granting the court the power to nullify laws passed by Congress.

In these initial discussions, there was no real distinction made between the power to create "inferior tribunals" and the power to appoint judges who would sit on the federal bench. Madison wanted both assigned to the legislature, be it Congress or only the Senate. To delegates objecting to a federal court system, only appointments mattered, but once they were forced to accept that Congress could create a series of federal courts, it became necessary to deal with appointment power separately.

The delegates attempted to do just that on July 18. Nathaniel Gorham immediately moved to have "Judges be appointed by the Execuve. with the advice & consent of the 2d branch," which he claimed had worked well in Massachusetts.[256] Wilson, although favoring the executive having unrestricted power, went along, but Luther Martin and Roger Sherman, both leery of executive power, objected. Mason made the point that if Supreme Court justices—the only judges that had been agreed to—were to preside over impeachment trials of the executive, they should not have been appointed by him. Morris agreed and Madison suggested perhaps the executive and one-third of the Senate might appoint judges, an idea that went nowhere.

The issues remained unresolved, and when the Committee of Detail's report was presented on August 6 the judiciary was still to consist only of a supreme court and "such inferior Courts as shall, when necessary, from time to time, be constituted by the Legislature of the United States," essentially Madison's original proposal. The power of appointment was reserved for the Senate, which "shall have power to make treaties, and to appoint ambassadors, and judges of the supreme court," another win for Madison.

Once appointed, judges were still to serve during "good behavior," and original jurisdiction was again limited to areas in which state courts were clearly inappropriate, such as maritime law, controversies between states, and cases involving ambassadors or public ministers. In one significant change, after the limits on original jurisdiction, the committee added that all the other jurisdiction "shall be appellate, with such exceptions and under such regulations as the Legislature shall make." And so, in addition to giving Congress the power to either establish a judiciary system or not, it was also given the power to alter federal courts' jurisdiction, this time including the Supreme Court. This power would be also included in Article III of the finished Constitution, which Chief Justice Marshall chose to ignore in his *Marbury* opinion.

When the judiciary was next taken up on August 27, Gouverneur Morris objected to assigning judicial appointments to the Senate because it would be "too numerous for the purpose." He added that, "If Judges were to be tried by the Senate … it was particularly wrong to let the Senate have the filling of vacancies which its own decrees were to create."[257] Wilson agreed, and the section was referred to another committee of five.

There is no record of this committee's deliberations, but when the plan emerged the Senate was no longer tasked with appointments. Instead, the committee adopted Gorham's suggestion and thus, "The President … by and with the advice and consent of the Senate shall appoint Ambassadors and other public Ministers, Judges of the supreme Court, and all other officers of the U. S. whose appointments are not otherwise herein provided for."[258]

On September 10, the draft Constitution was referred to the Committee of Style, which in effect meant Gouverneur Morris. In the final version, Article III contained only six paragraphs and was as notable for what was left out as for what was included. Missing was not only the role the courts would play in deciding constitutionality, a mandated roster of Supreme Court justices, and whether there would be inferior tribunals, but also any specifics on who could be appointed to the federal bench and how long they would serve.

Although the Constitution contained specific qualifications required to serve in the legislature or the executive, there was no indication of what, if any, qualifications would be required for judicial appointments. Strictly speaking, the chief justice of the Supreme Court need not even be a citizen.

The ambiguity was hardly an accident. Years later, in a note to a friend, Morris, who reminded his correspondent that the Constitution "was written by the fingers which write this letter," said he tried "be as clear as our language would permit," except for "a part of what relates to the judiciary. On that subject, conflicting opinions had been maintained with so much professional astuteness, that it became necessary to select phrases, which expressing my own notions, would not alarm others, nor shock their selflove, and to the best of my recollection, this was the only part which passed without cavil."[259]

Another glaring omission, one that has had enormous impact that has only increased over time, was a specific term of service for federal judges and how, if at all, they could be removed beyond impeachment. The phrase "serve during good behaviour" is, even by Morris's standard of ambiguity, virtually meaningless in that there is no interpretation that can be considered definitive.

There are two basic controversies regarding the phrase's meaning. The first is whether the delegates believed "good behavior" to be equivalent to "for life," and therefore the intention was that federal judges were to have no fixed term of office, nor could one be imposed legislatively. Since the Judiciary Act of 1789, the first piece of legislation passed by the First Congress, there has been no attempt to impose terms of service and so the nation has functioned since its outset as if "good behavior" and "for life" are interchangeable. Of course, in 1789, a Federalist president would be appointing Federalist judges to be confirmed by a Federalist Senate, so the incentive to limit their service was not great. In any event, most scholarship considers the terms congruent.[260]

Nonetheless, there is compelling evidence that the phrases had different meanings for the delegates. Alexander Hamilton, in his six-hour speech to the convention on June 18, proposed, "Let one branch of the Legislature hold their places *for life or at least during good-behaviour*. Let the Executive also be *for life*."[261] (Robert Yates was even stronger, writing that Hamilton said "good behavior or life.") George Mason, during the debate on the term of the executive on July 17, said, "He considered an Executive during *good behavior as a softer name only for an Executive for life*. And that the next would be an easy step to hereditary Monarchy."[262] If one can turn into the other, they could not have been equivalent to start. In the early debates about the term of the executive, Rufus King later wrote, "Madison proposed good behaviour, or Seven years with exclusion forever afterward."[263] Madison could in no way have meant "life" as an alternative to a hard limit of seven years.

The second controversy, a corollary of the first, has centered on whether the phrase creates grounds for removal other than by impeachment, such as an ordinary court proceeding or through action by the executive or the legislature. The evidence is that the delegates did not see good behavior as so weak a standard that Congress could pretty much ignore it.

On August 27, Dickinson moved that "after the words 'good behavior' the words 'provided that they may be removed by the Executive on the application (by) the Senate and House of Representatives.'" Gerry seconded.[264]

Although Sherman supported the motion, the other delegates did not. Morris "thought it a contradiction in terms to say that the Judges should hold their offices during good behavior, and yet be removeable without a trial." Rutledge saw it unacceptable on its face, and Wilson feared making judges "depend on every gust of faction which might prevail in the two branches of our Govt." The motion failed, only Connecticut voting aye. Whether a judge could be removed through ordinary legal proceedings was not discussed. Morris seemed to believe that a trial for removal need not have followed impeachment.

Beyond removal, however, if "good behavior" is not interchangeable with "for life," would it not follow that Congress can institute term limits on judges without the need for a constitutional amendment? Traditionally, scholars have insisted that an amendment would be required. For example, Jeffrey L. Fisher at Stanford Law School asserts, "Because Article 3 of the Constitution confers life tenure upon all federal judges, term limits would likely require a constitutional amendment."[265] Robert Peck, the Founder and President of the Center For Constitutional Litigation said, "Everyone agrees that [term limits] would be unconstitutional. That limits the tenure of a Supreme Court judge that is set by the Constitution for good behavior, which has always been interpreted as lifetime tenure."[266]

Not everyone agrees. A growing body of scholars believe statutory change would indeed be constitutional.[267] Members of a commission appointed by the Biden administration to study potential alterations in the Supreme Court's mandate were divided on whether term limits could be achieved legislatively and included three possible scenarios for change.[268] These proposals, however, as well as others proposed by legal experts, rely on semantics, interpretations of Article III that attempt to find holes in the wording. They do not go to the heart of the matter, that the men who drafted the Constitution saw a distinct difference in the two phrases, which makes Congressional imposition of term limits not only constitutional, but likely advisable.

In addition to Hamilton, Mason, and Madison's pronouncements, there is also indirect evidence that the judiciary was to be kept in check by one or both of the other branches. For four long, hot months in Philadelphia, where, for secrecy, the windows were bolted shut, guards were posted at the door, and the temperature reached 90 degrees, delegates who did not know and often did not like one another wrangled to try to find a means of government that would provide some centralized authority without granting any branch sufficient power to wield despotic power over either of the other branches or over the states. It stretches credibility to believe that in the midst of all this, the delegates would be willing to create one branch of government—the one they distrusted the most—that consisted of unelected, lifetime members with no checks on their authority or power, short of impeachment, which was made intentionally impracticable.[269]

Far more likely is that "good behavior" actually meant "as long as the justices are not corrupt or mix in politics." Although the evidence here is far more persuasive, unfortunately, the delegates, following a familiar pattern, chose to not spell out what would constitute "bad behavior." As written, Article III leaves Supreme Court justices free to rule on cases in which they had a financial, political, or religious interest, or even one in which, say, a family member was one of the attorneys.[270]

Although recent incidents of Supreme Court justices engaging in behavior that would violate a code of ethics—had one existed—such as Justice Clarence Thomas's potential involvement, through his wife, in the plot to overturn the 2020 presidential election, questionable behavior on the high bench is hardly new. In 1879, Associate Justice Ward Hunt suffered a massive stroke that left him partially paralyzed and unable to even attend Court sessions. Ignoring entreaties from his colleagues, he refused to resign unless he was granted a full pension, to which, because he lacked ten years' service and was not yet seventy, he was not entitled. After three frustrating years, to get him off the Court, Congress passed a special bill to grant Hunt his pension if he retired within thirty days. Hunt took the deal. Congress had made a smart move as Hunt lived another four years.

In 1972, Associate Justice William O. Douglas, as committed an environmentalist as ever sat on the Court, declined to recuse himself from a landmark land use case, *Sierra Club v. Morton*, although he held a lifetime membership in the Sierra Club, which was active when the suit was first filed, and had once served on its board of directors. In his historic dissent, Douglas claimed that trees and other natural resources have standing to bring suit, just as does a corporation, which is also an inanimate object.[271] His colleagues did not agree, which affected Douglas's belief in his own rectitude not one bit.

That judges on the federal bench have often approached the boundaries of conflict of interest and sometimes strayed over it is hardly a revelation. Perhaps an even greater threat to democracy is the willingness of many judges and Supreme Court justices to substitute their political, social, and even religious views for objective jurisprudence, a crisis that has grown more acute in recent years. Because of the failure of the convention delegates to delineate both the judiciary's powers and its limitations, the federal court system, and especially the Supreme Court, has evolved into a government within a government, accountable to no one, either in Congress, the presidency, or among the citizenry.

Chapter 10

Unreliable Narrator: The Federalist Essays

"Persuasion is achieved by the speaker's personal character when the speech is so spoken as to make us think him credible."
Aristotle

"There's something uniquely exhilarating about puzzling together the truth at the hands of an unreliable narrator."
Maria Semple, novelist.

On October 18, 1787, less than one month after the text of the new Constitution was first published in the *Pennsylvania Packet*, an article appeared in the *New York Journal* signed by "Brutus." Anticipating an election of delegates to a state ratifying convention, it was addressed "To the Citizens of the State of New-York," and began "When the public is called to investigate and decide upon a question in which not only the present members of the community are deeply interested, but upon which the happiness and misery of generations yet unborn is in great measure suspended, the benevolent mind cannot help feeling itself peculiarly interested in the result."[272]

After noting, "We have felt the feebleness of the ties by which these United-States are held together, and the want of sufficient energy in our present confederation, to manage, in some instances, our general concerns," Brutus went on to observe, "if the constitution, offered to your acceptance, be a wise one, calculated to preserve the invaluable blessings of liberty, to secure the inestimable rights of mankind, and promote human happiness, then, if you accept it, you will lay a lasting foundation of happiness for millions yet unborn; generations to come will rise up and call you blessed."

Then, for the remainder of the essay and in fifteen additional essays that stretched into April of the following year, Brutus persuasively and elegantly detailed why the new Constitution would achieve none of those aims, but rather would centralize power and eliminate the states as political entities. That, in turn, would "lead to the subversion of liberty," and threaten "to establish a despotism, or, what is worse, a tyrannic aristocracy."

Brutus had chosen his pseudonym with care. Although now popularly associated with the man who committed the ultimate betrayal of Julius Caesar (in the name of saving the Roman Republic from tyranny), late eighteenth-century readers were also familiar with the earlier Lucius Junius Brutus who, in the sixth century BC, led a successful revolt against the last Roman King, Tarquin the Proud, and became one of the founders of the Roman Republic. As was the custom at the time, the New York "Brutus" did not reveal his identity.[273]

Nine days after Brutus's essay appeared in the *Journal*, another essay was published in a rival newspaper, the *New York Independent Journal*, this one addressed "To the People of the State of New York," and signed by "Publius." Publius Valerius was an eminent statesman of the Roman Republic, whose fame and power crested after Lucius Junius Brutus died in battle trying to prevent Tarquin from retaking his throne. So popular was Publius Valerius with the citizenry of Rome, that he was granted the additional honorific, "Publicola," which according to Plutarch meant "people-cherisher."

Publius would write eighty-five essays, the last of which would appear in May 1788, all of them extolling the virtues of the new Constitution. Just after the final essay appeared, the entire body of work was published as a two-volume set entitled "The Federalist." The essays were translated into French soon after—just in time for the revolution there—and eventually into almost every other language. *The Federalist* has been in print ever since.

The *Federalist* essays have been called the "most important work in political science that has ever been written, or is likely ever to be written, in the United States. It is, indeed, the one product of the American mind that is rightly counted among the classics of political theory."[274] While the essays are certainly brilliant dissertations on both political theory and the permutations and ramifications of the new Constitution, they were also advocacy pieces, not even-handed discussions of Constitutional issues.

Like Brutus, Publius did not reveal his identity. Even as editions of *The Federalist* began to be read throughout Europe in the 1790s and early

1800s, the author's anonymity was maintained. Finally, in July 1804, as his duel with Aaron Burr drew near, Alexander Hamilton, in putting his affairs in order, included a brief note that revealed that the *Federalist* essays had been written on his initiative and that Publius was in fact three men—himself, James Madison, and John Jay. Jay had written five of the essays, and Madison and Hamilton had split the rest.[275]

Hamilton was undoubtedly provoked by Brutus's threat. According to the National Constitution Center, "Brutus's essays were so incisive that they helped spur Alexander Hamilton to organize … and co-author … *The Federalist Papers* in response."[276]

The first essay, written by Hamilton, began in the same manner as his opponent's. "You are called upon to deliberate on a new Constitution for the United States of America," he wrote. "The subject speaks its own importance; comprehending in its consequences nothing less than the existence of the UNION, the safety and welfare of the parts of which it is composed, the fate of an empire in many respects the most interesting in the world." Publius agreed with Brutus that arriving at the correct decision was vital. "It seems to have been reserved to the people of this country, by their conduct and example, to decide the important question, whether societies of men are really capable or not of establishing good government from reflection and choice." Publius further agreed that the stakes involved all humanity, present and future. "The crisis at which we are arrived may with propriety be regarded as the era in which that decision is to be made; and a wrong election of the part we shall act may, in this view, deserve to be considered as the general misfortune of mankind."[277]

While Publius spent significant time on every aspect of the plan, as well as the philosophic underpinnings of democratic government in general, Brutus targeted only those aspects that were most threatening and would therefore arouse the most Antifederalist sentiment. As such, he devoted fully five of his sixteen essays to the branch of government that had been defined the most vaguely in the Constitution—the judiciary.

On January 31, 1788, Brutus's eleventh paper opened, "The nature and extent of the judicial power of the United States, proposed to be granted by this constitution, claims our particular attention." Although Antifederalists were both at the time and subsequently accused of fearmongering, Brutus 11 provided an eerily prescient depiction of the post-*Marbury* judiciary. Noting that the judiciary under the new

Constitution would "be placed in a situation altogether unprecedented in a free country," Brutus explained that judges "are to be rendered totally independent, both of the people and the legislature, both with respect to their offices and salaries," which turned out to be exactly the Constitutional necessity that Chief Justice Marshall would insist on in the *Marbury* opinion.[278] The effect, Brutus would warn in his fifteenth essay, was "that the supreme court under this constitution would be exalted above all other power in the government, and subject to no control."

Article III, to Brutus, "vests the courts with authority to give the constitution a legal construction, or to explain it according to the rules laid down for construing a law," which will necessarily involve "a certain degree of latitude of explanation." Supreme Court justices will therefore "give the sense of every article of the constitution, that may from time to time come before them. And in their decisions they will not confine themselves to any fixed or established rules, but will determine, according to what appears to them, the reason and spirit of the constitution." There could be no checks and balances, he claimed, when "the opinions of the supreme court, whatever they may be, will have the force of law; because there is no power provided in the constitution, that can correct their errors, or control their adjudications. From this court there is no appeal." He added later, "And I conceive the legislature themselves cannot set aside a judgment of this court, because they are authorised by the constitution to decide in the last resort."[279]

The irony is that Article III did not grant the Supreme Court the powers Brutus enunciated, but nor did it forbid them. John Marshall, a Federalist, was thus able to use those omissions to put the Court in precisely the same position that Brutus, an Antifederalist, predicted.

Brutus 15 was published on March 20, 1788. Publius, again in the person of Hamilton, did not take up the judiciary until May in Federalist 78, but in his opening paragraph, he once again made plain that he was writing as a response. After noting that "the propriety of the [judicial] institution in the abstract is not disputed; the only questions which have been raised being relative to the manner of constituting it, and to its extent," Hamilton wrote, "to these points, therefore, our observations shall be confined."[280]

To reassure the people of New York, Hamilton described the judiciary far differently than had Brutus and, referring to Montesquieu, noted, "the judiciary is beyond comparison the weakest of the three departments of power; that it can never attack with success either of the other two; and that all possible care is requisite to enable it to defend itself against their attacks." History, of course, has hardly vindicated that point of view.

But weakness, if it even existed, was not impotence. Later, in Federalist 78, Hamilton at last took up the subject of judicial oversight and was unambiguous in his opinion. "No legislative act, therefore, contrary to the Constitution, can be valid," he asserted bluntly. Hamilton added:

> It is not otherwise to be supposed, that the Constitution could intend to enable the representatives of the people to substitute their *will* to that of their constituents. It is far more rational to suppose that the courts were designed to be an intermediate body between the people and the legislature, in order, among other things, to keep the latter within the limits assigned to their authority. The interpretation of the laws is the proper and peculiar province of the courts. A constitution is, in fact, and must be regarded by the judges, as a fundamental law. It therefore belongs to them to ascertain its meaning, as well as the meaning of any particular act proceeding from the legislative body.

This is precisely the power that Marshall would later claim for the Supreme Court, and it hews closely to the claim Justice Scalia made in 1996. But Hamilton's assertions come from a man absent from the Convention for two months, including the period in which the provisions of Article III were discussed. Asserting that the power of judicial nullification was implicit in Article III, Hamilton was merely advancing an argument he believed would help him achieve his aim, not stating fact. He was attempting to convince skeptical New Yorkers that the courts, represented "the people," and judicial nullification gave "the people"—us—power over the legislature—them.

Nonetheless, Marshall appreciated Hamilton's take, and would later use the *Federalist* to support his opinions. He first cited the essays in *Calder v. Bull* in 1798, and in 1821, in *Cohens v. Virginia*, he wrote, "It is a complete commentary on our constitution; and is appealed to by all parties in the questions to which that instrument has given birth. Its intrinsic merit entitles it to this high rank, and the part two of its authors performed in framing the constitution, put it very much in their power to explain the views with which it was framed."[281]

Chief Justice Marshall notwithstanding, the *Federalist Papers* were never intended to be even-handed discussions of Constitutional issues that "will explain the views with which it was framed," but were written with a very definite slant and a distinctly weighted point of view. James Madison, one the principal authors, admitted as much. "The immediate object of them was to vindicate & recommend the new Constitution to the State of N. Y. whose ratification of the instrument, was doubtful, as well as important."[282] The aim, therefore, was not truth, but persuasion.

Using *The Federalist Papers* to demonstrate intent without further critical analysis is akin to a prosecutor blindly accepting a defendant's proclamation of innocence while declining cross examination. While some, even most, of the testimony can be accurate, key portions may be misleading, incomplete, or even totally untrue.

The *Federalist*, then, is what is known in literature as an "unreliable narrator." Unreliable does not mean definitively false. In some cases, the essays may well provide proper insight into constitutional theory or the delegates' intent or both. But in other cases, they will not. The difficulty is determining which is which.

Hamilton's rosy assessment must be viewed with some skepticism. That becomes clear later in Federalist 78, when, to further deflect Brutus, he added, "Nor does this conclusion by any means suppose a superiority of the judicial to the legislative power. It only supposes that the power of the people is superior to both; and that where the will of the legislature, declared in its statutes, stands in opposition to that of the people, declared in the Constitution, the judges ought to be governed by the latter rather than the former." Compared to Brutus's hard-headed enunciation of practicalities, Hamilton seems absolutely Pollyannish. Not only do judges fail to consider "the will of the people" as a matter of course, but the very notion goes against the most basic rule of judicial conduct—judges are supposed to interpret the law, not contort it to match public sentiment. The justices have, of course, often contorted the law as a sop to public sentiment—so long as public sentiment coincides with their own.

Even more naively, Hamilton added, "It can be of no weight to say that the courts, on the pretense of a repugnancy, may substitute their own pleasure to the constitutional intentions of the legislature ... The courts must declare the sense of the law; and if they should be disposed to exercise WILL instead of JUDGMENT, the consequence would equally be the substitution of their pleasure to that of the legislative body."

Which is precisely what has occurred throughout American history and continues to occur even more acutely today.

Whether Hamilton misread the implications of leaving Article III indistinct or was making a transparent effort to convince a dubious public of what he did not himself believe will never be known. But his description of the Supreme Court as the "people's" branch of government could not have been more incorrect.

Brutus, however, had been prescient.

Chapter 11

The Will of a Few of the People: The Electoral College

"It's not the voting that's democracy; it's the counting."
Tom Stoppard

"The primary purpose of the Electoral College is to maintain the power of the states and to support the idea that the election is decided by the states. It's not decided by the general population, and it never was."
Rush Limbaugh

The most vexing practical issue for the delegates in Philadelphia was the design of the executive branch. While philosophic views and questions of economics and political power went into the problem, how the executive was defined would also bear significantly on the new government's functionality.

Although the states had both legislative and executive branches, not only did interplay between them vary from state to state, but members of both branches were, of course, from the same state. In a national government this would not be the case. While the first chief executive was universally expected to be George Washington, after he left office, tensions between the two branches had the potential of creating either substantial dysfunction or, at the other end of the spectrum, fertile ground for cabal. In addition, Washington was a Virginia slave owner and, adoration notwithstanding, northern states were certain to be reluctant to invest the executive with sufficient authority that he could single-handedly protect slave state interests.

Finally, after fighting a long and destructive war to free themselves from the authority of the British crown, the delegates were loath to create a new system of government in which a similarly despotic figure might be enabled. As such, it is likely that most of the delegates, regardless of other predilections, arrived in Philadelphia with the expectation of severe wrangling over both the powers to be granted to the executive and the means of appointing him, or them, to the office.

They were right.

Madison was doubtless aware of the contentiousness to come, because, in the Virginia Plan, he left the description of the executive vague. Of the original fifteen resolutions, only two were devoted to the head of state. In Resolution 7, the "national Executive" would be "chosen by the National Legislature for the term of __ years," and be ineligible for further service.

Powers of the office were also left undefined, beyond "a general authority to execute the National laws," and that "it ought to enjoy the Executive rights vested in Congress by the Confederation," although it was not clear what the specifics of those executive rights might be. Resolution 8 was a description of Madison's council of revision, on which he would expend so much political capital in the months ahead. Here, the executive, and a "convenient number of the National Judiciary," would compose the council, "with authority to examine every act of the National Legislature before it shall operate" and that a "negative thereon shall be final," unless overridden by an unspecified percentage of legislators.[283]

In using the term "executive," Madison was likely not implying a position of control, as the word is often used today, but rather employing it in a ministerial manner as had John Locke, who noted that because laws "have a constant and lasting force," they "need a perpetual Execution," so there should be a "Power always in being, which should see to the Execution of the Laws that are made, and remain in force."[284] An executive with only ministerial powers was also likely to appeal to many of the delegates who feared a national government descending into tyranny.

On June 1, the convention took up the first of these resolutions. Wilson immediately moved that the executive be a single person. South Carolinians John Rutledge and Charles Pinckney both agreed but would not allow the executive the power of "peace and war," which Pinckney said would lead to monarchy.[285]

Roger Sherman interjected that the executive should follow Locke's suggestion and be ministerial only. "He considered the Executive magistracy as nothing more than an institution for carrying the will of the

Legislature into effect, that the person or persons ought to be appointed by and accountable to the Legislature only, which was the depositary of the supreme will of the Society." Wilson also agreed that the executive's authority should be solely ministerial. "The only powers he conceived strictly Executive were those of executing the laws, and appointing officers, not appertaining to and appointed by the Legislature."

Since the delegates were also loath to grant the executive sufficient authority to approach that of a king, when Gerry proposed "annexing a council" to the executive, Randolph strenuously objected calling such a plan the "fetus of a monarchy." To break from the British model, Randolph proposed a three-person executive, to which Wilson demurred. (Mason initially favored a tripartite executive as well.)

With no agreement forthcoming, hardly unexpected, Wilson's motion was tabled, after which Madison proposed that the powers of the executive be discussed as a prerequisite, since "a definition of their extent would assist the judgment in determining how far they might be safely entrusted to a single officer." Madison proposed "with power to carry into effect, the national laws. To appoint to offices in cases not otherwise provided for, and to execute such other powers not Legislative nor Judiciary in their nature as may from time to time be delegated by the national Legislature." Limited as it was, this was strongest proposal yet submitted, with far greater and wider-ranging authority than Madison had included in his plan. But Pinckney immediately objected to the final clause, which was struck out by a 7-3 vote, Connecticut divided.

In these preliminary discussions, no delegate proposed granting powers to the executive that would in any way approximate those of the president today. Although the roads to achieve it differed, the delegates were unanimous that the national executive should not be permitted to lever his position into authoritarian power. But how much power and how extensive would be the limitations on that power could not yet be addressed.

The delegates next took up manner of appointment, term of office, and eligibility for additional terms, each a corollary of the search for the optimal means of executive control. Wilson proposed election of the executive by popular vote, observing that "Experience, particularly in N. York & Massts, shewed that an election of the first magistrate by the people at large, was both a convenient & successful mode."[286] Wilson's aim was to remove the states from the process of selecting the executive and thus create a genuinely independent branch of government. Sherman, one of the delegates who feared "too much democracy," disagreed, claiming that "An independence of the Executive on the supreme Legislative, was in his opinion the very essence of tyranny if there was any such thing."

Wilson backed off, moving to the term of office, for which he suggested three years with continued eligibility. Pinckney suggested seven, likely with no re-eligibility, since Sherman agreed with the three-year suggestion and spoke against a one-term limit. Mason backed Pinckney's suggestion of one seven-year term, to which Delaware's Gunning Bedford objected. In Rufus King's notes, but not in Madison's, it was here that Madison suggested "good behaviour, or Seven years with exclusion forever afterward." The seven-year proposal passed 5-4, with Massachusetts divided. Support, however, was lukewarm and the delegates surely realized this question would be revisited.

They then returned to the mode of appointment, with Wilson renewing his call for a popular vote. The question was once more put off.

The following day, Wilson tried a different method of ensuring executive independence. He suggested "the States be divided into districts and that the persons qualified to vote in each district for members of the first branch of the national Legislature elect members for their respective districts to be electors of the Executive magistracy." These electors would then meet and elect the "person in whom the Executive authority of the national Government shall be vested." Wilson did no better with this idea than his previous one, but the notion of independent electors had been introduced into the debate.[287]

Gerry, ever suspicious of centralized authority, although fearful of state cabals, "liked the principle of Mr. Wilson's motion," since he "opposed the election by the national legislature. There would be a constant intrigue kept up for the appointment. The Legislature & the candidates wd. Bargain & play into one another's hands, votes would be given by the former under promises or expectations from the latter, of recompensing them by services to members of the Legislature or to their friends." (Although not his intention, Gerry had stumbled on a quite accurate description of the relationship between legislators and lobbyists.) Hugh Williamson of North Carolina thought electors redundant to the state legislature and an unneeded expense.

With no one else in favor, Wilson's motion failed 8-2. On a motion for appointment by state legislatures for a seven-year term, the vote was reversed.

After a long monograph by Franklin was read into the record, which was "treated with great respect, but rather for the author of it, than from any apparent conviction of its expediency or practicability," Dickinson moved "that the Executive be made removeable by the National Legislature on the request of a majority of the Legislatures of individual States." This was first mention of removal and the motion was seconded by Gunning Bedford, and Sherman agreed that "the National Legislature should have power to remove the Executive at pleasure."

The discussion of removal mirrored that of appointment. Madison and Wilson both immediately objected since, "it would leave an equality of agency in the small with the great States; that it would enable a minority of the people to prevent ye removal of an officer who had rendered himself justly criminal in the eyes of a majority."[288]

The convention was hardly prepared to settle on either approach. The motions failed, but they were a precursor of future bickering about the source of the executive's appointment and, therefore, his authority.

As one scholar wrote, "In the eyes of such a nationalist as Wilson, even election by the legislature detracted from the national independent stature of the executive, whereas for Dickinson the states were not accorded adequate control over the nation's chief executive officer. The two viewpoints, in one shape or another, arose repeatedly during the numerous discussions the convention was to hold on the mode of electing an executive. Dickinson's comment on the composition of the legislature foreshadowed, at this early stage of the discussions, the growing dissatisfaction of the smaller states, with their diminished role in the organs of government."[289]

Discussion of the executive was largely quiescent until the June 15 introduction of the New Jersey Plan. At first blush, Paterson's proposal for appointing the executive seemed to be not that much different than Madison's. He granted Congress the power "to elect a federal Executive to consist of __ persons, to continue in office for the term of __ years...to be incapable of holding any other office or appointment during their time of service and for __ years thereafter; to be ineligible a second time, &

removeable by Congs. on application by a majority of the Executives of the several States."[290] But the similarities were deceptive since Paterson's upper house would now vote by states, giving the small states inordinate say in the choice.

The issues simmered for a month until, on July 17, the depth of the delegates' conundrum came into focus. The only agreement was that the executive should be a single person, which was agreed to unanimously without debate, although, with voting by state, whether Randolph and Mason acceded to the idea is not known. Immediately afterward, "to be chosen by the national legislature was taken up," and unanimity collapsed.

Gouverneur Morris pointed out that if the executive was both appointed and impeachable by Congress, "He will be the mere creature of the Leglsl." Morris again tried to sneak his freeholder preference in by equating them with "people at large," muddying the waters further by proposing that "national legislature" be struck and "citizens of the United States inserted." Morris did not elaborate on whether he thought only freeholders could be citizens, although from this statement it seems so. His reasoning was a bit convenient: "If the people should elect, they will never fail to prefer some man of distinguished character, or services; some man, if he might so speak, of continental reputation." Although he was likely referring to Washington, Morris thought similarly of himself. He added, "If the Legislature elect, it will be the work of intrigue, of cabal, and of faction: it will be like the election of a pope by a conclave of cardinals; real merit will rarely be the rifle to the appointment."

Sherman disagreed, once more refusing to place a great deal of trust in his fellow Americans. "The sense of the Nation would be better expressed by the Legislature, than by the people at large. The latter will never be sufficiently informed of characters, and besides will never give a majority of votes to any one man. They will generally vote for some man in their own State, and the largest State will have the best chance for the appointment."

Wilson defended his proposal, and Charles Pinckney attacked it, claiming "An Election by the people being liable to the most obvious & striking objections. They will be led by a few active & designing men." Of course, popular vote would rob the slave states of their hard-earned 3/5 bonus. Morris hit the shot back, insisting, "If the Executive be chosen by the Natl. Legislature, he will not be independent on it; and if not independent, usurpation & tyranny on the part of the Legislature will be the consequence."

At that point, Mason pointed out the absurdity of the back-and-forth. "At one moment we are told that the Legislature is entitled to thorough confidence, and to indefinite power. At another, that it will be governed by intrigue & corruption, and cannot be trusted at all." He was, however, of the opinion that ordinary citizens, even the elite among them, could not be trusted with the decision. "He conceived it would be as unnatural to refer the choice of a proper character for chief Magistrate to the people, as it would, to refer a trial of colours to a blind man."

Mason also failed to note the loss of influence of slave states in a popular vote. North Carolina's Hugh Williamson did not. He admitted that a popular vote would not be the favored method of slave states, as "slaves will have no suffrage."

Predictably, no one was persuaded to alter his views and here was the crux of the problem. Even in a ministerial role, an executive under a new constitution was likely to wield significant power, a departure from the Confederation, in which the only executive was the president of Congress, a purely ceremonial position. As such, none of the principal interest groups were willing to create an office that would unduly diminish their influence in the new government. Large states with no slaves would be best served by popular vote, while large states with slaves, such as Virginia, had to decide if the loss of the slave bonus they had gained in the House of Representatives was sufficient to allow them to accept a method that rewarded substantial white populations. Small states with no slaves would be against popular vote, especially since they had successfully fought for parity in the Senate, while smaller slave states would be the most disadvantaged by popular vote.

Given this unwieldy balance, it was easier to say no than yes, and so the motion to substitute the people for the national legislature failed 9-1.[291] Luther Martin tried to break the stalemate by reintroducing Wilson's notion of electors drawn from state-created districts, but that failed 8-2. The delegates then retreated to the previous fault line. "To be chosen by the Nationl. Legislature," passed unanimously, as did motions to grant the executive power "to carry into execution the national laws," and to "appoint to offices in cases not otherwise provided for."

But sighs of relief were not in the offing. The debate was not over. William Houstoun of Georgia moved "to be ineligible a second time" be removed from the executive's seven-year term. Sherman seconded and Morris spoke in favor.

Eliminating the one-term limit changed the game once more. Seven years seemed excessive to many of the delegates if it could be then followed by other seven-year terms. But prohibiting reappointment meant potentially losing an excellent head of state to term limits, as Gouverneur Morris pointed out. "The ineligibility proposed by the clause as it stood tended to destroy the great motive to good behavior, the hope of being rewarded by a re-appointment. It was saying to him, make hay while the sun shines." To the likely surprise of many delegates, Houstoun's motion eliminate the one-term limit passed 6-4, which sent the convention right back to debating the seven-year term.

James McClurg, a prominent Virginia physician held in high esteem by Madison and Jefferson, proposed to remove a fixed term of office and opt instead for "good behavior." This set off an extended discussion in which Morris expressed "great pleasure" in the idea, Sherman agreed, and Madison evoked Montesquieu in pointing out separation of power pitfalls, especially that if the legislature were to have any role in the appointment or re-appointment of the executive, the latter would be dependent on and thus beholden to the former. Mason then took the floor to state that good behavior could easily turn into rule for life and lead to hereditary monarchy.

Here again, no one was equating "good behavior" with "for life," except to express the fear that the first could disastrously lead to the second. None of the delegates who spoke during this exchange thought the terms interchangeable, nor did any other delegate join to discussion to say they were. They made clear service during good behavior in no way precluded the introduction of term limits.

Nonetheless, McClurg's motion failed by a 6-4 vote, as did a motion to strike "seven years" as the term of service. It seemed that every time the delegates attempted to come up with a formula for choosing the executive that would be acceptable to a sufficient number of their fellows, they were forced to retreat, a sort of rhetorical trench warfare.

The next day, July 18, did not show any progress. As they session opened, the delegates agreed unanimously to put off discussion of the executive until the following day. On July 19, the fireworks continued. Luther Martin opened the session by moving to restore the ineligibility clause, to which Gouverneur Morris responded with a speech that must have taken at least two hours, asserting the subject "was of so much importance that he hoped to be indulged in an extensive view of it." The speech was long on philosophy and short on specifics, except to propose a two-year term, the executive chosen by the people at large, by which, once again, Morris meant freeholders.[292]

Morris included an odd supposition. "He saw no alternative for making the Executive independent of the Legislature but either to give him his office for life or make him eligible by the people. Again, it might be objected that two years would be too short a duration. But he believes that as long as he should behave himself well, he would be continued in his place." He added a sweetener: "It deserved consideration also that such an ingredient in the plan would render it extremely palatable to the people."

When Morris finally took his seat, Randolph immediately rose to give a lengthy rebuttal, to which King gave a counter-rebuttal. Although King thought the people at large would "choose wisely," he proposed "that an appointment by electors chosen by the people for the purpose, would be liable to fewest objections." Electors were thus back in the mix, a notion to which Paterson ascribed as well. He suggested "that the Executive should be appointed by Electors to be chosen by the States in a ratio that would allow one elector to the smallest and three to the largest States."

Paterson was being quite cagey here. Given the population breakdown of the various states, 1:3 between the smallest and the largest would work in favor of the small states, which, with the exception of Georgia, were all in the North.

Wilson grabbed at this new proposal, not to endorse it, but rather to indicate that it actually supported his call for direct elections, which in fact it did not. "It seems to be the unanimous sense that the Executive should not be appointed by the Legislature, unless he be rendered in-eligible a 2d. time: he perceived with pleasure that the idea was gaining ground, of an election mediately or immediately by the people."

Madison agreed, sort of. "It is essential then that the appointment of the Executive should either be drawn from some source, or held by some tenure, that will give him a free agency with regard to the Legislature. This could not be if he was to be appointable from time to time by the Legislature." He added, "The people at large was in his opinion the fittest in itself," a reversal of what he proposed in the Virginia Plan.

But Madison once again was employing misdirection. "The right of suffrage was much more diffusive in the Northern than the Southern States; and the latter could have no influence in the election on the score of the Negroes. The substitution of electors obviated this difficulty and seemed on the whole to be liable to the fewest objections." He was not going to allow philosophy to create a system in which his state's slave bonus would be eliminated.

Electors and popular election, it seemed, were not at all the same thing, as Wilson had attempted to imply.

To say that the delegates were flailing about is an understatement. It seemed there was simply no permutation at this point that would gain the required level of support, even though the delegates, to a man, recognized that no product would be forthcoming without some agreement on the executive. And so, Morris's motion to reconsider the entire plan passed 9-1.

Seemingly in desperation, the delegates then leapt on the notion of electors. Ellsworth proposed a system similar to Paterson's 1-2-3 formula, with a total of 25 electors, of which the slave states would get only ten. Predictably, Rutledge demurred, but the motion was carried 6-3, with the three southernmost states in the negative. They then voted 8-2 to allow the state legislatures to appoint the electors, although this time the delegates balked at assigning a ratio.

That sent them right back to the second term ineligibility question, which failed 8-2. Finally, the seven-year term was replaced by six.

The next day, when the ratio was again taken up, Madison pointed out that before too long, every state would pass the threshold for three electors, which would make "all the states or nearly all the states equal."[293] Although Madison had raised what was eventually certain to be an insuperable objection, the delegates nevertheless attempted to agree on a workable ratio, finally settling for a proposal by Elbridge Gerry to divide the twenty-five electors such that free states would have a 16-9 advantage. Three of the five slave states voted aye, a bit of a surprise, except that, as they may have known, the question remained far from settled.

Only days later, Edmund Randolph, in discussing potential pitfalls of ratification, touched on the underlying reason agreement on specifics was so difficult to reach. "One idea has pervaded all our proceedings, to wit, that opposition as well from the States as from individuals, will be made to the System to be proposed. Will it not then be highly imprudent, to furnish any unnecessary pretext by the mode of ratifying it."[294] The difficulty was that different states would have different pretexts for rejection, leaving a very narrow path to obtaining agreement from nine states, which, from a practical standpoint, needed to include Virginia, Massachusetts, Pennsylvania, New York, and, likely South Carolina.

In the July 23 session, which also saw the arrival of New Hampshire's two delegates, the Convention, likely with great frustration, voted to reconsider the mode of electing the chief executive, and, at Gerry's suggestion "that the proceedings of the Convention for the establishment of a Natl. Govt. (except the part relating to the Executive), be referred to a Committee to prepare & report a Constitution conformable thereto." The Convention then voted to create the five-person Committee of Detail.

On July 25, as the convention was preparing to send the Committee of Detail off to do its work, the back and forth continued with no agreement. Finally, Madison, unable to hide his annoyance, interjected, "There are objections agst. every mode that has been, or perhaps can be proposed. The election must be made either by some existing authority under the Natil. Or State Constitution, or by some special authority derived from the people or by the people themselves." He repeated his objections in allowing the national legislature to make the choice. "Besides the general influence of that mode on the independence of the Executive, the election of the Chief Magistrate would agitate & divide the legislature so much that the public interest would materially suffer by it."[295]

Madison spoke at great length, and there were further attempts to attempt to find at least something concerning the executive that the delegates could agree on, but they simply again went over familiar ground. Ellsworth made a telling point. "The objection drawn from the different sizes of the States, is unanswerable. The Citizens of the largest States would invariably prefer the Candidate within the State; and the largest States wd. invariably have the man." The delegates once again left the hall no farther along than when they had arrived.

The following day, July 26, thc last mccting bcforc thc Committcc of Detail would convene, almost the entire session was devoted to the executive.[296] Mason opened by speaking extensively on the various proposals that delegates had considered, none of which had been adopted. Either in irritation, desperation, or both, he moved to return to the original idea of the executive chosen by state legislatures for a seven-year term with no right of reappointment.

Franklin spoke passionately against the motion:

> It seems to have been imagined by some that the returning to the mass of the people was degrading the magistrate. This he thought was contrary to republican principles. In free Governments the rulers are the servants, and the people their superiors & sovereigns. For the former therefore to return among the latter was not to degrade but to promote them and it would be imposing an unreasonable burden on them, to keep them always in a State of servitude, and not allow them to become again one of the Masters.

Franklin's idealism, which bypassed the obvious fact that slave states would never agree to a popular vote, was ignored. The Convention voted 7-3 to return to the default option, which had already proved unacceptable. The Committee of Detail, therefore, was dispatched to prepare its draft constitution with instructions to produce a definition of the chief executive that was certain to be rejected.

After more than two long, often meandering months, the delegates were back at the beginning.

If any of them thought Rutledge and his four colleagues might provide a magical solution to the problem, they would be disappointed. The committee's sole achievement was to provide the chief executive with a title. Section 10 of the report read, "The Executive power of the United States shall be vested in a single person. His stile shall be, 'The President of the United States of America;' and his title shall be, 'His Excellency.' He shall be elected by ballot by the Legislature. He shall hold his office during the term of seven years; but shall not be elected a second time."[297]

That, of course, was not the end.

On August 7, the debates almost immediately moved to Article III of the committee's report, "The legislative power shall be vested in a Congress, to consist of two separate and distinct bodies of men, a House of Representatives, and a Senate; each of which shall, in all cases, have a negative on the other," which lead quickly into discussion of the presidency.[298] Since Congress would choose the president, it meant that if the houses voted separately, the Senate would be granted a veto power on the House's choice and small states could effectively hold out for a president of their choosing or create chaos by refusing to accede to any choice acceptable to the House. The House, dominated by large states, could similarly frustrate the will of the small states. A solution would be to have Congress vote in a joint ballot, but that would also favor the large states, the only difference being that the small states would lose their veto.

Mason instantly pointed out the flaw, doubting "the propriety of giving each branch a negative on the other "in all cases." Morris suggested replacing "all cases" with "legislative acts."[299] Williamson agreed, but Sherman objected, favoring the idea of mutual veto power for appointments.

Gorham, opting for the best alternative for large states, proposed a joint ballot, correctly pointing out, "If separate ballots should be made for the President, and the two branches should be each attached to a favorite, great delay, contention & confusion may ensue." With a dollop of disingenuousness, he added, "The only objection agst. a joint ballot is that it may deprive the Senate of their due weight; but this ought not to prevail over the respect due to the public tranquility & welfare." Wilson, another large state delegate, thought that precisely correct.

Morris's motion failed but Madison's motion to strike out "in all cases" was successful, so, in the end, the convention had made no progress. The irony in this interchange was that most of the delegates were doubtless aware that leaving election of the president to the national legislature alone had little chance of being approved. It is an indication of just how bereft for solutions they were that they wasted time on a provision that was bound to be rejected. In any case, the executive would not again be seriously broached for almost three weeks, until, on August 24, the delegates had no choice but to make a serious effort to find a solution.

They began with a rare show of unity, but it was to approve a single president, who would be called "Your Excellency." The unanimity vanished when Rutledge proposed a joint ballot and Sherman opposed it as "depriving the States represented in the Senate of the negative intended them in that house."[300]

Gorham repeated his objection that "Great delay and confusion would ensue if the two Houses shd vote separately, each having a negative on the choice of the other." Jonathan Dayton of New Jersey countered. "If the amendment should be agreed to, a joint ballot would in fact give the appointment to one House." A motion was then made to replace the legislature with the people, which once again failed miserably.

The meandering continued until Madison pointed out, "If the amendment be agreed to the rule of voting will give to the largest State, compared with the smallest, an influence as 4 to 1 only, although the population is as 10 to 1." He was, in effect, telling the small states not to be greedy, which seemed to work because a joint ballot was approved 7-4.

After more quibbles, Morris—again—proposed removing the national legislature from the process entirely. To guard against "all the evils" he had brought up in previous debates and repeated here, "He moved that the President 'shall be chosen by Electors to be chosen by the people of the several States," which failed albeit by a narrow 6-5 margin. When Morris limited his motion to electors, it failed in a tie vote.

Although the delegates had agreed to continue discussion of the executive the following day, it took a week for the subject to come up again, although only to defer it once more, passing it on to a new committee of eleven. Immediately before adjournment, Madison reported, "On motion of Mr. Sherman it was agreed to refer such parts of the Constitution as have been postponed, and such parts of Reports as have not been acted on, to a Committee of a member from each State; the Committee appointed by ballot, being—Mr Gilman, Mr. King. Mr Sherman. Mr. Brearley, Mr. Govr. Morris, Mr. Dickinson, Mr. Carrol, Mr. Madison, Mr. Williamson, Mr. Butler & Mr. Baldwin."[301]

The reason for forming this committee was apparent. "Hoping to get out of Philadelphia, the delegates finally pushed the problem onto the docket of a special committee, chaired by David Brearley, charged with solving previously irresolvable issues ... With their eyes wandering to the exits, the Framers never focused on the absurdity of their job assignment."[302]

And the assignment was extensive. Among the items the committee was charged with resolving after more than three months of contention were: the power to declare war; choosing ambassadors; raising an army; responsibilities of the vice-president; and, of course, the means of selecting a president. Although the committee kept no notes that have survived, "with their eyes wandering to the exits," it did its work quickly. Beginning the following day, September 1, the committee began submitting its recommendations, the less inflammatory questions first.

On September 4, the committee got to the means of electing a president, and there was much that was shockingly new. The term was reduced from seven years to four, shorter than any previous proposal, with no prohibition of re-election. The national legislature was replaced by electors, "equal to the whole number of Senators, and Members of the

House of representatives to which the State may be entitled in the legislature."[303] Gone was the 1-2-3 formula, and instead was an arrangement that would give the smallest state three electoral votes, which granted it disproportionate power in the process.

Further, "The Electors shall meet in their respective States, and vote by ballot for two Persons, of whom one at least shall not be an inhabitant of the same State with themselves, and they shall make a list of all the Persons voted for, and of the number of votes for each, which list they shall sign and certify, and transmit sealed to the seat of the general Government, directed to the President of the Senate."[304] Whoever finished with the most votes would be president and the runner-up vice president. As to eligibility, "No Person except a natural born Citizen, or a Citizen of the U. S. at the time of the adoption of this Constitution shall be eligible to the office of President: nor shall any Person be elected to that office, who shall be under the age of 35 years, and who has not been in the whole, at least 14 years a resident within the U. S."

These changes were too much for Randolph and Charles Pinckney who "wished for a particular explanation & discussion of the reasons for changing the mode of electing the Executive." Morris listed the committee's reasons, which included "the danger of intrigue & faction if the appointmt, should be made by the Legislature" and "the inconveniency of an ineligibility required by that mode in order to lessen its evils." Morris added that no one had seemed satisfied with election by the national legislature, neglecting to mention that no one had been satisfied with any other method either.

Most delegates were surprisingly amenable to a plan they likely would have rejected earlier in the convention. As Madison was to write later, "The difficulty of finding an unexceptionable process for appointing the Executive Organ of a Government such as that of the U.S. was deeply felt by the Convention; and as the final arrangement of it took place in the latter stage of the Session, it was not exempt from a degree of the hurrying influence produced by fatigue and impatience in all such Bodies."[305]

The only real objection was allowing the Senate to make the choice if no candidate received a majority. Finally, on September 6, the day Hamilton returned, Sherman moved "To strike out the words 'The Senate shall immediately choose &c.' and insert 'The House of Representatives shall immediately choose by ballot one of them for President, the members from each State having one vote.'"[306] In what would have a total shock only weeks earlier, the convention agreed, voting 10-1 in favor.

The Electoral College was born.

Madison, who was appalled by the arrangement, later wrote. "The part of the arrangement which casts the eventual appointment on the House of Reps. voting by States, was, as you presume, an accommodation to the anxiety of the smaller States for their sovereign equality, and to the jealousy of the larger towards the cumulative functions of the Senate." He called for a constitutional amendment to correct a system that was "so great a departure from the Republican principle of numerical equality, and even from the federal rule which qualifies the numerical by a State equality and is so pregnant also with a mischievous tendency in practice."[307]

Many scholars agreed. "Out of the Brearley Committee came a new coalition structure, dominated by a powerful northern bloc of five small states from the Northeast and Middle Atlantic: New Hampshire, Connecticut, New Jersey, Delaware, and Maryland. They were joined by the only large northern state, Massachusetts, and by the weakest and most vulnerable of the southern states, Georgia, to form a controlling seven-state majority."[308]

Others were more even-handed. "The Electoral College, its creation, however, had little in its favor as an institution, as the delegates well appreciated … To a body of working politicians the merits of the Brearley proposal were obvious: everybody got a piece of cake. (Or to put it more academically, each viewpoint could leave the Convention and argue to its constituents that it had really won the day.)"[309]

For large states with no slave bonus, such as New York, selling the Electoral College became part of the challenge of getting the new Constitution ratified. Hamilton, in Federalist 68 took it on, attempting, as he would in Federalist 78, to extol the virtues of a flawed and tortuously arrived at provision of the new Constitution. Once again, the irony was that he had not been present during the debates, and the result was hardly one he would have endorsed given the sentiments he had expressed in his June 18 speech.

Nonetheless, he wrote, "The mode of appointment of the chief magistrate of the United States is almost the only part of the system, of any consequence, which has escaped without severe censure, or which has received the slightest mark of approbation from its opponents," a statement that was transparently untrue. He continued: "I … hesitate not to affirm, that if the manner of it be not perfect, it is at least excellent. It unites in an eminent degree all the advantages; the union of which was to be desired. It was desirable, that the sense of the people should operate in the choice of the person to whom so important a trust was to be confided."[310]

Hamilton was once again granting the "people" a say in the new government to which they had not been entitled and in this case had been specifically denied. (Of course, his definition of the "people" was extremely limited indeed.) In fact, if state legislatures chose to appoint the electors, as all but two would in the first presidential election, and electors could act of their own volition, the "people" would be twice removed from the process. He also avoided noting that electors appointed by state legislators would almost certainly come from the upper, likely creditor, class and therefore almost certainly choose of their own.

Hamilton defended the appointment of unbound electors by asserting:

> It was equally desirable, that the immediate election should be made by men most capable of analizing the qualities adapted to the station and acting under circumstances favourable to deliberation and to a judicious combination of all the reasons and inducements, which were proper to govern their choice. A small number of persons, selected by their fellow citizens from the general mass, will be most likely to possess the information and discernment requisite to so complicated an investigation.

But that forced him to address why, if the people were to make the choice, the people were not permitted to do so directly:

> It was also peculiarly desirable to afford as little opportunity as possible to tumult and disorder. This evil was not least to be dreaded in the election of a magistrate, who was to have so important an agency in the administration of the government as the President of the United States. But the precautions which have been so happily concerted in the system under consideration, promise an effectual security against this mischief. The choice of SEVERAL, to form an intermediate body of electors, will be much less apt to convulse the community with any extraordinary or violent movements, than the choice of ONE who was himself to be the final object of the public wishes.

Only months after Hamilton had extolled the virtues of the "excellent" system to the people of New York, he revealed that his true feelings were quite different. In a letter to James Wilson in January 1789, he wrote, "A degree of anxiety about a matter of primary importance to the new government induces me to trouble you with this letter. I mean the election of the President." What he feared was that because the provision had been so sloppily drawn, Adams, rather than Washington, would end as the nation's first president. "Everybody is aware of that defect in the constitution which renders it possible that the man intended for Vice President may in fact turn up President. Everybody sees that unanimity in Adams as Vice President and a few votes insidiously withheld from Washington might substitute the former to the latter. And everybody must perceive that there is something to fear from machinations of Antifederal malignity. What in this situation is wise?"[311]

Hamilton's fears were well founded. Although that eventuality did not arise in the first three presidential elections, in would in 1800, when Aaron Burr, Jefferson's vice-presidential candidate, came with a whisker of being named president rather than Jefferson himself. They had tied with seventy-three electoral votes each, and it took thirty-six ballots in the House of Representatives for Jefferson to prevail. Even so, Jefferson, secretary of state at the time and presiding over the House votes, was forced to resort to chicanery to gain the post, accepting as legitimate a number of electoral votes improperly submitted.[312]

Gouverneur Morris, who had defended the system in the convention, also revealed different views later on. Addressing the New York Senate in 1802, he gave a sense of why such a dangerous situation had been allowed to develop:

> The Convention not only foresaw, that a scene might take place similar to that of the last presidential election, but even supposed it not impossible, that at some time or other a person admirably fitted for the office of President might have an equal vote with one totally unqualified, and that, by the predominance of faction in the House of Representatives, the latter might be preferred. This, which is the greatest supposable evil of the present mode, was calmly examined, and it appeared that, however prejudicial it might be at the present moment, a useful lesson would result from it for the future, to teach contending parties the importance of giving both votes to men fit for the first office.[313]

In other words, if Morris is to be believed, the delegates *chose* to write the section in a manner that they realized would court disaster. In response, the Twelfth Amendment was drawn up and hastily ratified in 1804, requiring for separate electoral votes for president and vice president.

If the electoral vote section was ill drawn in theory, it was equally so in practice. Key details that had been ignored or sloughed over by the delegates quickly came to the fore, one which was in how electors would be selected. Madison pointed out that the voting by district mode, which was "mostly, if not exclusively in view when the Constitution was framed and adopted," was soon supplanted by "the general ticket and the legislative election," which he concluded was "the only expedient for baffling the policy of the particular States which had set the example."[314]

In fact, "until the 1830s, consistency in method was rare, as states constantly altered their mode of selecting electors between three common methods: selection of electors by the state legislature, selection of elector by popular election in districts, and selection of electors by popular election using an at-large, general ticket."[315]

In the election of 1824, the House of Representatives was once again called on to choose a winner, selecting John Quincy Adams over Andrew Jackson, even though Jackson had a plurality in both the popular and electoral vote. Jackson decried the result as a "corrupt bargain," a charge given increased weight as ascertaining the "'sense of the people' in presidential elections remained uncertain because states varied in their method of selecting electors. In particular, legislative selection of electors—the most frequently used method from 1804-1820—did not necessarily reflect the majority's preference in each state."[316]

As a result, at Madison's urging, a constitutional amendment was proposed to require by-district voting for electors, but it was not approved in Congress. Instead, states moved toward the general ticket method, which eliminated the threat of gerrymandered districts, although still leaving those who voted with no control over who the electors would choose for either office. Eventually, general ticket, which is winner-take-all, was almost universally adopted and is now in use in 48 of the 50 states. Maine and Nebraska employ a hybrid, with by-district voting for half of its electors and general ticket for the other half.

One of the greatest flaws of the Electoral College, that a candidate receiving fewer votes than his opponent will be awarded the presidency, has in recent years become a genuine threat to an effectively functioning democracy. Until 2000, it had only occurred three times: in 1824, in 1876, with Rutherford B. Hayes defeating Samuel Tilden, and in 1888, with Benjamin Harrison besting incumbent Grover Cleveland.) Since 2000, however, it has occurred twice more, both favoring Republican candidates, George W. Bush in 2000 and Donald Trump in 2016. An even starker example emerged in 2020, when Donald Trump came within 43,000 votes of tying Joe Biden in the Electoral College, and almost certainly winning in the Republican-controlled House of Representatives, even though Trump lost the popular vote by more than seven million.[317]

As it turned out, not only has the Electoral College become an instrument of minority rule, but lack of clarity of what states may or may not do in appointing slates of electors has created uncertainty as to whether the winner of the popular vote would gain a state's electoral vote.

In a sharply divided nation, which the United States has most surely become, each of these flaws works at the expense of the principles the Constitution is heralded to espouse.

Chapter 12

Arms and the (Common) Man: Whither a National Military

"I am not afraid of an army of lions led by a sheep;
I am afraid of an army of sheep led by a lion"
Alexander the Great

"The American republics have no standing armies to intimidate a discontented minority; but as no minority has as yet been reduced to declare open war, the necessity of an army has not been felt."
Alexis de Tocqueville

In 2020, the United States amassed $778 billion of military spending – three times as much as China, twelve times more than Russia, and exceeding the next nine top-spending countries combined.[318] Although those are staggering statistics, for decades military spending has been a large part of the federal budget. As a result, with the continued demand for weapons systems and myriad military logistical needs, a thriving domestic economy has, to some significant degree, become reliant on the defence budget remaining high. Although the amount of expenditure is often debated in Congress and during elections, few Americans question the need for a well-funded, well-equipped, well-staffed, modern military to protect the nation from threats and, at least in some cases, help worthy nations across the globe who have been attacked by a superior foe.

During the Founding period, the situation could not have been more different. Although the rebellious colonies had been forced to recruit soldiers to fight the British, "The army was ragtag, barely trained, half-starving, and woefully unequipped. The group was also hardly united for too much of the war and led by generals often squabbling, undermining, or fighting with each other."[319] What George Washington commanded was, in many ways, not really an army at all, but rather a hastily thrown group of militias and civilians who volunteered to fight without training, proper equipment, and often without pay. "There were no established protocols for exercising coordinated authority, for supplying and feeding the troops, for transportation, or any other of the myriad tasks necessary for a field army."

After the British defeat at Yorktown, for which at least equal credit must go the French, much of the army disbanded, many of the soldiers returning home unpaid only to find themselves in debt and with their property either seized or about to be. With a peace treaty yet to be concluded, however, the army was forced to retain sufficient officers and men to again repel the British if the need arose.

This did not sit well with most of the nation's leaders. A standing army was considered as much of a threat to liberty as a foreign invader. In 1776, for example, Samuel Adams wrote to a friend, "A Standing Army, however necessary it may be at some times, is always dangerous to the Liberties of the People. Soldiers are apt to consider themselves as a Body distinct from the rest of the Citizens … Such a power should be watched with a jealous Eye."[320]

Militias were by far the preferred means of defence. In 1774, John Hancock wrote, "From a well-regulated militia we have nothing to fear; their interest is the same with that of the state … They do not jeopardize their lives for a master who considers them only as the instruments of this ambition."[321]

Fear that a standing army could become a government unto itself was not lessened by a near insurrection in Newburgh, New York, in March 1783. The army was encamped seventy miles up the Hudson River from New York City, and with the peace treaty with the British still not concluded, the officers and men could not leave and go home, which many desperately wanted to do. In addition, discontent among over back pay, pensions, and lack of provisions had been rising. The officers had forwarded a petition to Congress, which said, "We have borne all that men can bear. Our property is expended, our private resources are at an end, and our friends are wearied out and disgusted with our incessant applications."[322] They had received nothing in return but hollow assurances.

On March 11, an address from "a fellow soldier" condemned Congress for its inaction and threatened to use force of arms to gain their objectives, or, if the war did not end, to simply lay down their arms and go home.

Washington was aghast that his soldiers would make such a threat, and he demanded a meeting with the officers on March 15.

There, Washington, in a moment of brilliance equal to anything he did on the battlefield, turned away the threat. "This dreadful alternative, of either deserting our Country in the extremest hour of her distress or turning our arms against it … has something so shocking in it, that humanity revolts at the idea," he told them. Before reading from a paper detailing the nation's desperate financial position, Washington withdrew a pair of spectacles. "Gentlemen, you must pardon me," he said, "I have grown gray in your service and now find myself growing blind."[323]

The officers were stunned and some wept. Many of their grievances would not be addressed by a virtually bankrupt nation, but the army remained peacefully in place until the peace treaty was ratified, after which they returned home, likely to the enormous relief of the Confederation Congress. (The issues continued to fester, however, as Shays's Rebellion would attest.)

But the issue of national defence remained and Washington was convinced that, Newburgh notwithstanding, militias were not the answer. In May 1783, writing from Newburgh, he made his proposals to Congress:

> A Peace Establishment for the United States of America may in my opinion be classed under four different heads:
>
> First. A regular and standing force, for Garrisoning West Point and such other Posts upon our Northern, Western, and Southern Frontiers, as shall be deemed necessary to awe the Indians, protect our Trade, prevent the encroachment of our Neighbours of Canada and the Florida's, and guard us at least from surprises; Also for security of our Magazines.
>
> Secondly. A well organized Militia; upon a Plan that will pervade all the States, and introduce similarity in their Establishment Manoeuvres, Exercise and Arms.
>
> Thirdly. Establishing Arsenals of all kinds of Military Stores.
>
> Fourthly. Academies, one or more for the Instruction of the Art Military; particularly those Branches of it which respect Engineering and Artillery, which are highly essential, and the knowledge of which, is most difficult to obtain. Also Manufactories of some kinds of Military Stores.

In addition to allowing militias a significant role, Washington was clever enough not to advocate for unbridled military expansion, noting, "Altho' a *large* standing Army in time of Peace hath ever been considered dangerous to the liberties of a Country, yet a few Troops, under certain circumstances, are not only safe, but indispensably necessary."[324]

Congress nonetheless refused to act on Washington's request. Distrust of a standing army went far too deep, especially among those who would later be Antifederalists. As Richard Henry Lee wrote to James Monroe in January 1784, "You are perfectly right, Sir, in your observation concerning the consequence of a standing army—that it has constantly terminated in the destruction of liberty. It has not only *been* constantly so, but I think it clear from the construction of human nature, that it will always *be* so." Lee also provided his alternative. "The spirit of the 4th section of the 6th article of the Confederation plainly discourages the idea of standing army, by the special injunctions concerning a well-regulated militia, which is indeed the best defence, and only proper security for a free people to venture upon."[325]

While Antifederalists, such as Lee and Patrick Henry would be expected to ferociously oppose a national army, even some strong nationalists, such as George Mason, had qualms. In 1776, when Mason drafted the Virginia Declaration of Rights, Section 13 read, "That a well-regulated militia, composed of the body of the people, trained to arms, is the proper, natural, and safe defence of a free state; that standing armies, in time of peace, should be avoided as dangerous to liberty; and that in all cases the military should be under strict subordination to, and governed by, the civil power."[326]

For a militia to be effective, of course, it needed to be armed. Lee was strong on that question as well. He would later write that a "militia shall always be kept well organized, armed, and disciplined, and include, according to the past and general usage of the states, all men capable of bearing arms … to preserve liberty, it is essential that the whole body of the people always possess arms, and be taught alike, especially when young, how to use them."[327] Henry had similar views. "Guard with jealous attention the public liberty. Suspect everyone who approaches that jewel. Unfortunately, nothing will preserve it but downright force. Whenever you give up that force, you are ruined … The great object is that every man be armed. Everyone who is able might have a gun."[328]

Henry's pronouncement notwithstanding, no Virginian—at least no white Virginian—advocated a universal right to bear arms, nor did almost anyone else. Free Blacks, of whom there were almost sixty thousand, more than half of those in the South, were legally enjoined from owning weapons, as were those of mixed race, and no one in a slave state suggested altering that arrangement. It was only in the context of the perceived future need of "citizen soldiers" – militia members – that armed civilians was discussed. Whether or not Americans—once again, white Americans—should have the inviolate right to keep weapons for self-defence, key to the current debate over gun ownership, was neither considered nor debated. Certainly, most of the delegates favored private gun ownership, given the tenor of the times, but that is not to say they thought such a provision should be enshrined in the new Constitution, nor that the right was to be free of government control.

In any case, avoiding a national military in favor of militias promised to be no easy task when Washington and those who had experienced both were bitterly opposed. "For one group, however, the lessons [of war] were clear. To most of the higher-ranking officers of the Continental Army, the heads of the special branches and administrative departments, and Washington's staff, the war proved that militia were unreliable and inefficient." Washington wrote, "They come in you cannot tell how, go, you cannot tell when; and act, you cannot tell where … They consume your provisions, exhaust your stores, and leave you at last in a critical moment."[329]

Still, although some of the delegates, such as Charles Cotesworth Pinckney, a former army general, recognized the need for a national military, few others felt the same. Their misgivings notwithstanding, when the convention began in May 1787, the nation's security was by no means assured. Not only was Shays's Rebellion fresh in the delegates' minds, but Native American tribes presented an ongoing threat, as did the British, who continued to occupy forts in the northwest in violation of thc 1783 peace treaty's terms.

Balancing the needs of a national defence with the antipathy to a permanent military force was yet another challenge for the delegates. In many ways, the problem was similar to what they faced with a national judiciary—overcoming the widespread fear that a national institution could be a source of tyranny and the tool of a despot. In addition, mandating a national army would threaten with conscription citizens who had already given years of their lives to fighting, which promised to be immensely unpopular.

In the Virginia Plan, Madison chose to bypass the question entirely. There was no mention of either national or state-based military force. The only oblique references were in Article 1, "Resolved that the Articles of Confederation ought to be so corrected & enlarged as to accomplish the objects proposed by their institution; namely, 'common defence [sic], security of liberty and general welfare,'" with no indication how common defence would be obtained, and in Article 11, "Resolved that a Republican Government & the territory of each State, except in the instance of a voluntary junction of Government & territory, ought to be guaranteed by the United States to each State," with no indication how that guarantee would be enforced.

Specific discussion of a national military would not come until after the Committee of Detail submitted its report, but on June 29, during a debate on suffrage and the role of the states in the new government, Madison noted, "A standing military force, with an overgrown Executive will not long be safe companions to liberty. The means of defence against foreign danger have been always the instruments of tyranny at home. Among the Romans it was a standing maxim to excite a war, whenever a revolt was apprehended. Throughout all Europe, the armies kept up under the pretext of defending, have enslaved the people."[330]

Although Madison often altered his views on subordinate issues to gain advantage on larger ones, he would echo his favor of well-regulated, armed civilian militias in Federalist 46.

> "Besides the advantage of being armed, which the Americans possess over the people of almost every other nation, the existence of subordinate governments, to which the people are attached, and by which the militia officers are appointed, forms a barrier against the enterprises of ambition, more insurmountable than any which a simple government of any form can admit of."[331]

In Congress in 1789, after a committee had been formed to draft what would become the Bill of Rights, he would voice similar sentiments. "The right of the people to keep and bear arms shall not be infringed. A well-regulated militia, composed of the body of the people, trained to arms, is the best and most natural defence of a free country."[332] (While this was a somewhat clearer statement than what eventually emerged as the Second Amendment, whether the people had a *constitutional* right to keep and bear arms for personal safety, unrelated to service in a militia remained ambiguous.)

At the convention, however, the subject was not broached for more than two months. In the Committee of Detail report, however, national defence could no longer be avoided. Article VII, Section 1, which listed the powers proposed for Congress, included:

> To subdue a rebellion in any State, on the application of its Legislature;
>
> To make war;
>
> To raise armies;
>
> To build and equip fleets:
>
> To call forth the aid of the militia, in order to execute the laws of the Union, enforce treaties, suppress insurrections, and repel invasions.[333]

Still, the delegates did not take up that provision for weeks. On August 18, Mason beginning the discussion. "He thought such a power necessary to be given to the Genl. Government. He hoped there would be no standing army in time of peace, unless it might be for a few garrisons. The Militia ought therefore to be the more effectually prepared for the public defence. Thirteen States will never concur in any one system, if the disciplining of the Militia be left in their hands. If they will not give up the power over the whole, they probably will over a part as a select militia. He moved as an addition to the propositions just referred to the Committee of detail, & to be referred in like manner, 'a power to regulate the militia.'"[334]

Mason's proposal was a hybrid. In addition to "a few garrisons," Mason's proposal would effectively nationalize state militias—not exactly what Washington had in mind and closer than the proposals of his fellow Virginians Lee, Henry, and Madison.

But Mason's proposal was not debated. Rather, the delegates veered off to discuss financial matters, mostly whether the new government would assume state debts, an appropriate segue since financing a new government was as big a concern as its potential to contribute to tyranny. It was not until later in the debate that Nathaniel Gorham moved to include "support" as well as "raise" armies, to which Gerry "took notice that there was (no) check here agst. standing armies in time of peace. The existing Congs. is so constructed that it cannot of itself maintain an army. This wd. not be the case under the new system. The people were jealous on this head, and great opposition to the plan would spring from such an omission." He warned that "preparations of force" were being put in place by states that would oppose a standing army.

Still, Gerry recognized the need to not rely solely on state militias. To solve the problem, rather than an "indefinite number" of national soldiers, "He proposed that there shall not be kept up in time of peace more than [blank] thousand troops. His idea was that the blank should be filled with two or three thousand." Luther Martin moved to support Gerry's idea, suggesting a cap on the numbers of national troops except after a declaration of war, but General Pinckney asked "whether no troops were ever to be raised until an attack should be made on us?"

After Gerry warned that without such a provision, "states may establish a military government," Dayton pointed out that "preparations for war are generally made in peace; and a standing force of some sort may, for ought we know, become unavoidable."

After the motion to cap the size of the army during peacetime was unanimously rejected, Mason tried to bridge the divide by again suggesting a nationalized militia, adding to Congress's powers a provision "to make laws for the regulation and discipline of the Militia of the several States reserving to the States the appointment of the Officers." Pinckney, who had experienced the dysfunction of an army comprised of polyglot units, agreed that uniformity was essential to a successful fighting force, something the states could not achieve alone.

But nationalizing the militia was going to engender serious opposition. Ellsworth groused, "The whole authority over the Militia ought by no means to be taken away from the States whose consequence would pine away to nothing after such a sacrifice of power." Sherman agreed and Dickinson added, "His opinion was that the States never would nor ought to give up all authority over the Militia. He proposed to restrain the general power to one fourth part at a time, which by rotation would discipline the whole Militia," a notion not altogether different than the arrangement for today's National Guard.

That struck Mason as a good idea. "Afraid of creating insuperable objections to the plan," he changed his motion to give Congress the power "to make laws for regulating and disciplining the militia, not exceeding one tenth part in any one year, and reserving the appointment of officers to the States."

Pinckney disagreed, stating "For a part to be under the genl. and a part under the State Govts. wd be an incurable evil," although he gave no reasons why. Madison, somewhat surprisingly, eschewed what would have been an effective compromise and sided with the general. His reason was odd as well. "If the States would trust the Genl. Govt. with a power over the public treasure, they would from the same consideration of necessity grant it the direction of the public force." Consequences from the misuse of funds might be destabilizing and cause a fiscal crisis but misuse of force by a national military could well prove fatal.

Ellsworth reminded the convention of main question here, as it was in any number of other provisions. "The States will never submit to the same militia laws."

But Pinckney thought the states would agree to a national militia because they needed to. "The States would see the necessity of surrendering [control of the militia]. He had however but a scanty faith in Militia. There must be also a real military force. This alone can effectually answer the purpose." Then referring to Shays's Rebellion, that had Ellsworth's Connecticut and all of New England in an uproar, he added, "The United States had been making an experiment without it, and we see the consequence in their rapid approaches toward anarchy."

But Sherman sided with his Connecticut colleague as did, in a bit of a surprise, Massachusetts's Gerry who called the plan a "black mark" and adding, "He had no such confidence in the Genl. Govt."

After more fruitless back and forth, the convention voted to do what they so often did—refer the question to yet another committee, choosing the same delegates that had served on the previous Grand Committee.

On August 21, the Grand Committee proposed, "To make laws for organizing arming and disciplining the Militia, and for governing such part of them as may be employed in the service of the US reserving to the States respectively, the appointment of the officers, and the authority of training the Militia according to the discipline prescribed by the U. States."[335]

The clause was not debated until August 23 and, perhaps Madison's comment about the delegates' fatigue applied here as well, because the disagreements were minor. It was clear, however, that most of delegates had come to recognize that some uniformity in the manner of training, discipline, and even armaments was essential. As such, Rufus King made an interesting point: "That by organizing the Committee meant, proportioning the officers & men- by arming, specifying the kind size and caliber of arms- & by disciplining prescribing the manual exercise evolutions &c." Madison clarified King's statement by adding, "that 'arming' as explained did not extend to furnishing arms," which, taken together would mean that while the citizenry should have the right "to keep and bear arms," the federal government reserved the right to define what those arms may be. King then "added to his former explanation that arming meant not only to provide for uniformity of arms, but included authority to regulate the modes of furnishing, either by the militia themselves, the State Governments, or the National Treasury."[336]

While, again, this debate did not touch on private ownership of weapons for self-defence, none of the delegates seemed to think this an issue that the Constitution would need to address. After a couple half-hearted attempts to alter the paragraph or water it down, the convention approved it as submitted.

In the final version, the convention side-stepped the standing army question by giving Congress the power "To raise and support armies, but no appropriation of money to that use shall be for a longer term than two years." Gerry tried to reduce two years to one, on the grounds that two years was tantamount to authorizing a standing army, but he was heartily voted down. At this point, the relief among the delegates was palpable and there was little chance of them attempting any change that would create further debate.

Congress was also authorized "To provide and maintain a navy," and "To make rules for the government and regulation of the land and naval forces," which were accepted without dissent.

That brought the convention to the militia, where, once again, controversy melted away as the delegates realized that they might actually gain a finished product. Each side had achieved something. For those who opposed a standing army, empowering Congress "To provide for calling forth the militia to execute the laws of the union, suppress insurrections and repel invasions" might obviate the need for one. For those who wanted to ensure that the national government would have military sufficient resources if the need arose, Congress was authorized "To provide for organizing, arming, and disciplining, the militia, and for governing such part of them as may be employed in the service of the United States, reserving to the states respectively, the appointment of the officers, and the authority of training the militia according to the discipline prescribed by Congress."

What was not included was more detail on what "arming" a militia might entail. Madison and Rufus King's suggestion that arms be standardized to facilitate both training and performance was not included, nor if arming the militia meant members bringing their own weapons, although everyone certainly believed that some members would. That left open the questions of whether civilians would be required to own weapons, allowed to own weapons, and what, if any, restrictions on owning weapons the government might impose.

Certainly, sentiment in the nation was very definitely in favor of an armed citizenry—at least an armed white citizenry—and not simply for militia service. Noah Webster, most famous for his dictionary, was also an ardent Federalist, having studied law under Oliver Ellsworth. Less than one month after the Constitution was signed, he wrote, "Before a standing army can rule, the people must be disarmed, as they are in almost every country in Europe. The supreme power in America cannot enforce unjust laws by the sword; because the whole body of the people are armed and constitute a force superior to any band of regular troops."[337]

The following year, Richard Henry Lee would write, "No free government was ever founded, or ever preserved its liberty, without uniting the characters of the citizen and soldier in those destined for the defence of the state … such area well-regulated militia, composed of the freeholders, citizen and husbandman, who take up arms to preserve their property, as individuals, and their rights as freemen."[338]

Still, it is difficult to separate Americans' feelings about an armed populace and the preference for a militia over a standing army. As Elbridgc Gerry would say in Congress, "What, Sir, is the use of a militia? It is to prevent the establishment of a standing army, the bane of liberty … Whenever Governments mean to invade the rights and liberties of the people, they always attempt to destroy the militia, in order to raise an army upon their ruins."[339]

But the desire for an armed citizenry and the need for citizen soldiers to be prepared to go into battle is not the same thing as guaranteeing that any American could own any weapons for any purpose without the possibility of government control or regulation. It also does not mean that the right to own guns for self-defence allows any citizen to carry any weapon in public because of an unstated or obscure threat. Absent a more detailed explanation of the role of both the militia and the weaponry that citizens, these questions would seem to have been delegated, like so many other open questions, to Congress to make the appropriate rules.

And the First Congress would do so, not with a law, but rather with an amendment to the Constitution, one of ten that were adopted from twelve that were proposed. Those ten, the "Bill of Rights," had become necessary after the convention, which had unanimously voted against the idea, had unwittingly left Antifederalists with an issue that could scuttle ratification. In order to get the Constitution approved, Madison, who had opposed a Bill of Rights in Philadelphia, was forced to quickly pivot, as were a number of other delegates who represented their states in ratifying conventions.

The wording of the second of those amendments, "A well regulated Militia, being necessary to the security of a free State, the right of the people to keep and bear Arms, shall not be infringed," did not make clarification of the militia clauses any easier. For more than two centuries, the amendment was seen to apply a guarantee to keep and bear arms only to ensure that national defence, in theory entrusted largely to militias, would be prepared when needed in times of need or crisis.

The Supreme Court seemed to affirm that meaning in 1939, when, James McReynolds, speaking for a unanimous Court in *United States v. Miller*, wrote "We construe the [Second] amendment as having relation to military service and we are unable to say that a sawed-off shotgun has any relation to the militia."[340]

Although McReynolds was merely repeating a generally thought sentiment, *Miller*, as the sawed-off shotgun might indicate, was an unusual case, stemming from a challenge to the 1934 National Firearms Act, itself a response to the carnage spawned by Prohibition-era gang wars, including the notorious St. Valentine's Day Massacre, in which seven members of Chicago's Bugs Moran gang were executed with machine guns on February 14, 1929 in a Lincoln Park garage by Al Capone's executioners. The law imposed taxes on the sale or transfer of a variety of hand and long guns, required that certain categories of firearms be registered, and restricted the movement of firearms across state lines.

In April 1938, Jack Miller and Frank Layton, two bank robbers on the run from both the law and their associates, were arrested and charged with transporting unregistered sawed-off shotguns across state lines. Miller had every reason to feel the need to carry a weapon—in 1935, he had turned state's evidence to avoid a prison sentence, about which his colleagues were none too pleased.

Miller, although an unlikely plaintiff, sued in federal court to void his arrest on Second Amendment grounds. The judge, a gun control advocate, sided with Miller, which resulted in Miller's release from prison, where any number of unhappy former associates were waiting for him. The decision was contrived—the judge assumed that Miller would flee and thus allow the government to win its appeal of Miller's dismissal virtually by default. His assumption proved correct. As soon as he was a free man, Miller promptly vanished.

As a result, when the government appealed the dismissal to the Supreme Court in January 1939, there was no one on the other side to contest its brief. Miller's and Layton's court appointed lawyer, working pro bono, refused to do any more work on their behalf. Oral arguments—or, rather, argument—were heard on March 30, 1939, and the decision was published only six weeks later.

McReynolds and the other justices deemed the meaning of the Second Amendment so obvious, so related to the need for citizen soldiers in a nation that had no standing army, that the argument that Miller or anyone else had the right to carry whatever weapon they wanted wherever they wanted was laughable. His nine-page opinion could not have been more dismissive.

(Jack Miller, however, was not around to learn of the verdict. Four days after oral arguments, his body was found with four bullet holes near Ketchum, Oklahoma. The crime remained unsolved. Layton, who had kept a much lower profile, was eventually given five years' probation for violating the National Firearms Act and died of natural causes in 1967.)

The *Miller* decision attracted little attention at the time, since almost no one interpreted the Second Amendment as anything other than an anachronism, rendered obsolete by the creation of a professional military.

That all changed in 2008, when in a bitterly contested 5-4 decision in

District of Columbia v. Heller, Antonin Scalia for the first time ruled that the Second Amendment also guaranteed an individual's right to keep gun in the home for self-defence.[341] He dismissed the Miller ruling with an inventive ploy, applying it not to an individual's right to keep and bear arms, but rather only to the weapon.

Scalia's opinion did not universally apply the amendment's guarantee to all weapons owned by all people in all settings, but ruled only that a gun kept in the home for self-defence by a private citizen was a protected right. "Although we do not undertake an exhaustive historical analysis today of the full scope of the Second Amendment," he wrote, "nothing in our opinion should be taken to cast doubt on longstanding prohibitions on the possession of firearms by felons and the mentally ill, or laws forbidding the carrying of firearms in sensitive places such as schools and government buildings, or laws imposing conditions and qualifications on the commercial sale of arms." As a result, although Congress has lacked the will to do so, any number of laws limiting the sale or use of firearms would not have infringed on the *Heller* decision.

Many of those potential limitations were short-circuited, however, when, in 2022, in his majority opinion in the New York case, *New York State Rifle & Pistol Association v. Bruen*, Clarence Thomas extended that right to, among other locations, streets, and shopping malls. In adopting the most expansive view of the Second Amendment in American history, Thomas and five of his colleagues ruled that, "that the Second and Fourteenth Amendments protect an individual's right to carry a handgun for self-defence outside the home."[342] The majority claimed that United States history had provided them precedent, although strict control laws were in common in, among other places, the Wild West, in such towns as Tombstone, Arizona.[343]

Regardless of whether the nation's founders believed that private individuals should have the right to own weapons, an amendment clearly written for one purpose has been shapeshifted into another and the original intent of the amendment has virtually disappeared from both jurisprudence and public discourse. As a result, Second Amendment law has descended into the preposterous notion of whether the founders believed that a man or woman, heavily armed, can stroll into a supermarket, movie theater, or public park with his or her hand on the grip of a holstered pistol in plain view of other citizens, including perhaps children. In some states, residents can do so without having obtained a permit for those weapons or training in their use and safe handling.

That leads to the question of if had Madison included "trained to arms" in the Second Amendment, would the meaning and the resulting jurisprudence have changed? "The right of the people to keep and bear arms shall not be infringed. A well-regulated militia, composed of the body of the people, trained to arms, is the best and most natural defence of a free country," might be interpreted as requiring gun owners to undergo at least some minimum training.

Although whether different wording would lead to a different interpretation is problematic, given that the Court seems determined to maximally broaden gun rights and maximally shrink gun safety, there is also the issue of in the current wording, "whether" also means "not control." Neither the *Heller* nor *Bruen* rulings stated that no controls under any circumstances would pass muster, but just where limits might be placed was not addressed. There have been many suggestions, including requiring gun purchasers to attend training sessions, or purchase liability insurance, or demonstrate an absence of mental illness counseling or substance abuse, but each of these could easily be ruled on being excessively burdensome on those who wish to own firearms.

In the end, absent a more specific definition of the founders' intentions regarding both a national military and private ownership of weapons, both gun rights and gun safety laws remain at the whim of Congress and the judiciary. Given the horrific record of gun violence and mass shootings in the United States, neither of those branches may be the optimal venue to define public safety.

Chapter 13

An Anti-Textualist Interlude: Necessary and Proper

"Congress has not unlimited powers to provide for the general welfare but is restrained to those specifically enumerated, and . . . it was never meant they should provide for that welfare but by the exercise of the enumerated powers."
Thomas Jefferson

"If opportunity doesn't knock, build a door."
Milton Berle

One of the most delicate questions facing the delegates was how much latitude to grant Congress. Under the Articles, Congress's authority was strictly circumscribed by Article II, according to which "Each state retains its sovereignty, freedom and independence, and every Power, Jurisdiction and right, which is not by this confederation expressly delegated to the United States, in Congress assembled." While such rigidity had proved unworkable and one of the principal reasons the Articles had failed, granting Congress too much flexibility under the new Constitution was generally assumed to threaten the autonomy of the individual states, which was unacceptable to all but the most ardent nationalists.

As a result, finding the proper balance between the two extremes would underlie many of the debates over not only what would become Article I, but by inference, the powers granted to the executive and the judiciary as well.

Virtually all the delegates favored granting Congress powers that were specifically delineated, with Hamilton once again the exception, proposing to invest Congress "with power to pass all laws whatsoever subject to the Negative hereafter mentioned," by which he meant the executive, which would "have a negative on all laws about to be passed, and the execution of all laws passed."[344] Hamilton's proposal had no support but the question of how much flexibility Congress would be allowed in the practical application of those powers it would be assigned remained unanswered.

Neither the Virginia nor the New Jersey Plan contained a formula to grant Congress sufficient authority to discharge its responsibilities without creating a body that could wield far too much power over state interests. In the Virginia Plan, Madison proposed giving Congress far more latitude than the states would agree to. Section 6 read, "That the National Legislature ought to be impowered to enjoy the Legislative Rights vested in Congress by the Confederation & moreover to legislate in all cases to which the separate States are incompetent, or in which the harmony of the United States may be interrupted by the exercise of individual Legislation; to negative all laws passed by the several States, contravening in the opinion of the National Legislature the articles of Union." [345]

On May 31, when the provision was discussed, there were immediate objections from South Carolina. "Mr. Pinckney, & Mr. Rutledge objected to the vagueness of the term incompetent, and said they could not well decide how to vote until they should see an exact enumeration of the powers comprehended by this definition." Pierce Butler "repeated his fears that we were running into an extreme in taking away the powers of the States, and called on Mr. Randolph for the extent of his meaning."[346] Roger Sherman objected as well.

That caused Randolph to backpedal. He "disclaimed any intention to give indefinite powers to the national Legislature, declaring that he was entirely opposed to such an inroad on the State jurisdictions, and that he did not think any considerations whatever could ever change his determination. His opinion was fixed on this point."

Madison chose to equivocate, once more attempting to be on both sides of an issue:

> He had brought with him into the Convention a strong bias in favor of an enumeration and definition of the powers necessary to be exercised by the national Legislature; but had also brought doubts concerning its practicability. His wishes remained unaltered; but his doubts had become stronger. What his opinion might ultimately be he could not yet tell. But he should shrink from nothing which should be found essential to such a form of Govt. as would provide for the safety, liberty and happiness of the Community. This being the end of all our deliberations, all the

> necessary means for attaining it must, however reluctantly, be submitted to.

Madison must have been persuasive, for the vote on "giving powers, in cases to which the States are not competent," passed 9-0, with Connecticut divided.

The New Jersey Plan was more vague. It expanded enumerated the powers of Congress and, for raising revenue, allowed the rules "to be applied to such federal purposes as they shall deem proper & expedient." Later in the plan, however, Paterson had included, "provided that none of the powers hereby vested in the U. States in Congs. shall be exercised without the consent of at least States, and in that proportion if the number of Confederated States should hereafter be increased or diminished."[347]

Charles Pinckney also proposed that the Articles approach be modified, although when and even if he did so to the delegates is unclear. He wrote that although, "Each State retains its Rights not expressly delegated ... no Bill of the Legislature of any State shall become a law till it shall have been laid before S. and H. D. in C. assembled and received their Approbation."[348]

On July 17, Delaware's Gunning Bedford moved to expand on the Virginia Plan proposal and that Congress's power extend "in all cases for the general Interests of the Union, and also in those Cases to which the States are separately incompetent, or in which the Harmony of the United States may be interrupted by the Exercise of individual Legislation."[349] Gouverneur Morris seconded and, with opposition to such a broad interpretation likely to be fierce when the plan was submitted to the states, Randolph was again forced to pull back.

> "This is a formidable idea indeed. It involves the power of violating all the laws and constitutions of the States, and of intermeddling with their police."

Bedford countered, "It is not more extensive or formidable than the clause as it stands: no State being separately competent to legislate for the general interest of the Union." His motion passed 6-4.

The following week, the Committee of Detail was created, with Congress's mandate broad indeed. In its report, Bedford's wording was simplified, although whether Congress's extensive mandate was more limited remained hazy. After a long list of enumerated powers, Article VII,

Section 1 read, "And to make all laws that shall be necessary and proper for carrying into execution the foregoing powers, and all other powers vested by this Constitution in the Government of the United States, or in any department or office thereof." The clause was adopted unanimously with virtually no debate on August 20, entering the Constitution almost verbatim from the committee's proposal.[350]

Many scholars have remarked that the clause appeared out of the blue. "The Necessary and Proper Clause was added to the Constitution by the Committee on Detail without any previous discussion by the Constitutional Convention. Nor was it the subject of any debate from its initial proposal to the Convention's final adoption of the Constitution."[351] Still, it did appear to have represented a general notion with which delegates had twice voiced approval. It is, however, also correct that a clause that seemed to grant Congress sweeping powers was not contested to any serious degree, although that would quickly change when the document was sent to the states for ratification.

> "The likely reason why the Necessary and Proper Clause received no attention by the Convention became clear during the debates in the ratification conventions, as did its public meaning. There, opponents of the Constitution pointed to this power as evidence that the national government had unlimited and undefined powers. In the New York Convention, for example, John Williams contended that it 'is perhaps utterly impossible fully to define this power.' For this reason, 'whatever they judge necessary for the proper administration of the powers lodged in them, they may execute without any check or impediment.'"[352]

Williams was not alone. In the Virginia ratifying convention, Patrick Henry found the implications of the clause is "dangerous, because it is unbounded: if it be admitted at all, and no limits be prescribed, it admits of the utmost extension. They say that everything that is not given is retained. The reverse of the proposition is true by implication. They do not carry their implication so far when they speak of the general welfare—no implication when the sweeping clause comes. Implication is only necessary when the existence of privileges is in dispute. The existence of powers is sufficiently established. If we trust our dearest rights to implication, we shall be in a very unhappy situation."[353]

In New York, Brutus once again zeroed in incisively on what he considered a grievous flaw. "The inference is natural that the legislature will have an authority to make all laws which they shall judge necessary for the common safety, and to promote the general welfare. This amounts to a power to make laws at discretion: No terms can be found more indefinite than these, and it is obvious, that the legislature alone must judge what laws are proper and necessary for the purpose." Again prescient, he added, "It is, perhaps, utterly impossible fully to define this power."[354]

As he did with the judiciary, Publius, this time both Hamilton and Madison, attempted to diffuse the criticism. Hamilton, in Federalist 33, did not spare hyperbole, exclaiming that "[It has] been the source of much virulent invective and petulant declamation against the proposed Constitution. [It has] been held up to the people in all the exaggerated colors of misrepresentation as the pernicious engines by which their local governments were to be destroyed and their liberties exterminated; as the hideous monster whose devouring jaws would spare neither sex nor age, nor high nor low, nor sacred nor profane." As to the clause itself, Hamilton could only offer subjective assurances that it was limited in scope and would remain so in practice. "[It is] only declaratory of a truth which would have resulted by necessary and unavoidable implication from the very act of constituting a federal government, and vesting it with certain specified powers. This is so clear a proposition, that moderation itself can scarcely listen to the railings which have been so copiously vented against this part of the plan, without emotions that disturb its equanimity."[355] Since Hamilton was writing anonymously, no one was aware that the assurances of the continuation of state sovereignty came from the man who had been accused with good cause of wanting to abolish the states entirely.

Madison, while less shrill, was equally subjective. Acknowledging that "Few parts of the Constitution have been assailed with more intemperance than this," he nonetheless asserted that "on a fair investigation of it, no part can appear more completely invulnerable. Without the SUBSTANCE of this power, the whole Constitution would be a dead letter." Ironically, later in the essay, Madison indicates that the clause was both superfluous and unnecessary. "Had the Constitution been silent on this head, there can be no doubt that all the particular powers requisite as means of executing the general powers would have resulted to the government, by unavoidable implication. No axiom is more clearly established in law, or in reason, than that wherever the end is required, the means are authorized; wherever a general power to do a thing is given, every particular power necessary for doing it is included."[356]

It is no accident that neither Hamilton nor Madison could mount a convincing argument for a limited definition of necessary and proper. Both "necessary" and "proper" are subjective adjectives, prone to individual interpretation and defying objectivity. As such, there seemed to be no way to employ them in strictly defining the boundaries of congressional action. Still, without some hard boundaries, Congress's power becomes virtually unlimited, which not even the most ardent nationalist would claim to have been the delegates' intention.

That contradiction therefore leaves textualist scholars scrambling to create limits on an open-ended phrase. As Robert Natalson frames the problem, "Among the unanswered questions about the Clause are how 'necessary' a law must be to the exercise of an enumerated power; what the meaning of 'proper' is; and whether the provision is an affirmative grant of power, a limitation on power, or a mere rule of construction." In other words, the question is "whether the Clause establishes an objective (judicially reviewable) standard for legislation or leaves legislation solely to congressional discretion."[357] Ironic is that, for Natalson, limits on the clause will be the purview of the courts under the power of judicial review, itself a power not specifically granted in Article III.

Thus, in order to find that a subjective phrase has an objective meaning, textualists, who claim to shun linguistic gymnastics, need to employ them here. Natalson goes on to say, "The Clause provides that a law 'shall be' necessary and proper. When the drafters wished to communicate a grant of unreviewable discretion, they used phrases such as 'shall think proper,' 'the Congress may,' and 'as he shall judge necessary and expedient.'" He is therefore using a subjective interpretation of a subjective phrase to come to what he wants to be an objective truth.

Almost immediately after the Constitution was adopted that lack of objectivity was put to a test, with the two Publius authors who had defended the limits on the necessary and proper clause, Hamilton and Madison, on different sides.

As far back as April 1781, Hamilton, never shy in his admiration of British institutions, thought to copy the Bank of England in the United States. He wrote to Robert Morris, who as Superintendent of Finance during the Revolution had helped establish the Bank of North America,

"The long and expensive wars of King William had drained England of its specie; its commerce began to droop for want of a proper medium; its taxes were unproductive and its revenues declined. The administration wisely had recourse to the institution of a bank; and it relieved the national difficulties. We are in the same, and still greater, want of a sufficient medium."[358]

The Bank of North America had been controversial, attacked for the high interest rates it had charged on its loans, and viewed by many farmers and debtors as a tool of rich speculators, an indictment not without merit. But Hamilton viewed it as essential. In his report on a national bank in December 1790, he wrote, "The aid afforded to the United States by this institution during the remaining period of the war was of essential consequence."[359]

But, under its most recent charter, the Bank of North America was not a true national bank, which was what Hamilton thought was desperately needed to support its currency, shore up the nation's credit, and provide a vehicle for economic growth. It had become, "the mere Bank of a particular State [Pennsylvania] liable to dissolution at the expiration of fourteen years, to which term the act of that state has restricted its duration, it would be neither fit nor expedient to accept it, as an equivalent for a Bank of the United States."

Hamilton did not think the bank a panacea, but it did deem it a necessity. In his letter to Morris, he wrote, "Most commercial nations have found it necessary to institute banks; and they have proved to be the happiest engines that ever were invented for advancing trade. Venice, Genoa, Hamburg, Holland and England are examples of their utility. They owe their riches, commerce, and the figure they have made at different periods, in a great degree to this source."[360] Hamilton would repeat those sentiments in his December 1790 report, in which he would also observe, "It is to be considered that such a bank is not a mere matter of private property, but a political machine of the greatest importance to the state," a pronouncement that was unlikely to assuage the fears of Antifederalists, who by then had almost all become Jeffersonians.

As a result, when the proposal reached Congress, there was deep and predictable opposition. Pennsylvania senator William Maclay wrote, "Yesterday the Secretary's [Hamilton's] report on the subject of a national bank was handed to us, and I can readily find that a bank will be the consequence. Considered as an aristocratic engine, I have no great predilection for banks. They may be considered, in some measure, as operating like a tax in favor of the rich, against the poor, tending to the accumulating in a few hands; and under this view may be regarded as opposed to republicanism."[361]

During the House of Representatives debates for establishing a bank on February 1, 1791, James Jackson of Georgia was "opposed to the principle of the bill altogether." He "calculated to benefit a small part of the United States, the mercantile class only; the farmers, the yeomanry will derive no advantages from it." Jackson then "read several passages from the *Federalist*," which, he asserted, proved that the bank would be "a monopoly of a very extraordinary nature; a monopoly of public moneys for the benefit of the corporation to be created," unaware that it was distinctly possible that the author of the passages he had quoted, who he thought of as an enemy, might well be sitting in the chamber with him, this time as his ally.[362]

The next day, it was Madison's turn. Without informing the House that he had been one of the principal authors of the *Federalist*, he proceeded in his usually orderly fashion to lay out the pros and cons of banks in general, before taking up whether the Constitution had granted Congress the power to charter a national bank.

In his list advantages, Madison included "the aid they afford to merchants, who can thereby push their mercantile operations further with the same capital … aids to merchants in paying punctually the customs … aids to the government in complying punctually with its engagements … diminishing usury … saving the wear of gold and silver kept in the vaults, and represented by notes … and facilitating occasional remittances from different places where notes happened to circulate." Under disadvantages, Madison mentioned "banishing precious metals" by taking them out of circulation, "exposing the public and individuals to all the evils of a run on the bank," the concentration of wealth, and the advantages to speculators who would be granted privileged ability to buy stock.

On balance, Madison concluded, "it did not make for a good for the public," which led him into his argument that the plan was unconstitutional anyway.[363]

"Reviewing the Constitution," he noted, "it was not possible in it the power to incorporate a Bank. Among the sections that would not supply justification was the necessary and proper clause. "Whatever meaning this clause may have, none can be admitted that would give unlimited discretion to Congress." This was true. "Its meaning must, according to the natural and obvious force of the terms and the context be limited to means necessary to the end, and incident to the nature of the specified powers." This was less so. Madison also neglected to mention that at no time did he express these sentiments in the convention, but simply acquiesced in the unanimous decision to include it as written, free of caveats.

He also neglected to mention that he had been one of the most ardent nationalists in Philadelphia and, while certainly not as extreme as Hamilton in that regard, he had not spent a good deal of time worrying about the diminution of state power. Here, however, as a Jeffersonian he was concerned that a national bank would intrude on the ability of states to create their own financial institutions. "In arguing that Congress could not grant corporate charters because the power was not enumerated in the Constitution, Madison was arguing against his own past record. The doctrine of implied powers had originated in his report to Congress of 1781. In the Federal Convention of 1787, he had co-sponsored a resolution granting Congress the power to incorporate bodies where the public interest dictated it, but the resolution had been tabled by the convention."[364]

Perhaps unwittingly, Madison also undermined the notion that there could be a definitive meaning to "necessary and proper." He lamented that "The proposed Bank could not even be called necessary to the Government; at most it could be but convenient." How to make the determination between "necessary" and "convenient" or who might be authorized to do so could be debated interminably, and in fact, would be even after one of Madison's intractable enemies, John Marshall, later insisted on appointing himself to provide the distinction.

Even among Madison's fellow Republicans in Congress, the issue was far from clear. Massachusetts's Fisher Ames observed, "Congress may do what is necessary to the end for which the Constitution was adopted provided it is not repugnant to the natural rights of man or to those which they have expressly reserved to themselves or to the powers which are assigned to the states ... By that instrument [the Constitution], certain powers are specifically delegated, together with all powers necessary and proper to carry them into execution. That construction may be maintained to be a safe one, which promotes the good of the society, and the ends for which the government was adopted, without impairing the rights of any man, or the powers of any State."[365]

In the end, objections to the bank came to naught and the First Bank of the United States was chartered for twenty years in 1791. Although the bank had many detractors, mostly from the agrarian south and west, they grudgingly accepted its existence, relieved when the charter expired in 1811. But the Second Bank of United States, chartered in 1816, would receive a far different reception.

The second bank was chartered for the same reasons as the first—a deteriorating economy and ballooning national debt, in this case byproducts of the War of 1812. Although the charter for the first bank had not been renewed in 1811 by President James Madison, it had helped stabilize the economy and provide desperately needed capital for investment. "The war with Britain, however, disrupted foreign trade. As one of the United States' largest trading partners, Britain used its navy to blockade U.S. trade with other nations. The war prevented U.S. farmers and manufacturers from exporting merchandise, blocked U.S. merchants and fisherman from sailing the high seas, and curtailed federal government revenues, which were derived mainly from tariffs on trade."[366]

By 1814, with the war raging, Madison, who no longer viewed a national bank as unnecessary or improper, reluctantly agreed to support the second bank's charter, as did many of his fellow Republicans. But as peace negotiations progressed, Madison withdrew his support and the first effort to create a second bank was rejected by Congress. The economy did not recover as quickly or profoundly as Madison had expected and, in April 1816, putting his objections aside, he approved the new bank's charter. "Constitutional questions of the authority of Congress to create such a bank, a talking point for the opposition during the war, were not pressed, but opposition based on states' rights doctrine did raise its head."[367]

As such, this time the bank's opponents did not merely sit on the sidelines and grumble, especially after the bank enjoyed a less than sterling performance caused by less than competent management. By 1818, the bank was "tottering on bankruptcy, the directors began to call in outstanding loans and press state banks to do the same." That was enough for many Republicans. "In response, some states—notably, Maryland and Tennessee, followed by Georgia, North Carolina, Ohio, and Kentucky—passed laws disfavoring the [the bank] in favor of state banks."[368]

Maryland went one step further. It imposed a tax on all banks or bank branches operating within the state's borders that had not been chartered by the Maryland legislature. That description fit only one bank, the Maryland branch of the Bank of the United States. When a clerk at the bank, James McCulloch, refused to pay the tax, Maryland sued. Unsurprisingly, the federal government, in the person of McCulloch, lost in state court.

That would eventually result in a showdown in the Supreme Court between the bank, represented by Daniel Webster, and the state of Maryland, represented by its attorney general, the Convention's gadfly, Luther Martin. Martin, totally unchanged, would argue that the Constitution had not granted the government the power to create the bank. Martin had also been Maryland's attorney general when Hamilton proposed the first bank but, as had everyone else, had declined to turn his objections into action.

And so, the necessary and proper clause, in all its seeming subjectivity, would be on trial. "The clause did not have any clear boundaries. These would have to be drawn around every act of Congress fitting the category. Were those boundaries merely political, or were they grounded in law? The legislative branch itself could not answer that question; it belonged to the courts. How far could the clause, and congressional legislation under it, advance into legislative territory claimed by the states? Was the clause an invitation for the federal government to destroy the sovereignty of the states?"[369]

Whether, in fact, the Constitution had been written to give the judiciary the power to determine if a law was "necessary and proper" is a dubious proposition. As with judicial review, allowing the courts to pass on laws based only on its own judgment would be to anoint unelected judges as quasi-legislators. But John Marshall never shrank from the opportunity to expand the Court's power, and he was not going to allow this opportunity to pass by.

In another lengthy opinion, Marshall, the strongest remaining Federalist in the national government, used the necessary and proper clause to once more enhance the authority of the national government at the expense of the states, and solidified the Court's pre-eminent role as arbiter in the bargain.

He began by demonstrating that the Constitution, as the "supreme law of the land," established unequivocally that in a conflict between a state and national government, the former must give way. Thus, "The States have no power, by taxation or otherwise, to retard, impede, burthen, or in any manner control the operations of the constitutional laws enacted by Congress to carry into effect the powers vested in the national Government."[370]

Although Marshall freely admitted, "Among the enumerated powers, we do not find that of establishing a bank or creating a corporation," he pointed out, "But there is no phrase in the instrument which, like the Articles of Confederation, excludes incidental or implied powers and which requires that everything granted shall be expressly and minutely described. Even the 10th Amendment, which was framed for the purpose of quieting the excessive jealousies which had been excited, omits the word 'expressly,' and declares only that the powers 'not delegated to the United States, nor prohibited to the States, are reserved to the States or to the people.'"

Having established Congress's latitude, it remained to determine how wide that latitude stretched, which of course brought the question of subjectivity back to square one. To Marshall, all the talk that "necessary and proper" were strictly circumscribed terms turned out to be hollow verbiage.

"The counsel for the State of Maryland," he wrote, "have urged various arguments to prove that this clause, though in terms a grant of power, is not so in effect, but is really restrictive of the general right which might otherwise be implied of selecting means for executing the enumerated powers." He went on that, to Maryland, "The word 'necessary' is considered as controlling the whole sentence, and as limiting the right to pass laws for the execution of the granted powers to such as are indispensable, and without which the power would be nugatory. That it excludes the choice of means, and leaves to Congress in each case that only which is most direct and simple."

This, to Marshall, was false. "Is it true that this is the sense in which the word 'necessary' is always used? Does it always import an absolute physical necessity so strong that one thing to which another may be termed necessary cannot exist without that other? We think it does not."

But what did it mean? Although for most men, an absolute definition would seem impossible, John Marshall was not most men. "To employ the means necessary to an end is generally understood as employing any means calculated to produce the end, and not as being confined to those single means without which the end would be entirely unattainable. Such is the character of human language that no word conveys to the mind in all situations one single definite idea, and nothing is more common than to use words in a figurative sense ... A thing may be necessary, very necessary, absolutely or indispensably necessary. To no mind would the same idea be conveyed by these several phrases."

From there, it was an easy matter to conclude that the "[necessary and proper] clause, as construed by the State of Maryland, would abridge, and almost annihilate, this useful and necessary right of the legislature to select its means. That this could not be intended is, we should think, had it not been already controverted, too apparent for controversy."

Marshall concluded, "After the most deliberate consideration, it is the unanimous and decided opinion of this Court that the act to incorporate the Bank of the United States is a law made in pursuance of the Constitution and is a part of the supreme law of the land."

And so, with Congress free to express the means by its powers would best executed, the assurances that the necessary and proper clause could not and would not provide open-ended power to the central government were largely stripped away.

> "In McCulloch, the Court adopted a generally broad and deferential test, and specifically rejected many of the narrow readings, such as the argument that 'necessary' mean 'indispensable' or even 'most direct and simple,' or the argument that the clause should be read as diminishing Congress's powers compared to what they would have been without the clause."[371]

What Marshall had succeeded in achieving, once again with an extremely deft use of language, was to demonstrate that no matter how much Hamilton and Madison disingenuously wished to portray the necessary and proper clause as applying only to explicitly enumerated powers, the Convention had, in truth, approved a passage that could easily be interpreted as granting Congress virtually limitless power.

Antifederalists, once again epitomized by Brutus, had been much closer to the truth.

Although no one on either side would have denied that in a checks and balances system, some boundaries must exist, where they should and would lie had been shown by Marshall to be totally subjective. In addition to creating an enormous gray area, it casts doubt on both “textualism” and “originalism” as legitimate means of approaching constitutional law.

Chapter 14

The Repair Shop: The Steep Road to Amendment

"Some men look at constitutions with sanctimonious reverence, and deem them like the ark of the Covenant, too sacred to be touched. They ascribe to the men of the preceding age a wisdom more than human and suppose what they did to be beyond amendment."
Thomas Jefferson

"Just when I discovered the meaning of life, they changed it."
George Carlin.

The Philadelphia delegates recognized that the unanimity required to make alterations in the Articles had left them fatally inadaptable to changing conditions and was one of the principal reasons that the convention in which they sat had been necessary. As such, a provision to provide for amendments was almost universally accepted as being an important feature of the new Constitution. "The members of the Philadelphia convention clearly wanted to create an amending system that, without rendering the Constitution unstable, would allow generally agreed-upon change to take place. They did not wish to ever see repeated the combination of constitutional inadequacy and inflexibility that had produced the governmental crisis they were confronting."[372]

Just how those amendments would be proposed, however, and how they would then be either accepted or rejected was yet another unknown.

Madison finessed the question in the Virginia Plan, stating only, "Resolved that provision ought to be made for the amendment of the Articles of Union whensoever it shall seem necessary, and that the assent of the National Legislature ought not to be required thereto." Eliminating the legislature in the amendment process served both to differentiate the plan from the sclerotic Articles and also ensured that Congress would not be able to grasp despotic power by, for example, abolishing the states.

When the provision came up for discussion on June 5, Charles Pinckney "doubted the propriety or necessity of it"—although he had included a similar provision in his own plan—while Gerry thought it vital. There was no debate and when the topic came up again on June 11, although several unnamed members again "did not see the necessity" of it, after Mason and Randolph spoke in favor of amendments adopted in "an easy, regular and Constitutional way" rather than "to trust to chance and violence," the first section of the provision was approved unanimously, with the section about avoiding the legislature, postponed. Legislative involvement or lack of it would not come up again until September.[373]

Paterson did not address amendments at all, nor did Hamilton, and the amendments question lay fallow with the Committee of Detail instructed only, "That provision ought to be made for the amendment of the articles of union, whensoever it shall seem necessary." The interim version produced in the committee was heavily notated. "(An alteration may be effected in the articles of union, on the application of two thirds nine <2/3d> of the state legislatures <by a Convn.>) <on appln. of 2/3ds of the State Legislatures to the Natl. Leg. they call a Convn. to revise or alter ye Articles of Union>"[374] Just which of the committee members suggested that formula or the fraction within it is unknown, but the version reported out contained both. "On the application of the Legislatures of two thirds of the States in the Union, for an amendment of this Constitution, the Legislature of the United States shall call a Convention for that purpose." When the provision was taken up on August 30, it passed unanimously without debate.

On September 10, however, things did not go so smoothly. Gerry asked to reconsider the clause as being a threat to state sovereignty. "This Constitution he said is to be paramount to the State Constitutions. It follows, hence, from this article that two thirds of the States may obtain a Convention, a majority of which can bind the Union to innovations that may subvert the State Constitutions altogether. He asked whether this was a situation proper to be run into."[375]

Hamilton seconded the motion but not because it threatened state sovereignty, about which he cared little. He feared just the opposite—that the clause as written would weaken national sovereignty, a danger he viewed as emanating directly from Congress's exclusion from the process:

> It had been wished by many and was much to have been desired that an easier mode for introducing amendments had been provided by the articles of Confederation. It was equally desirable now that an easy mode should be established for supplying defects which will probably appear in the new System. The mode proposed was not adequate. The State Legislatures will not apply for alterations but with a view to increase their own powers. The National Legislature will be the first to perceive and will be most sensible to the necessity of amendments, and ought also to be empowered, whenever two thirds of each branch should concur to call a Convention. There could be no danger in giving this power, as the people would finally decide in the case."

What Hamilton meant by the last sentence is hazy, unless he envisioned the resulting amendment convention as being either representative of the people—again using Hamilton's very limited definition—or that the result would need ratification within each state.

Madison, taking Hamilton a step further, also thought the terms in the committee's report vague, although they were more specific than he had offered. "How was a Convention to be formed? By what rule decide? What the force of its acts?"

Roger Sherman then "moved to add to the article 'or the Legislature may propose amendments to the several States for their approbation, but no amendments shall be binding until consented to by the several States.'" Gerry seconded but Wilson wanted to place "two-thirds" before "several States," which was defeated 6-5. When Wilson changed two-thirds to three-quarters, the motion passed without debate.

Madison then proposed a broader version. "The Legislature of the U- - S-- whenever two thirds of both Houses shall deem necessary, or on the application of two thirds of the Legislatures of the several States, shall propose amendments to this Constitution, which shall be valid to all intents and purposes as part thereof, when the same shall have been ratified by three fourths at least of the Legislatures of the several States, or by Conventions in three fourths thereof, as one or the other mode of ratification may be proposed by the Legislature of the U. S." Hamilton seconded.

That raised slaveowners hackles. In addition to demanding that, to request an amendment, 2/3 be raised to ¾, Rutledge exclaimed that he "never could agree to give a power by which the articles relating to slaves might be altered by the States not interested in that property and prejudiced against it." He proposed adding the caveat of prohibiting any amendments dealing with the slave trade or fugitive slaves until 1808. The convention agreed and the revised provision passed.

The issue was not settled, however. After the proposed final version emerged from the Committee of Style, on September 15, the last session before the document would be signed, Roger Sherman "expressed his fears that three fourths of the States might be brought to do things fatal to particular States, as abolishing them altogether or depriving them of their equality in the Senate." Taking a swipe at slave states, "He thought it reasonable that the proviso in favor of the States importing slaves should be extended so as to provide that no State should be affected in its internal police, or deprived of its equality in the Senate."[376]

Mason suggested throwing out the entire article. He "thought the plan of amending the Constitution exceptionable & dangerous. As the proposing of amendments is in both the modes to depend, in the first immediately, and in the second, ultimately, on Congress, no amendments of the proper kind would ever be obtained by the people, if the Government should become oppressive, as he verily believed would be the case."

But the delegates had come too far to turn back. Morris and Gerry proposed moving the states needed to call for an amendment from three-quarters back to two-thirds, which was agreed to. Other attempts to tinker with the wording failed until Sherman, in frustration with what he saw as endangering state sovereignty, moved to strike out Article V altogether, which was defeated 8-2.

Gouverneur Morris, in a rare attempt to find middle ground, then proposed "that no State, without its consent shall be deprived of its equal suffrage in the Senate." As Madison noted, "This motion being dictated by the circulating murmurs of the small States was agreed to without debate, no one opposing it, or on the question, saying no." With that, Article V was complete.

Although the delegates drafted Article V to be the sole means of updating the Constitution to meet changing conditions, and also to clarify language that might have been misinterpreted, fill in omissions, and correct errors, in the more than 235 years since the Constitution was ratified, after more than 11,000 proposed amendments, the Constitution has only been added to twenty-seven times, twenty-five if the two self-cancelling Prohibition amendments are left out.

Of those twenty-five, the first ten were appended almost immediately and were merely an explicit listing of rights the delegates thought implicit in the document, but the lack of which had given Antifederalists far more ammunition in the ratifying process than Federalists anticipated. It became clear even before the Constitution was accepted by the required nine states that, regardless of the restrictions in Article V, the absence of a "bill of rights" would need to be immediately addressed. "Our Founders designed the Constitution so that amending it would be hard, but not impossible. In fact, they ratified the document with many of the amendments that would become the Bill of Rights already in mind. George Washington dedicated a good chunk of his first inaugural address to the subject of amendments."[377]

"Hard but not impossible" is the key phrase. In well more than two centuries, again excluding the Prohibition amendments, the Constitution has been amended only fifteen more times, and it took a century and a half for the final ten to work their way into the Constitution, only one of them in the past fifty years, and that was an amendment originally proposed with the Bill of Rights in 1788.[378] One study determined that the United States Constitution is one of the two most difficult in the world to change.[379]

This was no accident. "The provisions of Article V have undoubtedly played a role in causing this low rate of amendment. The second round of approval by a supermajority of state legislatures or conventions seems especially daunting. By requiring the concurrence of both national and state legislatures, Article V comes close to requiring unanimity to approve any amendment as a practical matter."[380]

The delegates were forced to find balance between two poles and ended up tilting distinctly toward one of them. "If the constitution makes change too easy, there is a risk that the constitution will not structure politics, but will be hostage to it. But making change too difficult may cause political instability or force change to occur through a non-constitutional process. The procedure for change that the Framers provided in Article V appears to reflect a judgment that making change too easy is the greater danger."[381]

That "greater danger" was once more centered on the need of the states, especially the smaller states, to maintain the maximum degree of autonomy possible, while ceding the minimum to the new central government. The price for not doing so was, as before, rejection of the entire plan, which would throw the nation back into the near chaos that was rule under the Articles. Still, the question came down to balance since the nationalists were also capable of rejecting any plan that did not give the new government sufficient power to at least begin to address the nation's ills.

Madison took on the need for such a balance in Federalist 43, predictably claiming the delegates had found the correct one. "That useful alterations will be suggested by experience, could not but be foreseen. It was requisite, therefore, that a mode for introducing them should be provided. The mode preferred by the convention seems to be stamped with every mark of propriety. It guards equally against that extreme facility, which would render the Constitution too mutable; and that extreme difficulty, which might perpetuate its discovered faults."[382] Here, Madison may or may not have been anticipating the need for the Bill of Rights, which already seemed essential to ratification when he wrote the essay.

Those sentiments notwithstanding, eliminating discovered faults beyond providing a Bill of Rights promised to be difficult, as Madison must have been aware. Perhaps the reason the delegates chose to make amending the Constitution so cumbersome was that in the short-term the Federalists, who dominated the convention, would have sufficient control of the reins of government to be able gain both two-thirds majorities in each house of Congress and in three-quarters of the state legislatures. As competition for political power increased, however, overweight majorities would disappear and the difficulties in getting amendments adopted meant that the flaws that had been built into the original document had become that much harder to correct.

In Federalist 85, Hamilton, as he had done in all the essays, downplayed any potential problems and assured his readers that the amendment process was curative of the inability to draft a "perfect" document in Philadelphia. Ironically, he implied that the necessity of compromise had left many parts of the Constitution either incomplete or inadequate, the opposite of what Publius had asserted in the previous eighty-four essays. Including a formula for amending the document meant these deficiencies could be rectified, he contended, one problem at a time. His argument was more than a little idiosyncratic.

"But every amendment to the Constitution, if once established, would be a single proposition, and might be brought forward singly. There would then be no necessity for management or compromise, in relation to any other point no giving nor taking … And consequently, whenever nine, or rather ten States, were united in the desire of a particular amendment, that amendment must infallibly take place. There can, therefore, be no comparison between the facility of affecting an amendment, and that of establishing in the first instance a complete Constitution."[383]

For the most part, those amendments that did manage to achieve ratification have had a profound impact on both American government and American life. Of the remaining fifteen, four were devoted to voting rights, and an additional three to the conduct of elections. Three more dealt with presidential succession and term limits. Of the remainder, one authorizes an income tax, one prohibits suits against states, one limits increases of congressional compensation, one abolishes slavery, and one, the Fourteenth, is an enormous expansion of the federal government's ability to protect the rights of those living with the nation's borders.

Ensuring the vote for women, those eighteen or over, and, in theory, those of any race, has vastly altered both elections and the elected. Mandating that United States senators be elected by popular vote rather than appointed by state legislators has eliminated an obvious source of patronage and, again in theory, upgraded the quality of person who serves in the upper house. Authorization of income tax, as unpopular as it may be, created a source of funding for the government in which the wealthy were supposed to pay more than the poor. The Fourteenth Amendment has had such profound effect on both lawmaking and jurisprudence that it might almost be considered a second Constitution in itself.

But the most recent of those, guaranteeing the vote to those eighteen and over, was ratified in 1973, and the prospect of another amendment, especially one aimed at ensuring equal rights, is bleak. And so, voting rights, distorted electoral districts, an addition to the Second Amendment aimed at gun safety, terms limits for Supreme Court justices—assuming an amendment is needed—guarantees of citizenship, reform of the electoral college, and all the omissions in the Constitution that threaten democracy will be highly resistant to change.

The delegates to the Constitutional Convention, therefore, drafted a document which intentionally left a number of important holes and then created a mechanism inadequate to fill them.

But that does not mean they went unfilled.

The combination of a ponderous amendment process and John Marshall's seizure of the power to interpret the Constitution and disallow any law that the justices decide is in conflict with it has allowed the judiciary to become not only an arbiter but often a de facto Article V.

One need look no further than voting rights. In *Cruikshank*, Justice Bradley not only re-interpreted the Fifteenth Amendment but essentially rewrote it. Recent Supreme Court decisions, such as *Shelby County v. Holder*, and *Brnovich v. Democratic National Committee*, while not addressing the Fifteenth Amendment directly, significantly narrowed its scope on Tenth Amendment grounds. Giving preference to one amendment over another, especially on the questionable grounds that the Court ruled in *Shelby County* and *Brnovich*, could easily be seen as an off the books amendment process.

In response, voting rights advocates have proposed new laws guaranteeing voting rights to vulnerable populations, but they would face the same impediments that allowed the Court to end-run the Fifteenth Amendment in its previous decisions.

And so, although amending the Constitution was initially seen as a means of guaranteeing individual rights, it is dependent on an all but impossible rule of procedure and the potential antipathy of an imperious panel of Supreme Court justices in order to do so.

Chapter 15

Tyranny of Minority: American Democracy on the Brink

"The tyranny of the minority is infinitely more odious and intolerable and more to be feared than that of the majority."
William McKinley

"The tyranny of the minority cloaked in the mask of the majority."
Frank Herbert

Almost to a man, the delegates in Philadelphia favored minority rule—not just any minority, however, but one that was carefully controlled. Government leaders were to be drawn only from select classes and specific segments of the population, chosen by those of the same ilk. Policy, the theory went, would thus be formulated and implemented by those most suitable to make sound decisions. The malcontents who perpetrated Shays's Rebellion and others like them were to have at best a minimal say—even less if possible—in choosing who would control the nation, thus conforming to delegates' fear of "too much democracy." Carefully circumscribing who might populate government councils would thus allow the nation to move forward with intelligence and stability.

Without specific mechanisms in the Constitution to place controls on the participation of the lower classes, there was no guarantee that this strategy would be successful. The delegates seemed to assume that restrictions on both who could become a citizen and then which of those citizens were allowed to vote, neither of which the Constitution specifically addressed, would continue to maintain the rule of the economic and social aristocracy envisioned by delegates as different as patrician planter John Rutledge and Yankee merchant Roger Sherman.

In terms of actual governance, central to the delegates' approach was the belief—or the hope—that leaders drawn from the elites, even those with radically different philosophies, would be able to come to agreement on solutions to the nation's myriad problems in a reasonable manner, hashing out issues in the halls of government and achieving results that all would, if not be totally happy with, at least accept.

There was a second, far less appealing incarnation of minority rule that the nationalists had been forced to acknowledge. To avoid rejection by the states, the Convention had agreed to create a central government that, by apportioning senate seats by state and instituting an electoral college to choose the president, might one day be controlled by a coalition of the original small states and new ones admitted as the nation grew. That gave rise to the additional risk that governance might become as unwieldy under the Constitution as it had been under the Articles.

Federalists, such as Madison, Hamilton, Gouverneur Morris, and John Rutledge—among the strongest voices in Philadelphia—were aware of this potential outcome but had little choice. They were therefore gambling that the concessions granted to small states could be rendered moot even as the number of states grew, and that the dysfunction bred of by-state government that had plagued the nation earlier might be sidestepped. Thus, Benjamin Franklin's response of "A republic, if you can keep it," to a woman who asked what form of government the Constitution had mandated, is a good deal more trenchant than he is generally given credit for.

In Federalist 10, Madison, in perhaps the most famous of all the essays, attempted to persuade ordinary citizens that the Constitution had not only anticipated the risks in the new form of government, but had provided for them as well. He wrote that "a well-constructed Union," could "break and control the violence of faction."[384]

Noting that "Complaints are everywhere heard from our most considerate and virtuous citizens, equally the friends of public and private faith, and of public and personal liberty, that our governments are too unstable, that the public good is disregarded in the conflicts of rival parties, and that measures are too often decided, not according to the rules of justice and the rights of the minor party, but by the superior force of an interested and overbearing majority," Madison insisted that the new Constitution provided the means to avoid the "mortal diseases" of "instability, injustice, and confusion" in popular government.

He went on to postulate that while it would be impossible to remove the causes of the "mischiefs of faction," the Constitution offered the means to control their effects. Because of the nature of the human species, Madison reasoned, pure democracy would fall prey to these mischiefs and so the limited representative government endowed by the Constitution represented the only avenue of escape.

If Madison actually held this belief—no sure thing with the *Federalist* essays—he was either demonstrating naïveté about the inevitability of compromise in a conclave of elites or was hoping the people of New York would not notice how few of them would have a voice, even indirectly, in shaping the new government. Madison also neglected to mention that, if his plan were actualized, the vast majority of Americans would be forced to live with whatever a government in which they had no say had dictated to them.

Although Gouverneur Morris had failed in his repeated efforts to include in the Constitution a prohibition against all but freeholders being allowed to vote for the House of Representatives – the only organ of government in which "the people" would have any say – neither Madison nor any other delegate expected voting rolls to be thrown open to anywhere near a majority of the citizenry. In none of the thirteen states did what would be termed the lower classes have access to the ballot and, while strict freeholding requirements were likely to wither away, these were expected to be supplanted by the need to show payment of taxes, which could also include a minimum to weed out more of those who might contribute to discord.

The first presidential election in 1788 bore out both the Federalists' confidence and their success in limiting the size of the electorate. In a nation of more than three million people, even with slaves excluded, less than 200,000 were eligible to vote and less than 44,000 did, a participation rate of roughly 1.5 percent. Washington, to no one's surprise, was elected president, gaining a vote from each of the sixty-nine electors who participated. In the electors' other choice, John Adams, with thirty-four votes, finished second and became vice president. George Clinton, the only Antifederalist to receive electoral votes, received got only three.

During Washington's first term, those carefully laid Federalist plans to achieve consensus, already shown to be vulnerable during a contentious ratification campaign, would fray, a process that began when Thomas Jefferson returned from his five-year stay in France in September 1789. A key player in the descent into acrimony would be James Madison, the man whose idealized version of pluralist democracy had assured his fellow

Americans that the faction problem would be kept under control by limiting the size of the nation's leadership.

In Paris, Jefferson had witnessed the great events of the beginning of the French Revolution—which, unlike in the United States, would become a true revolution—from the Assembly of Notables in 1787 to the fall of the Bastille in July 1789 to the spectacle of Marie Antoinette being driven in her carriage through the streets shortly afterward with not a single Parisian along the route daring to cheer. By that time, he had been joined in France by Gouverneur Morris and, although they spent most days in each other's company, they saw the unfolding cataclysm quite differently.

Jefferson foisted the entire responsibility for the fall of the monarchy and the events that followed on the nobility in general and Marie Antoinette in particular. Writing decades later, he placed at her feet the unwillingness of the government to initiate reforms, and that "her inflexible perverseness and dauntless spirit, led herself to the guillotine, drew the king on with her, and plunged the world into crimes and calamities which will forever stain the pages of modern history."[385]

His take on the French queen was convenient, uninformed, and wrong. Marie Antoinette had little real power, especially in a court in which the titular leader was inept and possibly autistic. In fact, she did all she could to support the king and shield him from the machinations of his ministers. Nor was she responsible for France's fiscal crisis—brought on in large part by the nation's support of the American Revolution, money that was never repaid—and both she and the king attempted to initiate a tax on the aristocrats, but resistance was too strong.[386] But Jefferson needed a foil and Marie Antoinette, whose perceived excesses became a focal point of popular discontent, filled the bill nicely.

Morris's perspective could not have been more different. Morris "throws the blame of the subsequent horrors—including both Robespierre and Bonaparte—upon the destruction of the nobility; and in this opinion he lived and died. He wrote thus in his diary, after getting home one evening from Jefferson's house: 'Mr. Jefferson and I differ in our systems of politics. He, with all the leaders of liberty here, is desirous of annihilating distinctions of order. How far such views may be right respecting mankind in general is, I think, extremely problematical. But with respect to this nation, I am sure it is wrong, and cannot eventuate well.'"[387]

Jefferson left France reluctantly and only did so to accept the position of Secretary of State in Washington's administration, despite a previous vow to retire to Monticello. Once home, his populism buttressed by the radical changes he had witnessed across the Atlantic, rather than fearing the general population as did the Federalists, he intended to use them as springboard to power.

He would be forced to do so as a member of a staunchly Federalist administration, which included former allies turned bitter rivals, Vice President John Adams and Treasury Secretary Alexander Hamilton. Of the two, he viewed Hamilton, whose vision of a strong central government with a national bank to consolidate debt and promote economic growth was anathema to Jefferson, as the far greater threat. (Although he had grown none too fond of Adams either.)

In addition, Hamilton had a strong preference for the stability of Britain's aristocratic rule over the near anarchy that afflicted France. Jefferson, as he had indicated to Morris, felt that the revolution in France was an expression of republican principles and that the overthrow of the monarchy had been a necessary step in the creation of a society that would serve all the people, not just a select few.

Despite uncertain prospects—Hamilton was Washington's favorite, almost an adopted son—Jefferson, almost immediately from when he joined the government in March 1790, attempted to undermine Hamilton's Federalist philosophy and substitute it with his own. He openly and contemptuously opposed Hamilton's initiatives but made little headway. He and Hamilton came to loathe one another, and in the late spring and summer of 1792, with another presidential election looming, their feud was epitomized in a remarkable series of letters with Washington in the middle.

On May 23, Jefferson wrote a long missive to the president in which he attacked Hamilton's grim portrait of the United States economy and his plan to revive it. He accused the Treasury Secretary of contriving a crisis for self-serving reasons, and he repeated the accusation that Hamilton was attempting to turn the nation into a monarchy. "The ultimate object of all this is to prepare the way for a change from the present republican form of government to that of a monarchy of which the English constitution is to be the model. That this was contemplated in the Convention is no secret because its partisans have made none of it."[388] He lamented that "so many [Hamiltonians] have got into the legislature that, aided by the corrupt squadron of paper dealers who are at their devotion, they make a majority in both houses. The republican party, who wish to preserve the government in its present form, are fewer in number."

Washington had expressed a desire to retire when his term ended, but Jefferson urged him to remain and thus prevent Hamilton from seizing control of the government. "I, therefore, have no motive to consult but my own inclination, which is bent irresistibly on the tranquil enjoyment of my family, my farm, & my books. I should repose among them it is true, in far greater security, if I were to know that you remained at the watch, and I hope it will be so." (Jefferson would remain in the post until the end of 1793, and when he left, it was hardly to opt for the tranquil enjoyment of his family, farm, and books.)

Washington communicated Jefferson's accusations to Hamilton, who eventually replied on August 18: "I have not fortitude enough always to hear with calmness calumnies, which necessarily include me as a principal Agent in the measures censured, of the falsehood of which, I have the most unqualified consciousness. I trust that I shall always be able to bear, as I ought, imputations of errors of Judgment; but I acknowledge that I cannot be entirely patient under charges, which impeach the integrity of my public motives or conduct."[389]

That prompted Washington to write to Jefferson five days later. He both defended Hamilton and his policies and urged forbearance on Jefferson:

> How unfortunate, and how much is it to be regretted then, that whilst we are encompassed on all sides with avowed enemies & insidious friends, that internal dissentions should be harrowing & tearing our vitals … And without more charity for the opinions & acts of one another in Governmental matters—or some more infallible criterion by which the truth of speculative opinions, before they have undergone the test of experience, are to be forejudged than has yet fallen to the lot of fallibility, I believe it will be difficult, if not impracticable, to manage the Reins of Government or to keep the parts of it together: for if, instead of laying our shoulders to the machine after measures are decided on, one pulls this way & another that, before the utility of the thing is fairly tried, it must, inevitably, be torn asunder—And, in my opinion the fairest prospect of happiness & prosperity that ever was presented to man, will be lost—perhaps for ever![390]

Jefferson, likely livid over Washington siding with his sworn enemy, sent Washington an extraordinary response:

> When I embarked in the government, it was with a determination to intermeddle not at all with the legislature, & as little as possible with my co-departments. The first and only instance of variance from the former part of my resolution, I was duped into by the Secretary of the treasury and made a tool for forwarding his schemes, not then sufficiently understood by me; and of all the errors of my political life this has occasioned me the deepest regret.[391]

He went on to again accuse Hamilton of trying to control the legislature, the same charge Hamilton had leveled at him. "That I have utterly, in my private conversations, disapproved of the system of the Secretary of the treasury, I acknolege & avow: and this was not merely a speculative difference. His system flowed from principles adverse to liberty, & was calculated to undermine and demolish the republic, by creating an influence of his department over the members of the legislature. I saw this influence actually produced, & it's first fruits to be the establishment of the great outlines of his project by the votes of the very persons who, having swallowed his bait, were laying themselves out to profit by his plans."

Jefferson added that in his letters from France during the Convention, "You will there see that my objection to the constitution was that it wanted a bill of rights securing freedom of religion, freedom of the press, freedom from standing armies, trial by jury, & a constant Habeas corpus act. Colo. Hamilton's was that it wanted a king and house of lords. The sense of America has approved my objection & added the bill of rights, not the king and lords."

But Jefferson's attempt to change the nation's course did not stop at letter writing. In the days before his May 23 letter, in recognition that he would likely have no success thwarting Hamilton within the government, he moved to do so from without by initiating the founding of an actual political party. He had begun a year earlier in 1791, when he and Madison had taken a trip together, touring Lake Champlain, Connecticut, and Long Island, supposedly to "observe the vegetation and wild life of the region."[392] Madison, by this point, had also grown disillusioned with Hamilton's extreme nationalism and, during the sojourn, he and Jefferson met with Robert Livingston and George Clinton, two men against whom Madison, through Hamilton, had specifically aimed the *Federalist* essays.

Madison's conversion might not have been strictly policy oriented. "Some personal factors may have been involved. In the early 1790s, Madison was losing out to Hamilton as Washington's most trusted advisor."[393] Whatever his reasons, while traveling with Jefferson, Madison became part of a cabal.

At some point, they were joined by Aaron Burr, who was building his own political machine through his Tammany Society in New York City, and nothing Burr did was without underlayers. One of Hamilton's supporters wrote to him, "There was every appearance of a passionate courtship between the Chancellor [Livingston], Burr, Jefferson, and Madison when the two latter were in town."[394]

When Congress next sat, Madison had become the leader of the opposition and was energetically recruiting others to his new affiliation. By May 1792, Hamilton would write, "It was not until the last session that I became unequivocally convinced of the following truth: that Mr. Madison, cooperating with Mr. Jefferson, is at the head of a faction decidedly hostile to me and my administration; and actuated by views, in my judgment, subversive to the principles of good government, and dangerous to the union, peace, and happiness of the country."[395]

As the election of 1792 approached, Jefferson and Madison had not yet officially formed the party that would later be called the Democratic-Republicans. They had, however, begun the sort of organizing that would be necessary to do so and the coming election was an opportunity to act in concert with their allies.

Although unhappy with Washington's acceptance of Hamilton's program, they knew it would be folly to attempt to unseat him. But the man who finished second would be Vice President, and Madison and Jefferson were determined that it not again be John Adams. Neither could run for the spot themselves since the Constitution stipulated that each elector's two votes be for candidates from different states, and Washington was the only Virginian anyone was going to select. Instead, they threw their support to George Clinton. New York was an Antifederalist stronghold, and Clinton might successfully siphon off votes from other electors who were growing wary of what the Jeffersonians insisted were Federalist excesses.

They were only partially successful. The 1792 election actually saw a decrease in the popular vote to 28,000, less than one percent of the nation's free population. Washington, again tapped by every elector, received all 132 electoral votes, and Adams again finished second with seventy-seven. Clinton, however, received fifty electoral votes, not enough to become Vice President, but sufficient to indicate a change in the wind.

With Washington's first term cabinet in disarray, Madison's rosy assessment of the power of new government to achieve consensus was fully exposed as mere advocacy. The second term would be worse. Soon after Washington was sworn in February 1793, Jeffersonians began to form what became known as Democratic-Republican societies. The first two were formed in Philadelphia and drew their membership from very groups that had "traditionally denied a political voice." [396] As the societies began to proliferate, "The six leading classifications of members were "craftsmen, merchants, seamen, lawyers, governmental officials, and teachers and doctors as a group."[397]

The clubs, which initially claimed to be nonpartisan, were almost totally in support of Jefferson's agenda, including limited national government, opposition to the Bank of the United States, the embrace of revolutionary France, and antipathy toward Great Britain. Although, "Well before Thomas Jefferson's election [in 1800], these popular organizations had entirely disappeared from the national scene … the Democratic-Republican Societies left behind an altered political landscape. By serving as the first media of organized popular political dissent in the new republic, the Democratic-Republican Societies expanded the boundaries of political participation, helping to play out the logic of popular sovereignty."[398]

Thus, while not officially a precursor, these societies would ultimately coalesce into what became Jefferson's Democratic-Republican Party. "The significance of these groups, however, goes beyond their influence on the structure of early America. The Democratic-Republican Societies allow a glimpse of how Jeffersonians from many walks of life fused the variegated ideologies that pervaded early America, ideologies which historians have labeled 'liberal' and 'republican' … Optimistic, forward looking, and obsessed with the pursuit of individual material gain, ordinary Jeffersonians, according to this view, successfully challenged notions of hierarchy and deference." [399] And so, the societies' "methods of mobilizing the population in opposition to the government laid the foundation for national political parties."[400]

To make matters worse for Washington during his second term, with factionalism increasing, Jefferson, opting for the unthinkable, began to attack Washington personally, accusing him of being little more than Hamilton's puppet. "Tempers became strained; Washington accused Jefferson of having a low opinion of his intelligence and angrily declared he was the last man in the world who would tolerate the emergence of an American king."[401]

The acrimony did not abate, and in his farewell address, a letter published in September 1796, Washington attacked the rise of partisanship. Political parties, he wrote, "serve to organize faction; to give it an artificial and extraordinary force; to put in the place of the delegated will of the nation the will of a party, often a small but artful and enterprising minority of the community; and, according to the alternate triumphs of different parties, to make the public administration the mirror of the ill concerted and incongruous projects of faction, rather than the organ of consistent and wholesome plans digested by common councils and modified by mutual interests." [402] And, then, in a passage eerily prescient, Washington added, "However combinations or associations of the above description may now and then answer popular ends, they are likely, in the course of time and things, to become potent engines by which cunning, ambitious, and unprincipled men will be enabled to subvert the power of the people and to usurp for themselves the reins of government, destroying afterwards the very engines which have lifted them to unjust dominion."

With Washington declining to run, the 1796 election was a watershed, the first contested presidential race and the first in which candidates identified with a specific political party. Both the Federalists and Democratic-Republicans fielded multiple candidates, although the race was effectively between John Adams, running with South Carolina governor Thomas Pinckney, and Jefferson, running with Aaron Burr. Although there was still no differentiation between president and vice president in each elector's two votes—that would change after the election of 1800—Adams and Jefferson were certain to get the bulk of their respective party's votes, with the second split among the rest.

And so, in an outcome unique in American history, the president and vice president were members of different political parties, with Adams gaining 71 electoral votes, one more than he needed, Jefferson receiving 68. Turnout was almost three times larger than in 1792, but the nearly 67,000 popular votes remained a pittance in a nation whose population by then likely exceeded four million.

Adams's term, filled with turmoil, intrigue, and acrimony, justified Washington's fears, but of greater significance was that with the rise of political parties, the fundamental dynamic of government was altered, with pluralism replaced by the factionalism that both Washington and Madison had decried. And with that factionalism came a recognition that a clear route to attaining and holding power was to cultivate the very economic and social classes that the delegates in Philadelphia had spent so much time and energy maneuvering to exclude and then empowering them to choose members of Congress, and by extension the President.

As Jefferson was among the first to appreciate, achieving this aim in a truly pluralist environment would be difficult if not impossible. There would need to be too many messages and too many strategies, each aimed at a small, local group whose interests and individual needs would be too specific to create a unified, nationwide voting bloc. This, of course, was congressional structure Madison claimed to anticipate in Federalist 10, one in which shifting, issue-based coalitions could navigate their way through the thicket of raw partisanship.

But as Jefferson and a newly minted Madison recognized, it was possible to grab and hold power through a larger, more cohesive group whose message was broad and largely philosophical, emphasizing principles rather than specifics. Such an organization might well achieve what pluralism could not, the adoption of a full spectrum political agenda, allowing those elevated to power to implement whatever portions of that agenda they chose. As long as they fit into the overall ideology that the leaders had promulgated, local groups would likely be satisfied. Once such a road to political authority was realized, small, shifting coalitions would be rendered as obsolete as tricorn hats.

Thus, with aggressive organization and some measure of political discipline, even with only modest increases in voter eligibility, Jefferson succeeded in capturing the presidency in 1800. Then, as president, his populist instincts vindicated, he oversaw such a dramatic expansion of turnout that, by 1816, Federalists became doomed to extinction in the competition for national office.[403]

(Of course, the Federalist Party remained a power in national politics for another two decades with the Supreme Court controlled by John Marshall's iron rule. Jefferson had been proven correct about the party retiring into the judiciary as a stronghold. Andrew Jackson administered the final blow to Federalism in 1836 when he appointed Roger Brooke Taney to replace Marshall, who remained on the bench until his death at age seventy-nine.)

Although a strict two-party system took decades to gel, political parties became the dominant force in America during the first third of the nineteenth century. There was for a time some shift in both the dogma and membership of these parties, but with Abraham Lincoln's election in 1860, the current Democrat and Republican structure was set. (Ideologically, of course, there have been shifts within the parties, among them the Republicans having been once the party of equal rights and the defenders of Black Americans and Democrats the party of segregation and Jim Crow.)

Jefferson and Madison had thus thrown open the door to a new, unplanned environment for governance as well as the means to bypass the very limited controls in the Constitution. The restraints that Hamilton—and Madison—had so eloquently insisted were built into the system in the *Federalist* were thereby rendered moot.

This came as no surprise to Brutus and other Antifederalists, who had predicted that the Constitution was ill-drawn and ripe for exploitation. They in effect had accused Publius of running a bluff, covering a lack of substance and wrong-headed decisions with faulty logic and flowery verbiage. To them, it would have been no surprise that the Constitution became inadequate to meet challenges of a growing nation—it was, they had insisted, inadequate to meet the challenges of 1787.

In the end, the delegates had been willing to sacrifice completeness to achieve what they had most sought—a national government far stronger than had existed under the Articles, a means for national defence, and some consistency in the manner in which states could conduct their affairs. But the price was high. Slavery was protected, functionality was limited, the states would still wield significant and potentially dysfunctional power, and sectionalism continued to cleave the nation sufficiently that a civil war would be needed seventy-five years later to try to stitch it together.

Still, it is a testament to the desire of many, many Americans for fair, honorable government that at many points in United States history, the nation, both torturously and tortuously, has been successful in navigating past obstacles to genuine democracy that the Constitution had allowed to be erected in its path.

Regardless of whether the United States was created reflecting the prejudices of the day, be they racial, religious, or class oriented, the glory of this nation, what has made it the envy of the world, is its struggle over the ensuing two and a half centuries to expand the very rights that the founders sought to limit. One by one, previously banned groups were allowed into the political process, first in choosing the nation's leaders and then by becoming them. Property holding requirements to vote were eliminated in the first decades of the nineteenth century. Black Americans were guaranteed citizenship and the right to vote by the Fourteenth and Fifteenth Amendments and were allowed to become naturalized citizens in 1870. Women were granted the vote by the Nineteenth Amendment in 1920.

Equal rights struggled ahead as well. Chinese, Japanese, East Asians, Southern Europeans, and Native Americans were eventually prohibited by law from being denied what was termed in the Fourteenth Amendment the "privileges and immunities of citizenship." Catholics and Jews, once despised religious minorities, were permitted to aspire to any position in government they so desired and have become among the most prominent of the nation's leaders. (That the current Supreme Court, which has fought against inclusion, is dominated by the very brand of conservative Catholic that was once the focal point of religious prejudice by many of the nation's founders is the ultimate irony.)

Progress has not been straight line, as each of these expansions were opposed by groups determined to suppress reforms that would endanger their control; new roadblocks would be thrown up, and the conflict renewed on a different battlefield. America has, therefore, yet to be successful in achieving full equality for previously marginalized groups, nor has the progress the nation has made sufficient to eliminate bigotry, job and housing discrimination, and fair treatment under the law. Enormous problems remain and certain groups have to constantly fight both the legislatures and the courts to be treated with even a modicum of fairness. They are often prevented from succeeding.

Minority rule, traditionally the enemy of the expansion of equal rights, has once again become a powerful and aggressive force in American government. In this case, however, the ruling minority is not drawn from the groups the delegates envisioned, but rather from the ones the nationalists feared.

In the Senate, for example, the seat of confirmations for judicial and executive appointments, in 2020, more than fifty senators were elected from states with less than one-fifth of the population. This has created an enormous imbalance between urban and rural America, which has manifested itself, in a conservative/liberal divide. The Electoral College, another stronghold of the new minority, has occassionally been the misadventure many delegates feared in 1787 and now seems to virtually guarantee a series of minority-elected presidents.

This new minority, comprised largely of the very groups the delegates attempted to keep out of power, is pushing hard to initiate both a legal and philosophical return to many of the rules of governance the founding fathers foisted on the nation at the end of the eighteenth century but that have since been abandoned. Voting is to be limited, citizenship restricted, and the legal system structured to keep marginalized Americans from threatening white pre-eminence. Some of its goals are to incorporate principles the founders tried to prevent, such as religious dogma being substituted for jurisprudence, and warmed over theocracy substituted for democratic rule.

These trends have only manifested because the Constitution allowed them to be. Reversing them will be extremely difficult for the same reason, especially since the minority will fight tenaciously to maintain its supremacy, using the tools the Constitution provided. Maintaining minority rule demands a level of ruthless aggressiveness that is often not required of majorities. Where a majority may be able to squander some of its margin, a minority cannot.

The United States faces the ultimate dilemma—how to maintain progress in becoming a fairer, more inclusive democracy when its pre-eminent legal and political document can so easily be interpreted to enable the precise opposite?

Chapter 16

Filling in the Blanks: What Needs to Be Done

"We cannot solve our problems with the same thinking we used when we created them."
Albert Einstein

"Good laws lead to the making of better ones; bad ones bring about worse."
Jean-Jacques Rousseau

There are three ways to correct the inequities that were built into the Constitution: amendments, a new constitution, and working legislatively within the current framework. The first is impractical, the second inadvisable, and the third very likely fruitless without an aroused citizenry.

The amendment process, requiring overwhelming support majority in both Congress and state legislatures, will make it impossible for any amendment to be ratified that has a whiff of partisan overtones or will otherwise endanger minority rule. Therefore, to expect a constitutional amendment that will define electoral districts, solidify voting rights, alter or eliminate the Electoral College, restrict the authority of the Supreme Court, add conditions for ownership of firearms, outlaw abortion, or cement birthright citizenship is folly.

Making the amendment process as restrictive as it is presupposed either an overwhelming preponderance of one political point of view in national and state governments or a willingness by strong minority to put aside partisan interests for the good of the country. In a nation as divided as the United States now finds itself, neither of those conditions is likely to be present in the short or mid-range future.

An attempt to create a new constitution would only make matters worse for the same reasons. On its face, the idea is appealing. Given the Constitution's shortcomings, it would seem that Americans should attempt to redraft a more effective document, one in which areas of contention would be specifically addressed. For example, does the *right* to vote guarantee that the *ability* to vote be made equal for all citizens; does the right to bear arms exist without regard to the requirement that a militia be present; does the protection against illegal search and seizure protect a woman's right to abort an unwanted fetus; do religious beliefs allow some citizens to deny others services or legal protections?

The problem is that the very contentiousness that has wrenched American society apart would become the focus of any new constitutional convention. In addition, how delegates would be selected for such a convention and whether states would be represented based on population or as separate entities and how many votes each would be granted to decide on specifics might scuttle any plan for a new constitution before it got off the ground.

Even assuming some formula for empaneling a convention could be found, how could a nation that has lived under minority rule for virtually its entire existence expect that a ruling minority will voluntarily cede power? It is far more likely that any new plan would be far less effective at establishing majority rule than what we are living with today.

In the end, the very flaws that make the Constitution unworkable would render any attempt to update it unworkable as well. And so, if a new Constitution is not a reasonable option, Americans will need to find a means to use the existing document to solve the very deep problems that currently plague the nation.

The task will not be easy. Navigating through partisanship and overcoming minority rule could prove as daunting as attempting to amend the Constitution or rewriting it. But when the delegates to the Philadelphia convention chose to pass on the responsibility for filling in the gaps to Congress or state governments, they left little choice.

In the end, the responsibility for maintaining democratic institutions falls where it inevitably had to, with the "People of the United States." Only they have the power to overcome a deeply flawed Constitution and successfully continue the modern world's most profound experiment in creating a society in which fairness and equality may flourish.

Selected Bibliography

Websites:

Brennan Center. https://www.brennancenter.org/

CNN.com. https://www.cnn.com/2019/09/30/opinions/supreme-court-term-limits-law-roosevelt-vassilas/index.html

Court TV. http://www.courttv.com/archive/legaldocs/rights/scalia.html

Journals of the Continental Congress. https://memory.loc.gov

Letters of Delegates to Congress: https://memory.loc.gov/ammem/amlaw/lwdg.html

Library of Congress. American Memory. https://memory.loc.gov

National Archives: Founders Online. https://founders.archives.gov/

Papers of John Jay. https://www.americanheritage.com/jay-papers

Presidential Commission on the Supreme Court of the United States. https://www.whitehouse.gov/wp-content/uploads/2021/12/SCOTUS-Report-Final-12.8.21-1.pdf.

Politico. https://www.politico.com/news/magazine/2022/07/21/supreme-court-reform-term-limits-00046883

Quill Project. https://www.quillproject.net/resources/resource_item/56/3139

Teaching American History. https://teachingamericanhistory.org/

U.S. Senate https://www.senate.gov/civics/common/generic/Virginia_Plan_item.html

U.S. Congressional Documents and Debates, 1774 – 1875. 86National Constitution Center. https://constitutioncenter.org/the-constitution/historic-document-library/detail/brutus-essay-no-1

Yale University Avalon Project. https://avalon.law.yale.edu

WUSA9 https://www.wusa9.com/article/news/verify/can-congress-put-term-limits-on-supreme-court-justices-we-asked-five-legal-experts-court-packing-judges/65-2de67c84-910b-4a59-9824-f64d35866ae5

Books and Articles:

- "Alexander Hamilton on the Naturalization of Foreigners." *Population and Development Review*, March 2010, Vol. 36, No. 1.

- "Where We Have Been: The History of Gerrymandering in America." New America. https://www.newamerica.org/political-reform/reports/what-we-know-about-redistricting-and-redistricting-reform/where-we-have-been-the-history-of-gerrymandering-in-america/

Ackerman, Bruce. *The Failure of the Founding Fathers: Jefferson, Marshall, and the Rise of Presidential Democracy*. Cambridge, Mass: Harvard University Press, 2005.

Ackerman, Bruce and Fontana, David. "Thomas Jefferson Counts Himself into the Presidency." *Virginia Law Review*, April 2004, Vol. 90, No. 2

Adams, John. *The Adams Papers: Diary and Autobiography of John Adams*. L. H. Butterfield, ed. Cambridge, MA: Belknap Press, 1962.

Adams, William Howard. *Gouverneur Morris*. New Haven: Yale University Press, 2003.

Amar, Akhil Reed. *America's Constitution: A Biography*. New York: Random House, 2005.

Bacon-Foster, Corra. *Early Chapters in the Development of the Patomac Route to the West*. Washington, DC: Columbia Historical Society, 1912.

Barnett, Randy E. "The Original Meaning of the Necessary and Proper Clause." 6 University of Pennsylvania Journal of Constitution Law, 185 (2003), 183-221.

William Baude, Response, "Sharing the Necessary and Proper Clause," 128 Harvard Law Review Forum 39 (2014).

Beveridge, Albert. *Life of John Marshall*. Boston: Houghton Mifflin, 1919.

Blackstone, William. *Commentaries on the Laws of England*. Oxford: Clarendon Press, 1765-69.

Bradburn, Douglas. *The Citizenship Revolution: Politics and the Creation of the American Union, 1774-1804*. Charlottesville, VA: University of Virginia Press, 2009.

Carpenter, A. H. "Naturalization in England and the American Colonies." *The American Historical Review*, January 1904, Vol. 9, No. 2.

Chernow, Ron. *Alexander Hamilton*. New York: Penguin Press, 2004.

Clarkson, Paul and Samuel R, Jett. *Luther Martin of Maryland*. Baltimore: The Johns Hopkins Press, 1970.

Clinton, Robert Lowry. *Marbury v. Madison and Judicial Review*. Lawrence, KS: University Press of Kansas, 1989.

Cooke Charles. https://www.nationalreview.com/corner/no-good-behavior-is-not-a-meaningless-phrase/

Drutman, Lee. "What We Know About Redistricting and Redistricting Reform." https://www.newamerica.org/political-reform/reports/what-we-know-about-redistricting-and-redistricting-reform/

Durchslag, Melvyn R. "The Supreme Court and the Federalist Papers: Is There Less Here Than Meets the Eye?" 14 Wm. & Mary Bill Rts. J. 243 (2005).

Dyer, Walter A. "Embattled Farmers." The New England Quarterly, July 1931, Vol. 4, No. 3.

Elkins, Stanley and Eric McKitrick. *Age of Federalism: The Early American Republic, 1788-1800.* New York: Oxford University Press, 1993.

Elliot, Jonathan, ed. *The Debates in the Several State Conventions on the Adoption of the Federal Constitution.* Washington, DC, 1836.

Engdahl, David E. *Constitutional Federalism in a Nutshell.* St. Paul, Mn.: West Publishing Co. 1987.

Faber, Michael J. "The Federal Union Paradigm of 1788: Three Anti-Federalists Who Changed Their Minds." *American Political Thought*, Vol. 4, No. 4 (Fall 2015).

Farrand, Max, ed. *The Records of the Federal Convention of 1787*. Rev. ed. 4 vols. New Haven and London: Yale University Press, 1937.

Fiske, John. *The Critical Period of American History, 1783–1789. Boston: Houghton Mifflin, 1888.*

Fix, Michael. "Repealing Birthright Citizenship: The Unintended Consequences." https://www.migrationpolicy.org/news/repealing-birthright-citizenship-unintended-consequences.

Foner, Eric. *The Second Founding: How the Civil War and Reconstruction Remade the Constitution.* New York: Norton, 2019.

Ford, Worthington C. The Writings of George Washington. New York: G. P. Putnam's Sons, 1889.

Goldstone, Lawrence. *Dark Bargain: Slavery, Profits, and the Struggle for the Constitution.* New York: Walker & Company, 2005.

- *Not White Enough: The Long, Shameful Road to Japanese American Internment.* Lawrence, KS: University Press of Kansas, 2023.

- *On Account of Race: The Supreme Court, White Supremacy and the Ravaging of African American Voting Rights.* Berkeley, CA: Counterpoint, 2020.

Goldstone, Nancy. *In the Shadow of the Empress: The Defiant Lives of Maria Theresa, Mother of Marie Antoinette, and Her Daughters*. New York: Little Brown, 2021.

Griffin, Stephen M., "The Nominee Is ... Article V." (1995). Constitutional Commentary. 1020

Haney-Lopez, Ian. *White by Law: The Legal Construction of Race*. New York: NYU Press, 1996.

Haw, James. *John & Edward Rutledge of South Carolina*. Athens, GA: University of Georgia Press, 1997.

Hesson, Ted. "Can Trump revoke birthright citizenship? Nearly all on left and right say no."

https://www.politico.com/story/2018/10/30/trump-birthright-citizenship-plan-900891

Hill, Andrew T. "The Second Bank of the United States, 1816-1841." https://www.federalreservehistory.org/essays/second-bank-of-the-us

Hoff, Samuel B. "A Bicentennial Assessment of Hamilton's Energetic Executive." *Presidential Studies Quarterly*, Fall, 1987, Vol. 17, No. 4.

Hoffer, Peter Charles. *Daniel Webster and the Unfinished Constitution*. Lawrence, KS: University Press of Kansas, 2021.

Hoyt, Edward A. "Naturalization Under the American Colonies: Signs of a New Community." *Political Science Quarterly*, Vol. 67, No. 2

Hunter, Thomas Rogers. "The First Gerrymander? Patrick Henry, James Madison, James Monroe, and Virginia's 1788 Congressional Districting." *Early American Studies*, Fall 2011, Vol. 9, No. 3.

Isgur, Sarah. "It's Time to Amend the Constitution."

https://www.politico.com/news/magazine/2022/01/08/scalia-was-right-make-amending-the-constitution-easier-526780

Jensen, Merrill. *The New Nation: A History of the United States During the Confederation,1781-1789*. New York: Knopf, 1967.

Jillson, Calvin C. "Constitutional-Making: Alignment and Realignment in the Federal Convention of 1787." *The American Political Science Review*, September 1981, Vol. 75, No. 3.

Kaminski, John P. "Honor and Interest: John Jay's Diplomacy During the Confederation." New York History, Summer 2002, Vol. 83, No. 3.

Kettner, James H. *The Making of American Citizenship*. Chapel Hill: UNC Press, 1978.

Keyssar, Alexander. *The Right to Vote: The Contested History of Democracy in the United States*. New York: Basic Books, 2000.

Klarman, Michael. *The Framers' Coup: The Making of the American Constitution*. New York: Oxford University Press, 2016.

Kohn, Richard H. *Eagle and Sword: The Federalists and the Creation of the Military Establishment in America, 1783-1802*. New York: Free Press, 1975.

-"The Inside History of the Newburgh Conspiracy: America and the Coup d'Etat." The William and Mary Quarterly, April 1970, Vol. 27, No. 2.

Kramer, Larry. "Ever Since *Marbury*: Concluding Observations." http://www.law.nyu.edu/sites/default/files/NYU_Law_Magazine_2002.pdf

Kyvig, David. "Explicit and Authentic Acts: Amending the U.S. Constitution 1776-2015." Lawrence, KS: University Press of Kansas, 2016.

Lee, Richard Henry. *The Letters of Richard Henry Lee*. James Curtis Ballagh, ed. 2 vols. New York: Macmillan Co., 1911, 1914.

Levy, Leonard W. *Original Intent and the Framer's Constitution*. New York: Macmillan, 1988.

Link, Eugene Perry. *Democratic-Republican Societies, 1790-1800*. New York: Columbian University Press, 1942.

Littlefield, Douglas R. The Potomac Company: A Misadventure in Financing an Early American Internal Improvement Project." The Business History Review, Winter, 1984, Vol. 58, No. 4.

Locke, John. *Two Treatises of Government*. Peter Laslett, ed. Cambridge: Cambridge University Press, 1988.

Lutz, Donald S. "Toward a Theory of Constitutional Amendment." 88 Am. Pol. Sci. Rev. (1994)

Lynd, Staughton. "The Compromise of 1787." Political Science Quarterly, Vol. 81, No. 2, June 1966.

Lynch, Dennis Tilden. "'Boss' Tweed: The Story of a Grim Generation." London: Routledge, 2017.

Mason, Kate Rowland, G. Mason, Alexander Henderson, Daniel of St. Thomas Jenifer, T. Stone and Samuel Chase. "The Mount Vernon Convention." The Pennsylvania Magazine of History and Biography, January 1888, Vol. 11, No. 4.

Maclay, William. *The Journal of William Maclay*. ed. Kenneth R.Bowling and Helen E. Veit. Baltimore: Johns Hopkins University Press, 1988.

McDonald, Forrest. E Pluribus Unum: The Formation of the American Republic, 1776-1790. Boston: Houghton Mifflin, 1975.

- *Novus Ordo Seclorum: The Intellectual Origins of the Constitution*. Lawrence, KS: University Press of Kansas, 1985.

McKeown, M. Margaret. *Citizen Justice: The Environmental Legacy of William O. Douglas*. Lincoln, NE: Potomac Books, 2022.

Montesquieu, Baron de (Charles Louis de Secondat). The Spirit of the Laws. 1748. https://oll.libertyfund.org/title/montesquieu-complete-works-vol-1-the-spirit-of-laws

Morgan, H. Wayne. "The Origins and Establishment of the First Bank of the

United States." The Business History Review, December 1956, Vol. 30, No. 4.

Morris, Richard Brandon. *The Forging of the Union, 1781-1789*. New York: Harper & Row, 1987.

Natalson, Robert G. "The Constitutional Contributions of John Dickinson." Penn St. L. Rev. Vol. 108, 2003-2004.

- "The Agency Law Origins of the Necessary and Proper Clause," 55 Case W. Rsrv. L. Rev. 243 (2004).

Ohline, Howard A. "Republicanism and Slavery: Origins of the Three-Fifths Clause in the United States Constitution." The William and Mary Quarterly, October 1971, Vol. 28, No. 4.

Ottenberg, Louis. "A Fortunate Fiasco: The Annapolis Convention of 1786." *American Bar Association Journal*, August 1959, Vol. 45, No. 8.

Parton, James. *Life of Thomas Jefferson: Third President of the United States*. Boston: J. R. Osgood, 1874.

Pildes, Richard H. "Democracy, Anti-Democracy, and the Canon." Constitutional Commentary, (2000).

Priest, Claire. "The Colonial Courts and Secured Credit: Early American Commercial Litigation and Shays' Rebellion."

Rakove, Jack N. *Original Meanings: Politics and Ideas in the Making of the Constitution.* New York: Random House, 1996.

- "The Legacy of the Articles of Confederation." Publius, Autumn, 1982, Vol. 12, No. 4.

Reichley, A. James. *The Life of the Parties: A History of American Political Parties*. New York: Free Press, 1992.

Richman, Irving Berdine. "Citizenship of the United States. *Political Science Quarterly*, Vol. 5, No. 1, March 1980.

Rives, William C. *History of the Life and Times of James Madison*, 3 vols. (Boston: Little, Brown, 1859-68)

Roche, John P. "The Founding Fathers: A Reform Caucus in Action." *The American Political Science Review*, December 1961, Vol. 55, No. 4.

Roosevelt, Kermit. "Supreme Court justices should have term limits."
https://fixthecourt.com/wp-content/uploads/2020/10/Endorsers-of-H.R.-8424-10.23.20.pdf

Rosenbaum, Judith et al. "A Constitutional Perspective on Judicial Tenure." 61 *Judicature* 465, 474 (1978)

Ross Robert E. "Federalism and the Electoral College: The Development of the General Ticket Method for Selecting Presidential Electors." *Publius*, Vol. 46, No. 2 (Spring 2016).

Rossiter, Clinton, introduction. *The Federalist Papers.* New York: New American Library, 1961.

Schoenbachler, Matthew. "Republicanism in the Age of Democratic Revolution: The Democratic-Republican Societies of the 1790s." Journal of the Early Republic Summer,1998, Vol. 18, No. 2.

Slonim, Shlomo. "The Electoral College at Philadelphia: The Evolution of an Ad Hoc Congress for the Selection of a President." Journal of American History, June 1986, Vol. 73, No. 1.

Smith, Hayward H. "Revisiting the History of the Independent State Legislature Doctrine, 53 St. Mary's Law Journal, 445 (2022).

Snydor, Charles S. Gentlemen Freeholders: Political Practices in Washington's Virginia. Chapel Hill: UNC Press, 1953

von Spakovsky, Hans A. "Birthright Citizenship: A Fundamental Misunderstanding of the 14th Amendment."

Sparks, Jared, ed. *The Life of Gouverneur Morris, with Selections from His Correspondence and Miscellaneous Papers*. 3 vols. Boston, 1832.

Stahr, Walter. John Jay. New York: Hambledon and London, 2005.

Stevenson, Drury D. "Revisiting the Original Congressional Debates about the Second Amendment." Missouri Law Review. Forthcoming, posted 2022.

Szatmary, David P. *Shays Rebellion: The Making of an Agrarian Insurrection.* Amherst, MA: University of Massachusetts Press, 1980.

Trickey, Erick. "Where Did the Term 'Gerrymander' Come From?" Smithsonian, June 2017. https://www.smithsonianmag.com/history/where-did-term-gerrymander-come-180964118/

Tyler, Bruce. "The Mississippi River Trade, 1784-1788." *The Journal of the Louisiana Historical Association*, Summer, 1971, Vol. 12, No. 3.

Webster, Noah. *An Examination of the Leading Principles of the Federal Constitution*, October 10, 1787.

Winkler, Adam. *Gunfight: The Battle over the Right to Bear Arms in America.* New York: WW Norton, 2011.

Endnotes

[1] Jack Rakove. *Original Meanings: Politics and Ideas in the Making of the Constitution.* New York: Random House, 1996, 29.

[2] Franklin proposed calling the confederation "The United Colonies of North America," which would be "a firm League of Friendship with each other, binding themselves and their Posterity, for their common Defence against their Enemies, for the Security of their Liberties and Propertys, the Safety of their Persons and Families, and their mutual and general welfare." National Archives: Founders Online. https://founders.archives.gov/documents/Franklin/01-22-02-0069.

[3] National Archives. https://www.archives.gov/milestone-documents/lee-resolution.

[4] Robert Natalson. "The Constitutional Contributions of John Dickinson." Penn St. L. Rev. Vol. 108, 2003-2004, 420.

[5] Library of Congress: American Memory. https://memory.loc.gov/cgi-bin/ampage?collId=lljc&fileName=005/lljc005.db&recNum=131.

[6] Memory. https://memory.loc.gov/cgi-bin/ampage?collId=lljc&fileName=005/lljc005.db&recNum=132

[7] Archives. https://www.archives.gov/milestone-documents/articles-of-confederation.

[8] Jack Rakove. "The Legacy of the Articles of Confederation." *Publius*, Autumn, 1982, Vol. 12, No. 4, 51.

[9] Archives. https://www.archives.gov/milestone-documents/articles-of-confederation.

[10] ibid.

[11] Quoted in *The Adams Papers: Diary and Autobiography of John Adams*. L. H. Butterfield, ed. Cambridge, MA: Belknap Press, 1962 Vol. 2, 250. The South Sea was the Pacific Ocean. Although the grants would allow states that had obtained to claim all the land until the west coast, getting there was not likely to occur any time in the near future.

[12] Adams Papers. 2, 242.

[13] Adams Papers, 2, 249. Harrison would sire one future president, William Henry Harrison, and be great-grandfather to President Benjamin Harrison.

[14] Rakove, Articles, 49.

[15] ibid.

[16] U.S. Congressional Documents and Debates, 1774 – 1875. https://memory.loc.gov/cgi-bin/ampage?collId=lled&fileName=001/lled001.db&recNum=101.

[17] Letters of Delegates to Congress: Volume 9 February 1, 1778 - May 31, 1778. Thomas McKean to George Read. https://memory.loc.gov/cgi-bin/query/D?hlaw:2:./temp/~ammem_9Hbm.

[18] Paul S. Clarkson and R. Samuel Jett. *Luther Martin of Maryland.* Baltimore: The Johns Hopkins Press, 1970, 63.

[19] Journals of the Continental Congress. https://memory.loc.gov/cgi-bin/ampage?collId=lljc&fileName=018/lljc018.db&recNum=108&itemLink=D?hlaw:1:./temp/~ammem_SJbA::%230180109&linkText=1.

[20] John Fiske. *The Critical Period of American History, 1783–1789.* Boston: Houghton Mifflin, 1888, 94.

[21] John Adams Papers. Vol. 2, 245.

[22] Michael Klarman. *The Framers' Coup: The Making of the American Constitution.* New York: Oxford University Press, 2016, 16.

[23] For a detailed examination of the tripartite national economy, see Lawrence Goldstone. Dark Bargain: Slavery, Profits, and the Struggle for the Constitution. New York: Walker & Company, 2005.

[24] By 1779, the paper currency had lost an astonishing 95% of its face value.

[25] Washington to John Jay, quoted in Klarman, 19.

[26] Library of Congress. https://www.loc.gov/collections/continental-congress-and-constitutional-convention-from-1774-to-1789/articles-and-essays/to-form-a-more-perfect-union/identifying-defects-in-the-constitution/ Also, see Richard Brandon Morris. *The Forging of the Union, 1781-1789.* New York: Harper & Row, 1987, 92.

[27] Bruce Tyler. "The Mississippi River Trade, 1784-1788." *The Journal of the Louisiana Historical Association*, Summer, 1971, Vol. 12, No. 3, 258.

[28] Forrest McDonald. *E Pluribus Unum: The Formation of the American Republic, 1776-1790.* Boston: Houghton Mifflin, 1975, 81.

[29] Sarah Jay to her mother, December 12, 1779. American Heritage. https://www.americanheritage.com/jay-papers-i-mission-spain#3

[30] Walter Stahr, *John Jay*. New York: Hambledon and London, 2005, 136-7.

[31] Merrill Jensen. *The New Nation: A History of the United States During the Confederation,1781-1789.* New York: Knopf, 1967, 172.

[32] The Diplomatic Correspondence of the United States of America: From the Signing of the Definitive Treaty of Peace, September 10, 1783 to the Adoption of the Constitution, March 4, 1789. Being the Letters of the Presidents of Congress, the Secretary for Foreign Affairs--American Ministers at Foreign Courts, Foreign Ministers Near Congress--reports of the Secretary for Foreign Affairs on Various Letters and Communications; Together with Letters from Individuals on Public Affairs. United States Department of State. 1837. 3, 214

[33] ibid, 215.

[34] Journals, XXXI, 574-613.

[35] Jensen, 173

[36] Kate Rowland Mason. "The Mount Vernon Convention." The Pennsylvania

Magazine of History and Biography, Vol. 11, January 1888, 41.

[37] Clarkson and Jett, 64.

[38] Louis Ottenberg. "A Fortunate Fiasco: The Annapolis Convention of 1786." *American Bar Association Journal*, August 1959, Vol. 45, No. 8, 835.

[39] The company began construction of a series of bypass canals to skirt the waterfalls, but the project was abandoned. It was taken up again in the 1820s, which resulted in the Chesapeake and Ohio Railway, which operated into the 20th century until it was abandoned in the 1930s. Upset that route was the tentative site of a new highway, in 1954, Supreme Court Justice William O. Douglas lad an eight-day, 184-mile hike among the canal's towpath to call attention to the planned destruction of a wilderness area. As a result, the canal route was first declared a national monument and then, in 1971, designated as a national park. For the full story, see M. Margaret McKeown, *Citizen Justice: The Environmental Legacy of William O. Douglas.* Lincoln, NE: Potomac Books, 2022.

[40] Corra Bacon-Foster. *Early Chapters in the Development of the Patomac Route to the West.* Washington, DC: Columbia Historical Society, 1912, 51

[41] Bacon-Foster, 52

[42] Ottenberg, 837

[43] Morris, 255.

[44] *The New-York Packet. And the American Advertiser*, July 4, 1782.

[45] Papers of the Continental Congress, National Archives. https://founders.archives.gov/documents/Hamilton/01-03-02-0556

[46] Rakove, *Original Meanings*, 33

[47] Klarman, 75.

[48] Klarman, 83, 84

[49] Morris, 260.

[50] David P. Szatmary, *Shays Rebellion: The Making of an Agrarian Insurrection.* Amherst, MA: University of Massachusetts Press, 1980, 34.

[51] Claire Priest. Colonial Courts and Secured Credit: Early American Commercial Litigation and Shays' Rebellion. 2418

[52] Szatmary, 33.

[53] Szatmary, 53.

[54] He and Hancock handed the governorship back and forth for the entire decade.

[55] Dyer, Walter A. "Embattled Farmers." The New England Quarterly, July 1931, Vol. 4, No. 3, 464.

[56] They likely took the name from the Regulator movement in North Carolina in the 1760s, "a rebellion initiated by residents of the colony's inland region, or backcountry, who believed that royal government officials were charging them excessive fees, falsifying records, and engaging in other mistreatments. The movement's name refers to the desire of these citizens to regulate their own affairs." https://www.ncpedia.org/history/colonial/regulator-movement.

[57] Hampshire Gazette, September 20, 1786, 2.

[58] Szatmary, 59.

[59] Shays himself later denied he had ever been the leader of the rebellion and insisted all important decisions were made by committee.

[60] Szatmary, 84.

[61] Archives. Lincoln to Washington, December 1786. https://founders.archives.gov/documents/Washington/04-04-02-0374-0002

[62] Archives. Lincoln to Washington, February 1787. https://founders.archives.gov/documents/Washington/04-04-02-0374-0002#GEWN-04-04-02-0374-fn-0003-ptr

[63] Szatamry, 86.

[64] Shepard to Bowdoin, January 26, 1787. Records of the Court of general sessions of the peace for the county of Worcester, Massachusetts, from 1731 to 1737. https://archive.org/details/recordsofcourtof00mass

[65] "A fugitive in Vermont with a price on his head, and later a hapless wanderer, [Shays] died in poverty and obscurity in a little village in western New York long after the bitterness in Massachusetts had died out and the things he had fought for had come to pass." Dyer, 460.

[66] Henry Knox Letter to George Washington (October 23, 1786). In W. W. Abbott and Dorothy Twohig, eds., *The Papers of George Washington: Confederation Series, Volume 4: April1786-January1787*, vol. 4 (Charlottesville, VA University Press of Virginia, 1995). pp. 299-302.

[67] Quoted in Klarman, 92.

[68] Max Farrand, ed. *The Records of the Federal Convention of 1787*. Rev. ed. 4 vols. New Haven and London: Yale University Press, 1937, iii: 547.

[69] New Hampshire did eventually send two delegates, who needed to borrow the money for expenses, but they did not arrive in Philadelphia until the end of July.

[70] Farrand, iii: 550

[71] Farrand, i:21. What follows is from the version Randolph introduced on May 29.

[72] Worthington C. Ford. *Writings of George Washington*. Vol. XI, 158-9. New York: G. P. Putnam's Sons, 1889.

[73] Forrest McDonald. *Novus Ordo Seclorum: The Intellectual Origins of the Constitution*. Lawrence, KS: University Press of Kansas, 1985, 186.

[74] Farrand, i:18.

[75] The records of the Convention are notoriously incomplete. The official record, kept by Major William Jackson, contains little more than a list of motions and the resulting votes. A number of delegates kept journals, most notably Madison, whose detailed notes scholars have relied on since their publication in 1840. But Madison made major revisions during his lifetime and so must be taken as subjective, especially when it comes to Madison's record of his own speeches. Robert Yates of New York also kept detailed notes, but Yates left less than halfway through the proceedings and did not return. Still, when Madison's notes are compared to those of Yates and others, the inconsistencies tend to be nuanced, which might slightly alter the view scholars develop on certain delegates, but do not preclude an accurate

analysis of the proceedings. That is particularly true of an analysis of what the delegates failed to include in the Constitution, since the philosophy of this speaker or that becomes less important than the omissions in the document themselves. Madison's record has never been thought not to capture the overall spirit and nature of debates. For the genesis and develop of Madison's notes, see: https://founders.archives.gov/documents/Madison/01-10-02-0001

[76] Farrand, i:23.

[77] Farrand, i: 27

[78] Farrand, i:48.

[79] Farrand, i:23-24.

[80] Farrand, i:30

[81] Farrand, i:34

[82] Farrand, iii:195

[83] These debates were interspersed with questions of whether Congress's mandate gave the convention the power to alter the unicameral legislature at all. The legitimacy issue would arise periodically in the first weeks, but no one seriously suggested that the convention be adjourned.

[84] Farrand, i:35

[85] Farrand, i:83

[86] Farrand, 1:36

[87] Pinckney was not as young a genius as he pretended. He was actually thirty, the same age as Hamilton, but he tried to pass himself off as being only twenty-four, perhaps thinking it would inspire awe. It did not.

[88] Farrand, i:131

[89] Farrand, i:132-33.

[90] McDonald, *E Pluribus Unum*, 166

[91] The June 11 debates are in Farrand, i:196-208.

[92] Italics added.

[93] "The three-fifths clause also affected the selection of presidential electors because the number from each state equaled the total of its representatives and senators. Article II, Section 1. The electoral college was agreed to in the Convention after the three-fifths principle was approved. Once it was decided that the president would not be elected by the national legislature, some Southerners preferred a system of electors instead of the direct election of the president in order to enhance the influence of southern states whose slave populations could not vote." Howard A. Ohline. "Republicanism and Slavery: Origins of the Three-Fifths Clause in the United States Constitution." The William and Mary Quarterly, October 1971, Vol. 28, No. 4, 563

[94] Farrand, i:242-245.

[95] The June 16 debates are in Farrand, i:249-280

[96] Farrand, i:257-258. These quotes are from Lansing's fellow anti-nationalist New Yorker, Robert Yates. In Madison's notes, Lansing's remarks are more measured, although he does note that Lansing made specific reference to the

new national government's ability to void state laws.

[97] Hamilton's speech is in Farrand, i:282-311

[98] Although "good behavior" has been interpreted by most scholars as meaning "for life," especially in Article III, Hamilton both in here and later in the debates, made plain that he did not consider the terms synonymous. Neither did George Mason, James Madison, Rufus King, and likely few of the other delegates since not one of them ever indicated they thought the terms interchangeable.

[99] Farrand, i:363.

[100] Rakove. *Original Meanings*, 64.

[101] Farrand, i:328

[102] Farrand, iii:54

[103] Both Yates and Lansing would depart in early July, but, unlike Hamilton, neither would return. Hamilton, then the only New Yorker present, could not vote because a minimum of two delegates were required to cast a vote for a state. And so, for the final two months of the Convention, New York cast no votes.

[104] https://www.nps.gov/inde/learn/historyculture/hamilton-speaks.htm

[105] The June 30 debates are in Farrand, i:481-508 Some historians, such as Gordon Wood, claim that Madison was speaking only for effect, and that slavery was less of a factor that it would seem from his pronouncement. Given his subsequent statement proposing specific remedies for the sectional divide, this seems unlikely.

[106] Farrand i:522

[107] The July 5 debates are in Farrand, i:526-537

[108] The July 6 debates are in Farrand, i:539-547

[109] Farrand i:548, 551

[110] The July 9 debates are in Farrand i:559-562

[111] The July 10 debates are in Farrand i:566-574

[112] If slaves had not been counted for apportionment, Adams likely would have won 72-69.

[113] On July 13, the day after the three-fifths clause was approved in Philadelphia, in New York, Congress enacted "An Ordinance for the government of the Territory of the United States northwest of the River Ohio." The Northwest Ordinance, as it came to be known, was passed with only one congressman opposed, Abraham Yates Jr. of New York, the older brother of Robert Yates. All southern congressmen present voted in favor. The ordinance banned slavery in the vast northwest territories, but limited the area to five new states. A number of the delegates in Philadelphia, some in Congress, shuttled back and forth between Philadelphia and New York and so the details of the debates in each body were well known. For an excellent explanation of the relationship, see Staughton Lynd. "The Compromise of 1787." Political Science Quarterly, Vol. 81, No. 2, June 1966.

[114] The July 13 debates are in Farrand, i:600-606

[115] In the end, direct taxes, the other side of the compromise, were instituted rarely and are now obsolete, so the census was now only used for apportionment.
[116] See for example, Dennis Tilden Lynch. "'Boss" Tweed: The Story of a Grim Generation." London: Routledge, 2017.
[117] https://www.vox.com/2019/7/11/20689015/census-citizenship-question-trump-executive-order
[118] Ibid.
[119] https://www.supremecourt.gov/opinions/18pdf/18-966_bq7c.pdf
[120] https://www.pewresearch.org/fact-tank/2020/07/24/how-removing-unauthorized-immigrants-from-census-statistics-could-affect-house-reapportionment/
[121] https://www.theatlantic.com/ideas/archive/2021/05/citizenship-census-redistricting-apportionment/618975/
[122] Austin Cross. "Yes, the census-bureau-helped-make-the-japanese-american-internment-possible https://laist.com/news/yes-the-census-bureau-helped-make-the-japanese-american-internment-possible
[123] https://www.census.gov/history/www/through_the_decades/overview/1920.html
[124] See Alexander Keyssar. *The Right to Vote*: *The Contested History of Democracy in the United States*. New York: Basic Books, 2000, 306-322.
[125] Center for the Study of the American Constitution. https://csac.history.wisc.edu/document-collections/religion-and-the-ratification/religious-test-clause/religious-tests-and-oaths-in-state-constitutions-1776-1784/
[126] Constitutional Rights Foundation. https://www.crf-usa.org/bill-of-rights-in-action/bria-8-1-b-who-voted-in-early-america
[127] Charles S. Snydor. *Gentlemen Freeholders: Political Practices in Washington's Virginia*. Chapel Hill: UNC Press, 1953, 21
[128] https://founders.archives.gov/documents/Hamilton/01-01-02-0057#ARHN-01-01-02-0057-fn-0023-ptr. William Blackstone. *Commentaries on the Laws of England in Four Books*. Book 1, Chapter 2, 142.
[129] Farrand i:299
[130] John Adams to James Sullivan, 26 May 1776. https://founders.archives.gov/documents/Adams/06-04-02-0091
[131] John Locke had been a forward-thinking physician with a special interest in pediatrics before branching out to write Two Treatises on Government, in which he proposed that all citizens have an inherent right to "life, liberty, and property," which was bastardized by Thomas Jefferson in the Declaration of Independence. Jefferson substituted "pursuit of happiness" for "property" to avoid dealing with the contentious question of the status of slaves.
[132] quoted Keyssar, 3.
[133] *Papers of Thomas Jefferson*. Julian P. Boyd, ed. (Princeton: Princeton University Press, 1950), v. 1, 504.
[134] https://www.loc.gov/exhibits/jefferson/60.html.
[135] James Haw. *John & Edward Rutledge of South Carolina*. Athens, GA: University of Georgia Press, 1997, 257-8

[136] Committee of Detail Report. https://www.quillproject.net/resources/resource_item/56/3139

[137] Antonin Scalia, for example, once said, "The only good Constitution is a dead Constitution." New York Times, February 14, 2016.

[138] The August 7 debates are in Farrand, ii:196-212.

[139] Farrand, ii:123

[140] In Virginia's ratification debates, Madison would go further in making the case for limited suffrage. "In future times, a great majority of the people will not only be without landed, but any other sort of property. These will either combine, under the influence of their common situation—in which case the rights of property and the public liberty will not be secure in their hands—or, what is more probable, they will become the tools of opulence and ambition; in which case there will be equal danger on another side."

[141] Federalist 52. https://avalon.law.yale.edu/18th_century/fed52.asp

[142] Eric Foner. *The Second Founding: How the Civil War and Reconstruction Remade the Constitution.*" New York: Norton, 2019, 99

[143] Circuit Court of the United States. District of Louisiana. The United States v. Cruikshank et al. *The American Law Register* (1852-1891), Vol. 22, No. 10, New Series Volume 13 (October 1874), 680.

[144] For an excellent discussion of Giles, see Richard H. Pildes. "Democracy, Anti-Democracy, and the Canon." Constitutional Commentary, (2000) and Lawrence Goldstone. *On Account of Race: the Supreme Court, White Supremacy and the Ravaging of African American Voting Rights*. Berkeley, CA: Counterpoint, 2020.

[145] James H. Kettner. *The Making of American Citizenship.* Chapel Hill: UNC Press, 1978, 213

[146] The Citizenship Revolution, 7

[147] https://www.archives.gov/founding-docs/declaration-transcript

[148] Kettner, 214-6

[149] Kettner, 219

[150] Charles S. Snydor. *Gentlemen Freeholders: Political Practices in Washington's Virginia.* Chapel Hill: UNC Press, 1953, 21

[151] Federalist 42. https://avalon.law.yale.edu/18th_century/fed42.asp. Italics in the original

[152] In the finished Constitution, this clause, slightly altered, appeared in Article IV, Section 2, the same section as the Fugitive Slave Clause. "The Citizens of each State shall be entitled to all Privileges and Immunities of Citizens in the several States." In both cases, the clause protected the "property" of slaveholders when traveling to a free state.,

[153] Kettner, 221

[154] Other than by secret ballot, it is uncertain how the voting was done, whether by state or by individual. As James O. Stewart notes, "Jackson's journal describes the Convention having 'produced to ballot' for that panel, while Madison called it 'a ballot for a committee.' As a practical matter a five-

member committee could not be chosen by having each state delegation choose a member, so all of the delegates voted—either by states or as individuals—for those committee members…the available texts from the convention provide no definitive answer." https://allthingsliberty.com/2018/09/who-picked-the-committees-at-the-constitutional-convention/ But in every vote that was state by state, Jackson recorded the result, which he did not do here. Most likely, then, is that the delegates voted for five-man committees as individuals.

[155] The July 26 debate is in Farrand, ii:118-128

[156] Washington's expense account was anything but moderate, amounting to almost a half million dollars, which more than made up for his noble gesture in refusing payment for his services.

[157] https://www.quillproject.net/resources/resource_item/56/3139. Technically, the use of "he," which also appears in the finished document, might be thought to eliminate women from holding the office, particularly to those who consider themselves "originalists," or "textualists." Certainly, the delegates never anticipated women being president. It has been argued that in 1787, "he" was a pronoun that in this context could mean either gender, but it is difficult see how those who argue that the Constitution must interpreted verbatim or according to original intent cannot believe that only a man can hold the office.

[158] Pinckney, "Observations on Our Plan of Government." Farrand.

[159] The August 8 debate is from Farrand ii:215-226

[160] Mercer, like fellow Maryland delegate Luther Martin, would leave the convention early and refuse to sign the Constitution.

[161] "Every member of the Senate shall be of the age of thirty years at least; shall have been a citizen of the United States for at least four years before his election; and shall be, at the time of his election, a resident of the State for which he shall be chosen."

[162] The August 9 debate is from Farrand ii:230-244

[163] During the debates, immigration was considered to come only from Europe. While the delegates could not have foreseen later immigration from Asia, they were aware that some from the Caribbean would try to enter the United States.

[164] The August 13 debates and in Farrand ii:267-281

[165] Hamilton had again dropped in on the proceedings but would leave just as quickly. In the few days that he was present, as New York's only delegate, he could again not vote.

[166] Farrand, i:256

[167] Farrand, i:245

[168] Kettner, 225

[169] Whether legal and political rights went hand-in-hand would remain unsettled until the ratification of the 14th Amendment and even afterward, what constituted "privileges and immunities of citizenship" would remain a source of debate and controversy.

[170] 3--4 Feb. 1790 Annals 1:1111

[171] https://founders.archives.gov/documents/Madison/01-13-02-0018

[172] https://www.statutesandstories.com/blog_html/naturalization-act-of-1790-first-immigration-act-by-the-first-congress/

[173] See Lawrence Goldstone. *Not White Enough: The Long, Shameful Road to Japanese American Internment.* Lawrence, KS: University Press of Kansas, 2023; and, Ian Haney-Lopez. *White By Law: The Legal Construction of Race.* New York: NYU Press, 1996.

[174] Once again, nowhere more so than during the heyday of New York's Tweed Ring, when immigrants were naturalized almost instantly—if they would vote Democratic. As above see Dennis Tilden Lynch. "'*Boss' Tweed: The Story of a Grim Generation.*"

[175] William Maclay. *The Journal of William Maclay.* ed. Kenneth R.Bowling and Helen E. Veit. Baltimore: Johns Hopkins University Press, 1988, 208

[176] Kettner, 233.

[177] *Dred Scott v. Sandford*, 60 U.S. 393 (1856) https://supreme.justia.com/cases /federal/us/60/393/

[178] Two years after the Fourteenth Amendment, Congress passed and President Grant signed the Naturalization Act of 1870, of which the final section read, "The naturalization laws are hereby extended to aliens of African nativity and to persons of African descent." This was a remarkable extension of opportunity since it did not restrict naturalization to Black immigrants who were related to former slaves, but to any African who wished to become an African American. But the doors to United States citizenship had not been thrown open. It was not until 1943 that naturalization was extended to immigrants from China and nine years after that to immigrants from Japan.

[179] 83 US 36 (1872)

[180] Michael A. Ross. "Justice Miller's Reconstruction: The Slaughter-House Cases, Health Codes, and Civil Rights in New Orleans, 1861-1873."

[181] See for example Hans A. von Spakovsky. "Birthright Citizenship: A Fundamental Misunderstanding of the 14th Amendment."
https://www.heritage.org/immigration/commentary/birthright-citizenship-fundamental-misunderstanding-the-14th-amendment.

[182] https://www.cnn.com/2018/10/30/politics/birthright-citizenship-executive-order-trump-paul-ryan/index.html

[183] Ted Hesson. "Can Trump revoke birthright citizenship? Nearly all on left and right say no."
https://www.politico.com/story/2018/10/30/trump-birthright-citizenship-plan-900891

[184] https://www.congress.gov/bill/117th-congress/house-bill/140

[185] Michael Fix. "Repealing Birthright Citizenship: The Unintended Consequences."
https://www.migrationpolicy.org/news/repealing-birthright-citizenship-unintended-consequences

[186] The six states with the smallest populations, Alaska, North Dakota, South Dakota, Wyoming, Vermont, and Delaware, have less people than Cook County, Illinois.

[187] Farrand i:254

[188] Farrand i:337

[189] The August 9 debates are in Farrand ii:230-244

[190] Jonathan Elliot ed. *The Debates in Several State Conventions on the Adoption of the Federal Constitution.* Washington, DC, 1836, vol. 2, 50.

[191] Elliot, Debates. Vol. 4, 58.

[192] Farrand iii:195

[193] Thomas Rogers Hunter. "The First Gerrymander? Patrick Henry, James Madison, James Monroe, and Virginia's 1788 Congressional Districting." *Early American Studies*, Fall 2011, Vol. 9, No. 3, 785.

[194] Henry was unsurpassed in the courtroom. In a cross examination during a murder trial involving the elite Randolph family, Henry asked an elderly woman who had claimed to have witnessed a shocking scene in a bedroom, although the door was closed, "And just which eye did you use to peek through the keyhole, Mrs. Page?" The courtroom erupted in laughter and his client was acquitted.

[195] "The Virginia Convention, 2–27 June 1788 (Editorial Note)" https://founders.archives.gov/documents/Madison/01-11-02-0057.

[196] Hunter, 785

[197] Some scholars later posited that Henry did not gerrymander the seat, but nor was he upset that of the seven counties in the district, five were Republican and another was split. Farquhar County, next to Madison's Orange and linked by both history and tradition, was placed in a different district.

[198] William C. Rives, *History of the Life and Times of James Madison*, 3 vols. (Boston: Little, Brown, 1859-68), 2:655.

[199] Washington to Madison, November 17, 1788. https://founders.archives.gov/documents/Madison/01-11-02-0255

[200] Hunter, 797

[201] Farrand iii:88. The other two were Virginians Mason and Randolph.

[202] https://archive.csac.history.wisc.edu/elbridge_gerry_in_ma_convention.htm

[203] https://www.smithsonianmag.com/history/where-did-term-gerrymander-come-180964118/

[204] https://www.smithsonianmag.com/history/where-did-term-gerrymander-come-180964118/

[205] "'Gerrymander' Born in Massachusetts." https://www.massmoments.org/moment-details/gerrymander-born-in-massachusetts.html

[206] Erick Trickey. "Where Did the Term 'Gerrymander' Come From?" Smithsonian, June 2017. https://www.smithsonianmag.com/history/where-did-term-gerrymander-come-180964118/ The author claims the term originated at a Boston dinner party and not Russell's office.

[207] Lee Drutman. "What We Know About Redistricting and Redistricting

Reform." https://www.newamerica.org/political-reform/reports/what-we-know-about-redistricting-and-redistricting-reform/

[208] https://history.house.gov/Blog/2019/April/4-16-Apportionment-1/

[209] Although the word is now pronounced with a soft "g," as in Jerry, Gerry's name was actually pronounced with a hard "g," as in Gary.

[210] 328 U.S. 549 (1946) The chief justice chair was vacant after the death in April 1946 of Harlan Fiske Stone and Robert Jackson was in Germany prosecuting at the Nuremberg war crimes trials.

[211] 369 U.S. 186 (1962)

[212] 377 U.S. 533 (1964)

[213] "Where We Have Been: The History of Gerrymandering in America." New America. https://www.newamerica.org/political-reform/reports/what-we-know-about-redistricting-and-redistricting-reform/where-we-have-been-the-history-of-gerrymandering-in-america/

[214] Hayward H. Smith. "History of the Article II Independent State Legislature Doctrine." 29 Fla. St. U. L. Rev. (2002) 734.

[215] Richard Goodwin wrote the speech under intense time pressure and finished it so near to when it was to be delivered that Johnson read from a typewritten copy rather than a teleprompter.

[216] Statutes at Large. 79 Stat. 437. The wording was such that it significantly strengthened the 25th Amendment, which Joseph Bradley and Oliver Wendell Holmes, among others, had so weakened.

[217] https://www.justice.gov/crt/introduction-federal-voting-rights-laws-0

[218] New York Times, September 22, 2011, 20.

[219] https://ecf.dcd.uscourts.gov/cgi-bin/show_public_doc?2010cv0651-83

[220] https://www.brennancenter.org/sites/default/files/legal-work/2012.5.18%20DC%20Court%20of%20Appeals%20Opinion%20and%20Order.pdf

[221] The Tenth Amendment sates, "The powers not delegated to the United States by the Constitution, nor prohibited by it to the States, are reserved to the States respectively, or to the people."

[222] https://www.supremecourt.gov/opinions/12pdf/12-96_6k47.pdf

[223] https://www.brennancenter.org/our-work/policy-solutions/effects-shelby-county-v-holder

[224] 5 US 137 (1803)

[225] Scalia speech quoted in http://www.courttv.com/archive/legaldocs/rights/scalia.html.

[226] Robert Lowry Clinton, for example, stated categorically that "the idea of limiting legislative power by judicial nonapplication of statutes in certain cases was clearly understood." Clinton, *Marbury V. Madison and Judicial Review*, 56. Forrest McDonald asserted that there was "general agreement" that the courts would "have the power to strike down legislative acts if they were in violation of the Constitution." *Novus Ordo Seclorum*, 254

[227] Larry Kramer. "Ever Since *Marbury*: Concluding Observations." http://www.law.nyu.edu/sites/default/files/NYU_Law_Magazine_2002.pdf

[228] Virginia Declaration https://avalon.law.yale.edu/18th_century/virginia.asp

[229] Federalist 41. https://avalon.law.yale.edu/18th_century/fed41.asp

[230] http://www.mass.gov/legis/const.htm

[231] Blackstone, *Commentaries*, Introduction, Sec III, p.90-1 www.yale.edu/lawweb/avalon/blackstone/introa.htm#3.

[232] When Marshall was a teenager, his father had purchased a full set of Blackstone's *Commentaries*, which Marshall read in their entirety.

[233] Montesquieu, *Spirit*, Book XI, Section 6, www.constitution.org/cm/sol_11.htm.

[234] Farrand, i:21 Significantly, section 8 of the plan is listed after that which defines the executive (section 7) but before the judiciary (section 9) a clear indication that Madison although the council of revision would contain judges, he considered it distinct from the judiciary itself. The exact wording is: "The Executive and a convenient number of the National Judiciary, ought to compose a Council of revision with authority to examine every act of the National Legislature before it shall operate, & every act of a particular Legislature before a Negative thereon shall be final; and that the dissent of the said Council shall amount to a rejection, unless the Act of the National Legislature be again passed, or that of a particular Legislature be again negatived by of the members of each branch."

[235] The June 4 debates are in Farrand, i:96-114

[236] Therefore, to use this pronouncement as an indication that the delegates favored the power Marshall claimed in Marbury, which some scholars have done, is simply wrong.

[237] This debate in Farrand Records, v.1, 97-103. Yates's notes are a valuable counterbalance to Madison's and the analysis of what went on in the statehouse might have been far different had he stayed.

[238] By 7-3, the convention voted for a single executive, thwarting Mason who had held out for three.

[239] Mason, trying to resurrect his three-person executive, claimed that he would have less concern if the executive consisted of more than one person. "If more than one had been fixed on, greater powers might have been entrusted to the Executive. He hoped the attempt to give such powers would have its weight hereafter as an argument for increasing the number of the Executive."

[240] Since Virginia only had six delegates at the Convention (George Wythe had gone home due to illness) Madison and Mason, the states two most powerful delegates, were unable to convince a single colleague, including Edmund Randolph, the titular author of the Virginia Plan, to support a council of revision instead. Had even one other Virginian voted no, the state's vote would have been "divided."

[241] The July 21 debates are in Farrand, Records, ii:73-80.

[242] Albert Beveridge. *Life of John Marshall.* Boston: Houghton Mifflin, 1919, vol. III, pp. 114-5

[243] But Luther Martin left the convention in disgust at the end of August to become

---

an opponent of the Constitution in the Maryland ratifying debates. Yet, despite the source, this statement is also cited as proof of the delegates' acceptance of judicial review. See Robert Lowry Clinton, *Marbury v. Madison*, 60

[244] Madison made clear the following year that he viewed a council of revision as necessarily encompassing both branches. "A revisionary power is meant as a check to precipitate, to unjust, and to unconstitutional laws. These important ends would it is conceded be more effectually secured, without disarming the Legislature of its requisite authority, by requiring bills to be separately communicated to the Exec: & Judicy depts If either of these object, let 2/3, if both ¾ of each House be necessary to overrule the objection; and if either or both protest agst a bill as violating the Constitution, let it moreover be suspended notwithstanding the overruling proportion of the Assembly, until there shall have been a subsequent election of the H. of Ds and a re-passage of the bill by 2/3 or ¾ of both Houses, as the case may be. It sd not be allowed the Judges or ye. Executive to pronounce a law thus enacted unconstitul & invalid.

In the State Constitutions & indeed in the Fedl one also, no provision is made for the case of a disagreement in expounding them; and as the Courts are generally the last in making ye decision, it results to them by refusing or not refusing to execute a law, to stamp it with its final character. This makes the Judiciary Dept paramount in fact to the Legislature, which was never intended and can never be proper." Madison, October, 1788. "Observations on the 'Draught of a Constitution for Virginia'" http://memory.loc.gov/cgi-bin/query/r?ammem/mjmtext:@FIELD(DOCID+@lit(jm050096))

[245] Leonard W. Levy. *Original Intent and the Framer's Constitution.* New York: Macmillan, 1988, 100.

[246] "John Adams' Federalists" is something of a misnomer, since there were large numbers of Federalists under the spiritual leadership of Alexander Hamilton, often called "High Federalists," who detested Adams almost as much as Jefferson and plotted actively for his defeat. Under the circumstances, that Adams did as well as he did was amazing.

[247] Jefferson to John Dickinson, December 19, 1801. Multiple sources.

[248] It is testament to how little Supreme Court justices had to do that the first, John Jay, and the third, Ellsworth, both accepted diplomatic posts in Europe without feeling the need to resign from the Court. (The second, Rutledge, was never confirmed.)

[249] 1 Stat. 73

[250] Marshall did in fact recuse himself from a companion case, *Stuart v Laird*, which had promised to be far more incendiary.

[251] "The man who made the court supreme" was coined by Marshall biographer Albert Beveridge, the same man who noted that the power of judicial review had been intentionally omitted from Article III.

[252] Farrand, i:29

[253] The June 5 debate is in Farrand i:119-129

[254] William Pierce wrote, "The 16 lords of Sessions in Scotland are the Judicial-they are appointed by the Barristers or Doctors. They elect the most learned, Doctor, because he has the most business wh. they may divide when he becomes a Judge."

[255] Farrand i:242

[256] The July 18 debate is in Farrand ii:41-49

[257] The August 27 debates are in Farrand ii:429-433

[258] Farrand, ii:495

[259] *The Life of Gouverneur Morris, with Selections from His Correspondence and Miscellaneous Papers*. Edited by Jared Sparks. 3 vols. Boston, 1832. 3:322-3

[260] See, for example, Judith Rosenbaum *et al.*, A Constitutional Perspective on Judicial Tenure, 61 Judicature 465, 474 (1978) or Charles Cooke, https://www.nationalreview.com/corner/no-good-behavior-is-not-a-meaningless-phrase/

[261] Farrand, i:289 italics added.

[262] Farrand, ii:35 italics added

[263] Avalon Project. https://avalon.law.yale.edu/18th_century/king.asp#b2

[264] This exchange in Farrand, ii:428-9

[265] https://www.politico.com/news/magazine/2022/07/21/supreme-court-reform-term-limits-00046883

[266] https://www.wusa9.com/article/news/verify/can-congress-put-term-limits-on-supreme-court-justices-we-asked-five-legal-experts-court-packing-judges/65-2de67c84-910b-4a59-9824-f64d35866ae5

[267] See, for example, https://fixthecourt.com/wp-content/uploads/2020/10/Endorsers-of-H.R.-8424-10.23.20.pdf for list of law professors advocating reform by statute or Kermit Roosevelt, "Supreme Court justices should have term limits." https://www.cnn.com/2019/09/30/opinions/supreme-court-term-limits-law-roosevelt-vassilas/index.html

[268] Presidential Commission on the Supreme Court of the United States. https://www.whitehouse.gov/wp-content/uploads/2021/12/SCOTUS-Report-Final-12.8.21-1.pdf. 130-140

[269] As if to prove the point, in 1804, Samuel Chase became the only Supreme Court justice ever to be impeached. His alleged crime was allowing his loyalty to the Federalist Party to influence his behavior on the bench. Although Congress was by then fully in control of his enemies, he was acquitted.

[270] The source of the term limit misunderstanding may have been that, to the delegates, the issue did not seem at all vital. Serving as a Supreme Court justice was assumed to entail "riding circuit," a particularly odious task in a nation largely backwoods, requiring long, bumpy rides over poorly maintained roads—if roads even existed—followed by uncomfortable stays in inferior lodging serving often inedible food. As a result, being appointed

to the Supreme Court did not seem like an especially plum job, nor one that a well-heeled 18th century gentleman would be prone to keep for any length of time. In addition, because the need to prevent federal courts from treading on state prerogatives had impelled the delegates to limit federal jurisdiction, most assumed the United States Supreme Court would not have all that much to do.

Before Marshall's appointment, that turned out to be true. There were so few cases that the first two confirmed chief justices, John Jay and Oliver Ellsworth, accepted diplomatic assignments in Europe without feeling the need to resign their seats on the bench.

[271] For the best discussion of Douglas and the Sierra Club case, see M. Margaret McKeown. *Citizen Justice: The Environmental Legacy of William O. Douglas*. Lincoln, NE: Potomac Books, 2022.

[272] https://teachingamericanhistory.org/document/brutus-i/ The election would not be called until February 1788, but, in a departure from usual voting rules, every free male citizen over twenty-one would be eligible, thus making public opinion far more important than in most contsts. The convention itself would not begin until June 1788.

[273] His identity has never been definitively established. Most speculation centers around Robert Yates, the convention delegate who had left in early July, although some credit another noted antifederalist, Melancton Smith.

[274] *The Federalist Papers*. Alexander Hamilton, James Madison, John Jay. With an introduction, table of contents, and index of ideas by Clinton Rossiter. (New York: Mentor, 1961.

[275] Although seventy-three of essays have clear authorship—Jay five, Hamilton fifty-one, and Madison twenty-nine—the remaining twelve are disputed. Hamilton claimed them as his own, but, after Hamilton's death, when the authorship became public, Madison insisted they were his. Some forensic work and a computer analysis of the language sides with Madison.

[276] https://constitutioncenter.org/the-constitution/historic-document-library/detail/brutus-essay-no-1

[277] Federalist 1. https://avalon.law.yale.edu/18th_century/fed01.asp

[278] Brutus 11. https://teachingamericanhistory.org/document/brutus-xi/

[279] Brutus 15. https://teachingamericanhistory.org/document/brutus-xv/

[280] Federalist 78. https://avalon.law.yale.edu/18th_century/fed78.asp

[281] 19 U.S. (6 Wheat.) 264 at 418 (1821)

[282] Letter from James Madison to James K. Paulding (July 23, 1818), in 8 The Writings of James Madison, 410, 410 (Galliard Hunt ed., 1908).

[283] https://www.senate.gov/civics/common/generic/Virginia_Plan_item.htm

[284] John Locke. *Two Treatises of Government.* Peter Laslett, ed. Cambridge: Cambridge University Press, 1988, 364-5

[285] That power was purely legislative in the Articles, as was everything else. The June 1 debates are in Farrand, i:63-75

[286] In addition to those two, only New Hampshire used popular vote. The remaining states used some variety of legislative appointment for their

executive officers.

[287] The June 2 debates are in Farrand i:79-92

[288] A prescient observation given the two failed impeachments of Donald Trump.

[289] Shlomo Slonim. "The Electoral College at Philadelphia: The Evolution of an Ad Hoc Congress for the Selection of a President." Journal of American History, June 1986, Vol. 73, No. 1, 39

[290] Farrand i:244

[291] Only ten states were present at this point. New Hampshire's two delegates had not yet arrived and New York's three delegates, including Hamilton, had left.

[292] The July 19 debates are in Farrand, ii:51-59

[293] The July 20 debates are in Farrand ii:61-70

[294] The July 23 debates are in Farrand, ii:

[295] The July 25 debates are in Farrand ii:108-115.

[296] The July 26 debates are in Farrand, ii:116-128.

[297] https://www.quillproject.net/resources/resource_item/56/3139. The question of how state legislatures would make their choice seemed to have been debated by committee members, with equal lack of resolution. "One document of the Committee of Detail in the Farrand collection hints that the committee experienced considerable difficulty in settling the matter. Randolph, a member of the committee, had originally written that the executive shall be elected 'by joint ballot.' Subsequently, 'joint' had been crossed out, and Randolph had added to an emendation of South Carolina's John Rutledge the words '& in each Ho. havg a Negative on the other.' However, the final report of the Committee of Detail, issued on August 6, reverted to the simple form adopted by the convention plenum, namely, 'He shall be elected by ballot by the Legislature.'" Slonim, 48-9.

Electoral College at Philadelphia 49 "The President of the United States") read as follows: "He shall be elected by ballot by the Legislature. He shall hold his office during the term of seven years; but shall not be elected a second time."33

[298] Committee of Detail Report. https://www.quillproject.net/resources/resource_item/56/3139

[299] The August 7 debates are in Farrand ii:197-212

[300] The August 24 debates are in Farrand, ii:400-407

[301] Farrand ii:481

[302] Bruce Ackerman and David Fontana. "Thomas Jefferson Counts Himself into the Presidency." Virginia Law Review, April 2004, Vol. 90, No. 2, 557

[303] The September 4 debates are in Farrand, ii:494.

[304] John Dickinson later claimed to have warned the committee members that the "powers which we have agreed to vest in the President were so many and so great," that its legitimacy depended on popular vote, and that afterward Madison sat down and sketched out the electoral scheme, but neither Madison nor anyone else confirmed that assertion.

[305] James Madison to George Hay, August 23, 1823. Writings 9:147-55

[306] Farrand ii:527.

[307] Madison to Hay, August 23, 1823. Writings 9:147-55

[308] Calvin C. Jillson. "Constitutional-Making: Alignment and Realignment in the Federal Convention of 1787." American Political Science Review, September 1981, Vol. 75, No. 3, 608

[309] John P. Roche. "The Founding Fathers: A Reform Caucus in Action." American Political Science Review, December 1961, Vol. 55, No. 4, 810

[310] Federalist 68. https://avalon.law.yale.edu/18th_century/fed68.asp

[311] Papers 5:247-49

[312] For the story of that episode, see Bruce Ackerman, *The Failure of the Founding Fathers: Jefferson, Marshall, and the Rise of Presidential Democracy.* Cambridge, Mass: Harvard University Press, 2005.

[313] Life 3:174—75

[314] Madison to Hay, August 23, 1823. Writings 9:147-55

[315] Robert E. Ross. "Federalism and the Electoral College: The Development of the General Ticket Method for Selecting Presidential Electors." Publius, Vol. 46, No. 2 (Spring 2016), 151.

[316] Ross, 159.

[317] In addition, in fourteen other elections, the man named to be president gained less than a majority of the popular vote, with third party candidates drawing enough support to keep the winner under fifty percent.

[318] https://worldpopulationreview.com/country-rankings/military-spending-by-country

[319] https://www.mountvernon.org/library/digitalhistory/digital-encyclopedia/article/continental-army/

[320] Richard H. Kohn. *Eagle and Sword: The Federalists and the Creation of the Military Establishment in America, 1783-1802.* New York: Free Press, 1975, 2.

[321] Kohn, *Eagle*, 6.

[322] Richard H. Kohn. "The Inside History of the Newburgh Conspiracy: America and the Coup d'Etat." *The William and Mary Quarterly*, April 1970, Vol. 27, No. 2, 189.

[323] https://www.gilderlehrman.org/sites/default/files/inline-pdfs/t-2437.09443.pdf

[324] May 2, 1783. *Writings 26:374--76*

[325] *The Letters of Richard Henry Lee.* Edited by James Curtis Ballagh. 2 vols. New York: Macmillan Co., 1911--14. 2:287--88

[326] https://www.archives.gov/founding-docs/virginia-declaration-of-rights. That the phrasing is much the same as the Second Amendment is not an accident.

[327] Lee. *Federal Farmer* 18, January 25, 1788, https://teachingamericanhistory.org/document/federal-farmer-xviii/

[328] Elliot, *Debates*, iii:45

[329] Kohn, *Eagle*, 10-11

[330] Farrand, i:465

[331] Federalist 46, https://avalon.law.yale.edu/18th_century/fed46.asp

[332] James Madison, *I Annals of Congress 434*, June 8, 1789
[333] Committee of Detail Report. https://www.quillproject.net/resources/resource_item/56/3139
[334] The August 18 debates are in Farrand, ii:324-33.
[335] Farrand ii:356
[336] Farrand ii:385
[337] Noah Webster, *An Examination of the Leading Principles of the Federal Constitution*, October 10, 1787. https://teachingamericanhistory.org/document/a-citizen-of-america-an-examination-into-the-leading-principles-of-america/
[338] Richard Henry Lee, *Charleston Gazette*, September 8, 1788.
[339] Rep. Elbridge Gerry of Massachusetts, *I Annals of Congress 750*, August 17, 1789
[340] 307 US 174 (1939)
[341] 554 U.S. 570,
[342] 597 U.S. (2022)
[343] For a comprehensive and highly readable history of gun control in the United States, see Adam Winkler. *Gunfight: The Battle over the Right to Bear Arms in America.* New York: WW Norton, 2011.
[344] Farrand, i:291, 292
[345] Farrand, i:21
[346] The May 31 debates are in Farrand, i:47-61
[347] Farrand, i:243-4.
[348] https://www.usconstitution.net/plan_pinck.html. Pinckney's plan may never have been formally presented to the convention, nor its contents debated. Only later did Pinckney publish the plan and there is significant question as to whether it was drawn up before, during, or after the convention.
[349] Farrand, ii:26
[350] The final version was, "To make all Laws which shall be necessary and proper for carrying into Execution the foregoing Powers, and all other Powers vested by this Constitution in the Government of the United States, or in any Department or Officer thereof."
[351] Randy E. Barnett. "The Original Meaning of the Necessary and Proper Clause" 6 U. PA. J. Const. L. 183-221 (2003), 185.
[352] Barnett, 185.
[353] Elliott, iii:436–37.
[354] Brutus V. https://teachingamericanhistory.org/document/brutus-v/
[355] Federalist 33. https://guides.loc.gov/federalist-papers/text-31-40#s-lg-box-wrapper-25493387
[356] Federalist 44. https://guides.loc.gov/federalist-papers/text-41-50#s-lg-box-wrapper-25493408
[357] Robert G. Natelson, "The Agency Law Origins of the Necessary and Proper Clause," 55 Case W. Rsrv. L. Rev.
(2004), 244, 249.

[358] Hamilton to Robert Morris, April 30, 1781. https://founders.archives.gov/documents/Hamilton/01-02-02-1167

[359] https://founders.archives.gov/documents/Hamilton/01-07-02-0229-0003#ARHN-01-07-02-0229-0003-fn-0152-ptr

[360] Hamilton to Robert Morris, April 30, 1781.

[361] Journal of William Maclay, 355

[362] Annals of the Congress of the United States, First Congress, Third Session, 1940-1.

[363] Annals, 1944-5.

[364] H. Wayne Morgan. "The Origins and Establishment of the First Bank of the United States." The Business History Review, December 1956, Vol. 30, No. 4, 485.

[365] Annals, 1956.

[366] Andrew T. Hill. "The Second Bank of the United States, 1816-1841." https://www.federalreservehistory.org/essays/second-bank-of-the-us

[367] Peter Charles Hoffer. *Daniel Webster and the Unfinished Constitution.* Lawrence, KS: University Press of Kansas, 2021, 59.

[368] Hoffer, 59.

[369] Hoffer, 62.

[370] McCulloch v. Maryland, 17 US 316 (1819)

[371] William Baude, Response, "Sharing the Necessary and Proper Clause", 128 Harvard Law Review Forum
(2014), 42

[372] David Kyvig. "Explicit and Authentic Acts: Amending the U.S. Constitution 1776-2015." Lawrence, KS: University Press of Kansas, 2016, 55.

[373] Farrand, i:202-3.

[374] Farrand, ii:148.

[375] This debate is in Farrand, ii:558-9

[376] This debate is Farrand, ii:629-31

[377] Sarah Isgur. "It's Time to Amend the Constitution." https://www.politico.com/news/magazine/2022/01/08/scalia-was-right-make-amending-the-constitution-easier-526780

[378] The 27th Amendment, which was originally submitted in 1788 with the ten that later became the Bill of Rights, states, "No law, varying the compensation for the services of the Senators and Representatives, shall take effect, until an election of Representatives shall have intervened."

[379] Donald S. Lutz, Toward a Theory of Constitutional Amendment, 88 Am. Pol. Sci. Rev. (1994) 362

[380] Stephen M Griffin. "The Nominee Is ... Article V." Constitutional Commentary, 1995, 172.

[381].Griffin. 171.

[382] Federalist 43. https://avalon.law.yale.edu/18th_century/fed43.asp

[383] Federalist 85. https://avalon.law.yale.edu/18th_century/fed85.asp

[384] Federalist 10. https://avalon.law.yale.edu/18th_century/fed10.asp

[385] From the "Autobiography," now printed in Volume I of the "Writings of

Jefferson," edited by Paul Leicester Ford. https://flexpub.com/epubs/pg28653-images/OEBPS/@public@vhost@g@gutenberg@html@files@28653@28653-h@28653-h-4.htm.html#Footnote_32_32.

386 See Nancy Goldstone. *In the Shadow of the Empress: The Defiant Lives of Maria Theresa, Mother of Marie Antoinette, and Her Daughters.* New York: Little Brown, 2021.

387 James Parton. *Life of Thomas Jefferson: Third President of the United States.* Boston: J. R. Osgood, 1874, 329.

388 Jefferson to Washington, May 23, 1792. https://founders.archives.gov/documents/Washington/05-10-02-0268.

389 Hamilton to Washington, August 18, 1792. https://founders.archives.gov/documents/Washington/05-11-02-0004

390 Washington to Jefferson, August 23, 1792. https://founders.archives.gov/documents/Washington/05-11-02-0009

391 Jefferson to Washington, September 9, 1792. https://founders.archives.gov/documents/Washington/05-11-02-0049. Jefferson is referring to legislation proposing national assumption of state debt, which Jefferson opposed but felt tricked into supporting.

392 A. James Reichley. *The Life of the Parties: A History of American Political Parties.* New York: Free Press, 1992, 31.

393 Reichley, 33.

394 Reichley, 31.

395 Reichley, 42.

396 George Washington's Mount Vernon. https://www.mountvernon.org/library/digitalhistory/digital-encyclopedia/article/democratic-republican-societies/

397 Eugene Perry Link. *Democratic-Republican Societies, 1790-1800.* New York: Columbia University Press, 1942, 73.

398 Matthew Schoenbachler. "Republicanism in the Age of Democratic Revolution: The Democratic-Republican Societies of the 1790s." Journal of the Early Republic Summer,1998, Vol. 18, No. 2, 238.

399 Schoenbachler, 239.

400 George Washington's Mount Vernon. https://www.mountvernon.org/george-washington/the-first-president/washington-vs-jefferson/

401 George Washington's Mount Vernon. https://www.mountvernon.org/george-washington/the-first-president/washington-vs-jefferson/

402 Washington Farewell Address. https://www.govinfo.gov/content/pkg/GPO-CDOC-106sdoc21/pdf/GPO-CDOC-106sdoc21.pdf

403 Although voter turnout increased to only 75,000 in 1800, it almost doubled in 1804, and reached almost 200,000 in 1808, 300,000 in 1812. Turnout dropped off considerably in in 1816 and 1820, but by then, the Democratic-Republicans were so powerful that the nation had effectively one-party rule. By 1828, with the two-party system in ull bloom, voter turnout exceeded one million.

Index

D

E

F

G

H

I

J

K

L

M

N

O

P

R

Y

www.ingramcontent.com/pod-product-compliance
Lightning Source LLC
Chambersburg PA
CBHW050239270326
41914CB00041BA/2041/J
9781680538434